DUBBING AND SUBTITLING
WORLD CONTEXT

Dubbing and Subtitling in a World Context

EDITED BY

Gilbert C. F. Fong

AND

Kenneth K. L. Au

The Chinese University Press

Dubbing and Subtitling in a World Context
  Edited by Gilbert C. F. Fong and Kenneth K. L. Au

© **The Chinese University of Hong Kong**, 2009

ISBN: 978–962–996–356–9

THE CHINESE UNIVERSITY PRESS
The Chinese University of Hong Kong
SHA TIN, N.T., HONG KONG
Fax: +852 2603 6692
    +852 2603 7355
E-mail: cup@cuhk.edu.hk
Web-site: www.chineseupress.com

Printed in Hong Kong

Contents

—ɯ—

Introduction

Kenneth K. L. Au

—ന്ത—

With the rapid internationalization of distribution of films and TV programmes, people in different countries are able to watch audiovisual products in different languages and cultures. The proliferation of new forms of entertainment such as DVD and pay-per-view TV also creates a huge demand for the professional service of dubbing and subtitling, which are indispensable tools to help viewers with little knowledge in the foreign language to overcome the language barriers.

Dubbing and subtitling can be subsumed under the broader discipline of audiovisual translation (AVT), which is much more than mere interlingual transfer as pictures, music, sounds and other non-verbal elements are also involved in the process, making it a kind of multi-semiotic transfer. In addition to the language transfer and the technicalities of the production (such as the use of time-code for subtitling), socio-cultural factors should not be overlooked as the life-style and value systems of the people are reflected in the films and TV programmes.

Every day, professional translators all over the world have been working hard and have accumulated substantial experience after countless hours of subtitling and dubbing practice. On the other hand, more and more translation scholars have conducted academic studies on the subject matter and produced fruitful results (Luyken 1991; Dollerup and Lindegaard 1993; Gottlieb 1997; Ivarsson and Carroll 1998; Karamitroglou 2000; Gambier and Gottlieb 2001; Orero 2004; just to name a few). It is time for academics and professionals in the industry to have a dialogue to share their insights and experience.

The present volume is mostly a collection of selected papers presented at the International Conference on Dubbing and Subtitling in a World Context organized by the Department of Translation of the Chinese University of Hong Kong in mid October 2001, the first major conference on subtitling and dubbing in Asia. During the three-day conference, scholars and professionals from China, Japan, Korea, Taiwan, the Philippines, Italy, Belgium, Finland, Sweden, Australia, and Hong Kong shared their views on and insights in subtitling and dubbing. Subtitling equipment suppliers, film distributors, managers from translation agencies and other professionals of the field were invited to speak at a sharing session at Sai Wan Ho Amenities Centre in Hong Kong, followed by a round-table discussion by professionals and stakeholders with frank exchanges on the various facets of the industry.

The papers collected in this book are categorized into three sections in the book: (1) history of the profession; (2) theory; and (3) practice. The first four papers in the first section are about the history of subtitling and dubbing in Europe and East Asia. In "The History of Subtitles in Europe," **Jan Ivarsson** traces the development of subtitles in Europe, from intertitles in 1903 to the subtitles used today. The second part of the paper is devoted to a detailed description of the evolution of the various techniques in the production of subtitles for films and TV programmes: the mechanical and thermal processes, the chemical process, use of laser burning, caption generators, time-code readers and personal computer.

Qian Shaochang's "Screen Translation in Mainland China" outlines the three major stages of subtitling in China: before 1949, between 1949 to 1978, and after 1978. Political and socio-cultural factors have been playing an important role in the choice of imported films and TV programmes for translation. Qian also notes that the "inconceivable sensation" of imported television programmes in China in the 1980s died down after the mid 1990s due to certain political and socio-cultural factors.

In "Subtitling in Japan," **Karima Fumitoshi** gives a brief history of subtitling in Japan. The livelihood of Japanese movie narrators (who were called *benshi*) was threatened with the arrival of subtitled movies. He also points out that "the chief function of the subtitler is to make the dialogue correspond to the intention of the director."

Lee Young Koo's "The History of Subtitling in Korea" first outlines the history of Korean filmmaking industry from the difficult days in the 1950s to the prosperous growth in recent years. The second half of his paper discusses some practical problems in translating some film titles and subtitles into Korean.

The papers in Section Two cover some theoretical issues of subtitling and dubbing. In his paper "The Two Worlds of Subtitling: The Case of Vulgarisms and Sexually-oriented Language," **Gilbert C. F. Fong** addresses the intrinsic dualism of subtitling: the audience "is experiencing double—he is seeing a movie and reading about it at the same time." So the subtitle translator has to negotiate the differences between the two worlds, and make a decision among the three approaches in cultural transfer, namely, foreignisation, naturalization and neutralization. There is some insightful discussion on the choice of these approaches, illustrated with interesting examples of the sexually-oriented language subtitled in the local dialect of Hong Kong, Cantonese.

Also included in this section is **Fong**'s other paper "Let the Words Do the Talking: The Nature and Art of Subtitling," which explores the basic issues of the spatial and temporal constraints of the art, and elaborates on the linguistic and stylistic features of the cross-media transference with interesting examples of translating puns and song lyrics. It also firmly asserts the applicability of *skopos* theory to subtitling because subtitles have a clearly defined *skopos*: "to serve the needs of the audience who are the end-users."

In "A Functional Gap between Dubbing and Subtitling," **He Yuanjian** investigates the representational disparity between the two forms of audiovisual translation. While there is over-representation of source language features in film subtitling, target-language-specific features are more commonly found in dubbing scripts. He accounts for the contrast by incorporating Sari Eskola's (2001) stimuli theory into the textual processing model of James S. Holmes (1978).

Chuang Ying-ting's "Subtitling as a Multi-modal Translation" studies the concept of multi-modality in the process of subtitle translation, and concludes that the equivalence relationships range from one-to-one to many-to-many, in terms of the concept of semiotic mode. She points out that different semiotic modes contribute different kinds of meaning to the text of film. The translator should distribute or integrate the meanings to the various modes so as to create equivalent wholeness between the source and target texts. The translation of multi-modal texts, such as subtitling, requires not only a one-way decoding and encoding process, but multiple ways of translating.

In "A Critical Evaluation of a Chinese Subtitled Version of Hitchcock's *Spellbound*," **Chapman Chen** makes a detailed analysis on the subtitled film and concludes that a good subtitler should pay attention to the four constraints of subtitling proposed by Paola Guardini, namely, technical, textual, intralinguistic and extra-linguistic.

Section Three of this volume is devoted to papers covering the different aspects of the practice of dubbing in various countries. In "I Translate, You Adapt, They Dub," **Sergio Patou-Patucchi** discusses the problems found in dubbing and subtitling activities in Italy, including the incompetence of some poorly trained translators. He observes that "dubbing becomes a medium of political control and censorship." He calls for collaboration with the Academy to develop a "cross-disciplinary consciousness."

Zhang Chunbai notes the constraints of translating film dialogue for dubbing in his paper "The Translation of Film Dialogues for Dubbing," namely, the irreversibility of utterances, and the matching of lip movements, gestures and movements with the dubbed sound. Therefore the translator should aim at producing a dubbed film version with immediate comprehensibility and pragmatic equivalence.

Loss of meaning seems to be the necessary evil in many translations. **Lu Danjun** in "Loss of Meaning in Dubbing" addresses a subtle difficulty in dubbing, namely, the inability of expressing foreign accents and local dialects. Interesting linguistic contrasts between characters evident in the original film will be totally lost when dubbed in another language.

Veteran subtitle expert in Hong Kong, **Rupert Chan** shares his substantial experience in adapting, dubbing and surtitling/subtitling for theatre performance, TV programmes and movies in his paper "Dubbing and Subtitling—Art or Craft?" Interesting examples are cited to illustrate the subtlety involved in Chinese-English subtitling and dubbing practice.

In "Translation Imperative: Synchronise Discipline and

Technique," **Janet Tauro** highlights some areas for improvement in the production and consumption of Filipino audiovisual translation and calls for "the synchronization between the academic community and television industry." The paper also showcases the imbalance in resource allocation of the Filipino media: they prefer to spend more on programme promotion than on improving the quality of subtitles.

Kari Jokelainen's "Translating Understanding and Non-understanding through Subtitling" is an interesting case study of subtitling across several languages and cultures. The film in question is a comedy with situations where the characters speak Polish, French, Hungarian, Icelandic, and English. The translator has to make sensible decisions (using italics, for example) in the subtitling process so as to suit the needs of the situations.

Hong Kong filmmaker and distributor **Shu Kei** gives an interesting account of how he joined the subtitling profession in "Translating Subtitles for the Hong Kong Audience: Limitations and Difficulties." He also traces the three-phase development of subtitling production: the burning method, laser-subtitling and the more expensive optical method. The challenges posed by Cantonese, the local dialect in Hong Kong and the issue of censorship are also discussed.

In "Surtitling for *Xiqu* (Chinese Opera) in the Theatre," **Jessica W. Y. Yeung** describes the technicalities of surtitling in the performance of the culture-specific theatrical form. She then makes a detour to phenomenology to illustrate the importance of surtitles to the overall theatrical experience.

A good training programme for subtitlers is a pre-requisite for subtitling quality. In "The Pedagogy of Subtitling," **Corinne Imhauser** introduces the post-graduate subtitling course at ISTI (*Institut Supérieur de Traducteurs et Interprétes*), Belgium, which helps students develop both technical skills and linguistic skills. Some practical drills are suggested for a subtitling class by using affordable ordinary equipment.

The conference is but a starting point of sharing among professionals and academics. We believe that international cooperation and constant interaction among stakeholders will be helpful to the development of audiovisual translation, in terms of professional insights and academic excellence.

In the course of preparing this volume, we received great help from all contributors whose enthusiastic supports are indispensable to the publication of this volume. Some of them even took the trouble to rewrite some parts of the paper to make it update. To them, we owe our indebtedness. Our thanks are also extended to Carmen Yu, Maisie Chow, Amy Siu, Teresa Wang, Jennifer Eagleton and Shelby Chan, who shared the heavy burden of proofreading all the manuscripts for publication.

References

Dollerup, Cay and Annete Lindegaard (eds.). 1993. *Teaching Translation and Interpreting 2: Insights, Aims, Visions.* Amsterdam: John Benjamins.

Gambier, Yves and Henrik Gottlieb (eds.). 2001. *(Multi) Media Translation: Concepts, Practices, and Research.* Amsterdam: John Benjamins.

Gottlieb, Henrik. 1997. *Subtitles, Translation & Idioms.* PhD Thesis, Copenhagen: University of Copenhagen.

Ivarsson, Jan and Mary Carroll. 1998. *Subtitling.* Simrishamn: TransEdit.

Karamitroglou, Fotios. 2000. *Towards a Methodology for the Investigation of Norms in Audiovisual Translation: The Choice between Subtitling and Revoicing in Greece.* Amsterdam: Rodopi.

Luyken, Georg-Michael. 1991. *Overcoming Language Barriers in Television: Dubbing and Subtitling for the European Audience.* Manchester: European Institute for the Media.

Orero, Pilar (ed.). 2004. *Topics in Audiovisual Translation.* Amsterdam: John Benjamins.

SECTION ONE

The Historical Perspective

1

The History of Subtitles in Europe

Jan Ivarsson

—ɯ—

Almost since the invention of films, efforts have been made to convey the dialogue of the actors to the audience. It began with what we now call *intertitles* (first seen in 1903 as epic, descriptive titles): texts, drawn or printed on paper, filmed and placed between sequences of the film. They came to be called *subtitles* quite early on, as they were used in the same way as subtitles in newspapers. From the beginning, it also happened (but rarely) that the subtitles were placed in the image, e.g. in *College Chums* (1907) or the French films *Judex* or *Mireille* (1922).

In the era of intertitles, it was easy to solve the translation problem. The original titles were removed, translated, filmed and inserted again. Or a speaker was used to give a simultaneous interpretation of the intertitles, like the French *bonimenteur* or the Japanese *benshi*. But from 1927 on, with the invention of sound film, the audience could hear the actors. Since then, the titles inserted between scenes disappeared and the problem assumed new dimensions.

From Intertitles to Subtitles

Of course, one could make several language versions, or have the film post-synchronised (dubbed) into another language. However, some film producers and distributors found this technique complex and expensive.

Why not use titles as before, but inserted in the picture? They thus became what we now call subtitles, and since this technique was comparatively cheap (subtitling only costs between a tenth and a twentieth as much as dubbing), it became the preferred method in the smaller language areas, such as the Netherlands and the Scandinavian countries.

The main problem in the early days of film subtitling was to place the subtitles on the distribution copies, as the negative was usually in safe keeping in the country of origin. In fact, the very first "subtitles" saw the light of day already during the silent film era. In 1909, M. N. Topp registered a patent for a "device for the rapid showing of titles for moving pictures other than those on the film strip." With this method, the projectionist showed the subtitles on the screen below the intertitles using a sciopticon (a kind of slide projector). However, this was never much more than a curiosity, although similar techniques, with the titles on a film strip instead of slides, have been used from time to time up to the present day (Brant 1984: 30).

Norway, Sweden, Hungary and France quickly took the lead in developing techniques for subtitling films. However, the first Nordic country to subtitle seems to have been Denmark: in 1929, Al Jolson's *The Singing Fool* was shown in Copenhagen with subtitles (Gottlieb 1994: 20–22).

The Optical Method

To start with, attempts were made to breathe new life into the technique invented in 1909. For example, there was manual projection of slides with texts printed directly onto the screen. But very soon, methods of copying photographed titles onto the film copy itself came into use. A frame containing the title was kept in position while the film negative and the positive print strip were fed forward and exposed.

Later on, this process was made automatic. Exposed "blank" frames were inserted between the title frames and the titles were fed forward by means of a counter to ensure that the subtitles were of the right length and came in the right place. Using this method, one could also tint the titles to make them more easily legible.

One problem with the method was that, since the film negative was usually not available, it was necessary to photograph the whole film to obtain a negative, with a consequent loss of focus and substantial increase in the noise level—a serious drawback in the early days of sound films.

But sometimes the film negative could be obtained, and it was soon realised that, if a large number of copies were required, the most efficient method was to photograph the titles onto a separate film of the same length as the original, with the in-and-out cue frames synchronised with the sound.

The film negative and the roll with the titles were then copied simultaneously, an operation that took much less time than repeating the slow exposure procedure frame by frame.

Film Subtitling Using Mechanical and Thermal Processes

In 1930, a Norwegian inventor, Leif Eriksen, took out a patent for a method of stamping titles directly onto the images on the film strip, first moistening the emulsion layer to soften it. The titles were typeset in the usual way and printed on paper; each subtitle was then produced by very small letterpress type plates made through a photographic process (the height of each letter being only about 0.8 mm). Later, in 1935, a Hungarian inventor, O. Turchányi, registered a patent for a method whereby the plates were heated to a sufficiently high temperature to melt away the emulsion on the film without the need for a softening bath. However, both these processes were difficult to control and the results were often erratic, with poorly defined letters. The ridges of emulsion that arose around the letters were also very susceptible to wear, and the deeply embossed letters naturally accumulated dirt very quickly. Despite these drawbacks, this technique is still used by some film laboratories in Eastern Europe and South America.

The Chemical Process

In 1932, R. Hruska, an inventor in Budapest, and Oscar I. Ertnæs in Oslo (later in Stockholm) simultaneously took out patents on an improved technique for impressing the titles directly onto the film copies.

A very thin coating of wax or paraffin was applied to the emulsion side of the finished film copy. The printing plates were placed in a kind of printing press, into which each plate was fed and heated to a temperature of nearly 100°C and one by one pressed against the paraffin coating at the bottom of the frame that corresponded to the beginning of the dialogue line. The paraffin under the letters melted and was displaced, exposing the emulsion. This process was repeated with all the frames on which this subtitle was to appear, corresponding to the duration of the speech. The same procedure was carried out with the next subtitle and so on throughout the film.

After the printing process, the film was put through a bleach bath, which dissolved the emulsion that had been exposed, leaving only the transparent nitrate or acetate film. The etching fluid and the paraffin were then washed away. This process produced clearly legible white letters on the screen, although the edges of the letters were slightly ragged due to the variable consistency of the paraffin and variations in the penetration of the etching fluid.

Later on, this process too was automated by means of a counter, which fed the plates forward, counted the frames on the roll and ensured that the subtitles came in the right place and were of the right length. This was the cheapest process when less than ten copies of a film were to be subtitled.

The chemical and optical processes described above are still used in the film industry today, more or less as before, except that the plate-making process has been modernised. In the early days, the titles were typeset (usually with a Linotype machine), printed on paper, photographed and then plates were made for each set. Later, with the adoption of new techniques in the printing industry, came phototypesetting (e.g. Cinétype) and still later computerised typesetting. Nowadays computers are usually used for the production of the titles themselves, and they can be time coded and "simulated" on a videocassette for proofreading purposes. Basically, however, the chemical and optical processes used for subtitles have changed very little in the last sixty years. They are still largely manual and work-intensive, and the quality of the result varies considerably.

The Norwegian-Swedish film laboratories Filmtekst in Oslo, Ideal Film in Stockholm and the Kagansky brothers' Titra-Film in Paris held the most important patents. As a result, they dominated the European subtitling market from 1933 right up to the mid-50s.[1]

Laser Subtitling

The latest development in this field is the use of lasers to burn away or vaporise the emulsion. This makes both typesetting and plates unnecessary. The technique has been developed by Denis Auboyer in Paris and by Titra-Film in Paris and Brussels, and has, with great success, been in commercial use since 1988.

In this process, a computer controls a very narrow laser beam, in the same way as in a modern typesetting machine, i.e. the beam virtually writes the text in such a way as to result in vaporization of the emulsion without damage to the acetate film underneath. It takes the beam less than a second to write a subtitle consisting of two lines, after which the next frame is fed forward. Where no subtitles are to appear, the film is fast-wound to the next operative frame. The sharpness of the letters is excellent, the contours being enhanced by a slight shading as a result of heat-darkened edges.

The titles themselves are computer typeset and can be cued on the video display by means of time coding or frame-counting.

Laser subtitling is cheaper than the chemical process, but requires costly investment in equipment. However, the method is highly automated and needs very little manual labour.

Subtitling for Television

Films for the cinema were soon shown on television. On August 14, 1938, the BBC broadcast Arthur Robison's *Der Student von Prag* in a subtitled version. (This was probably also the first scheduled showing of a film in the history of television.)

But it was soon discovered that the prints with subtitles intended for the cinema caused a number of problems. The titles, legible enough in the cinema, were very difficult to read on the television screen. One reason for this is the difference in the speed at which the audience can read subtitles on television as compared with the cinema. But the main reason is that the picture on a TV set has a narrower contrast range than that on a cinema screen. What was needed, therefore, was a method for incorporating subtitles produced for television into untitled film copies or videotapes.

Optical Film Subtitles for Television

In countries where the optical process was used for subtitling films, the first method that was tried was to use the existing subtitle film strip and run it in parallel with the original untitled film in a second film scanner. The title images were mixed electronically into the film images, so that to the viewers it looked as if the titles were on the film, except that now it was possible to control the whiteness of the letters. If a roll with the subtitles was not available, one could be ordered from a company that made subtitles for films. This method is still used occasionally today.

At about the same time, work started on the development of a rather crude, but cheap and reliable, optical subtitling process for television. The method used was to write the titles on paper, make one-frame stills of each title with a film camera, put the resulting film negative in a scanner and then either have the translator feed in the titles manually, one at a time, synchronizing them with the programme, or use an automatic system to feed in the titles, more or (usually) less reliably, with the help of punched-out marks on the edge of the film.

The title images (with white titles against a black background, the whiteness and blackness being controlled to ensure optimum readability) were then mixed into the programme images and transmitted or taped as necessary. Where no subtitles were to appear, exposed frames—blank frames—were placed between the subtitle frames. To make sure that the titles would be clearly visible even against light backgrounds, black bands—"letter boxes"—in many countries were laid over the bottom part of the picture throughout the film.

Quite soon, some improvements were made on this method. For example, the titles were written in more attractive proportional typefaces on offset composers, i.e. simple typographical setting machines, which also allowed the use of italics and kerning, squeezing the letters together. The titles were written on punch cards, which could be inserted in a feed mechanism and either photographed onto a roll of film or displayed directly by means of a TV camera with image inversion (black shown as white and vice versa). This "rapid subtitling" method was used mainly for news items or when time was short for other reasons. Thus, photographing the subtitles and developing the film were no longer necessary, but the feeding system was not entirely reliable, and sometimes the machine supplied several cards at a time or none at all.

Both techniques allowed manual feeding of the subtitles during recording or transmission or, as with film subtitling, automatic feeding by means of a frame counter. An automatic adjustment let the background appear only behind the subtitles, and the black box was there solely while the subtitles were being shown and disappeared when they ended.

Caption Generators

With the introduction of various types of caption generators (such as Aston, Capgen, Logica, Vidifont) to insert captions directly on the television image by electronic means, subtitles could be generated directly in the transmitted picture itself. This apparatus also made it possible to dispense with the black box as a background for the subtitles and instead use shaded or coloured letters.

However, caption generators, which were intended for various kinds of captions or titles and offered a wide range of typographical variation, proved impractical for subtitling in large quantities. They were difficult to operate; their word processing functions were very rudimentary and above all, they were extremely expensive.

Subtitling Equipment

It was therefore only natural that efforts be made to produce dedicated subtitling equipment, and this was achieved in the second half of the 1970s, more or less simultaneously in several places. Two major systems were developed, both based on the use of a word processor with a special subtitling program that made it possible to write the subtitles in a form identical to that shown on the television screen.

The first system is based on the teletext principle (Oracle, from the U.K., and Antiope, from France, are two examples). A computer generates concealed signals in the image data, in response to which, a simple character generator in the receiver creates the characters and mixes them into the television picture when a specified teletext page is selected.

The second system uses a computer-controlled character generator in the transmitter—much less sophisticated and much cheaper than a caption character generator. When the subtitler cues in a new subtitle, the characters are generated by electronic means and mixed into the transmitted image. Examples of such systems are the BBC's Television Electronic Characters (TEC) system, which appeared in 1976, the SVT–TeleEkonomi's system, which was developed by Bengt Modin and came into operation in 1981, and the Screen Electronic system, which appeared at about the same time.

Time Codes

Logically, the next question that had to be answered was: why are the titles fed manually when time codes, which have so many other functions in television, can do the job?

When a videotape is time-coded, a "clock" is recorded on the tape which tells you to the nearest 1/25 of a second when a particular frame will appear on the screen. This time code may be recorded lengthwise along the tape on one of the soundtracks, as in the case of the Longitudinal Time and Control code (LTC code; the EBU standard is used in Europe and the SMPTE standard in the US and Japan) or crosswise, concealed in the lines outside the visible part of the screen, in the case of the Vertical Interval Time and Control code (VITC). In both cases, the code can be read while the videotape is running, and either displayed (in the TV picture or on a special display) and/or used to start or stop a certain process, e.g. to show a selected subtitle as desired. The VITC code has the advantage of being usable even when the tape is not running and will not be damaged (like the longitudinal code) when the tape is "cut," since each frame contains the complete code.

Soon a further advance was made, which made it possible to install the complete subtitling system on a personal computer, thus allowing the subtitler to carry out the whole job, including the cueing of the subtitles in the right place in the programme, in a continuous operation and in his own home or office.

Subtitling Today

Nowadays, therefore, a subtitler with access to state-of-the-art equipment sits in front of a personal computer, which is connected to a videotape recorder with a monitor. The computer is equipped with a time code reader and a word processing program specially designed for subtitling, which displays the titles as they will appear on the television or film screen. He will run a time-coded videocassette for a few seconds or longer, time his subtitles, write them on the computer and cue them in the appropriate place. The time code that is recorded on the tape is written to the disk alongside the subtitle, thus ensuring that the in and out cues for the subtitles make them appear in the right place. When the subtitler has written all the subtitles for the programme or film, he proofreads the text and then lets the videotape run the subtitles, looks at the result and makes any corrections that may be necessary.

Alternatively, he will get a copy of the film with pre-recorded time codes on a DVD disk or on his computer's hard disk (by way of the Internet) and work from this in the same way.

His task is now accomplished. The floppy disk can be handed in and, with any luck, it will be checked by a colleague. All that needs to be done now is to insert the disk in the computer of the transmission unit or film subtitling machine and let the time code on the master tape run the subtitles. If the equipment used is the very latest available, the subtitler can even use the Net to transmit the result of his labour to the hard disk of the transmission unit.

Of course, all this costly equipment is not strictly necessary, and the subtitler who only translates a few television programmes or films a year can still do his job in the traditional way: watch the programme or film, time his subtitles with the help of an audio tape and a script if there is one, write down the subtitles on paper, check his work with the images on the screen, hand it in to be written onto a floppy disk and cue them manually during recording or transmission (or perhaps time-code them at the television company).

If he works for a film importer, the chances are that he will still have to work from a "master list," translating the dialogue according to a predetermined format, perhaps without even seeing the film.

Subtitles Outside the Screen

But why not move the subtitles out of the image and show them on a separate display below the screen, with a display of the LED type or a separate projector?

This is actually the last development in subtitling technology. To have the subtitle just outside the image may seem too revolutionary, and some hold that such subtitles are harder to read than the "normal" ones. But the fact is that the eyes do not have to move much more than at present—the emplacement of the subtitle in relation to the image center and the borders of the total surface is virtually identical. Moreover, the practice of showing subtitles below the screen has already been successfully adopted, especially in film festivals.

Note

1. According to interviews given by O. Ertnaes's daughter and Mme Nina Kagansky, Paris. See also Brant, pp. 53–63. Her thesis contains a detailed description of all the stages in both the optical and chemical processes.

References

Brant, Rosemary. 1984. *The History and Practice of French Subtitling.* MA thesis, University of Texas, Austin. Ann Arbor: United Microfilms International Dissertation Information Service, 1989.

Gottlieb, Henrik. 1994. *Tekstning. Synkron Billedmedieoversættelse* (Danske Afhandlinger om Oversættelse nr. 5), Center for Oversættelse, Københavns Universitet.

Ivarsson, Jan. 1992. *Subtitling for the Media. A Handbook of an Art.* Stockholm: TransEdit.

Ivarsson, Jan and Mary Carroll. 1998. *Subtitling.* Simrishamn: TransEdit.

Kagansky, Nina. 1995. *TITRA FILM. Une chronique cinématographique et familiale.* Paris: Titra Film.

Machado, José. 1993. *La traduction au cinéma et le processus de sous-titrage de films.* PhD thesis, Université de Paris III.

Letters patent at the Swedish Patent and Registration Office, Stockholm.

2

Screen Translation in Mainland China

Qian Shaochang

—ɯ—

Screen Translation Before 1949

Before 1949, mainland China had virtually no screen translation. There was no television. In certain cinemas in a few big cities audiences who did not know foreign languages might listen to simultaneous interpretation through earphones (ingeniously translated as *yi yi feng* 譯意風 in Chinese) attached to the seat. In old Shanghai, in my memory, only certain big cinemas, such as the Cathay (國泰), the Grand (大光明), the Majestic (美琪), and the Roxy (大華, now known as 新華), had simultaneous interpretation facilities. But listening to the simultaneous interpretation was far from being a pleasure, for it was usually poor and frequently interrupted. Personally, I preferred not using the earphones since I was able to understand the original dialogue, having been educated at St. Francis Xavier's College and St. John's University in the 1940s.

Dubbing versus Subtitling

Generally speaking, studios and television stations in China do not subtitle films. People sometimes watch subtitled Western films imported from Hong Kong, Taiwan or Singapore. But they prefer dubbed films to subtitled ones.

The primary reason for this is that most of the population is poor at foreign languages. A few years ago I conducted a little quiz in a class of ten graduate students specialising in English to test their level of listening comprehension. I asked them to translate into Chinese a short one-minute passage of dialogue chosen from the American television series *Falcon Crest*. I first explained to them the roles of the three main characters: Angie, Jason and Richard, and their interactions with each other. Then I played the videotape of the passage three times. The results indicated that their rate of comprehension ranged from 50 to 80 per cent. In mainland China, the postgraduate students of English at the Shanghai International Studies University are regarded by the public as being strong in English. Thus you can imagine the English level of the public in general. Before 1949, an English course was a requirement in most high schools. After 1949, especially after the Korean War that began in 1950, Russian took the place of English. When China and the Soviet Union became enemies in the early 1960s, no more foreign languages were taught in most schools. China gradually resumed English teaching after opening up to the outside world in 1978, but the listening and speaking abilities of most English-learners are poor for lack of practice.

Chinese people, including government leaders, are now increasingly aware of the importance of English, and a nationwide English-learning campaign is now going on. On 30 July 2001, *China Daily*, China's English language national newspaper, carried a report that describes China's English-learning craze:

> Tens of thousands of people across China – ranging from young kids to the mayor of Beijing and senior State leaders – have discovered new and very practical reasons for learning English. The catalyst was the decision made on 13 July by the International Olympic Committee (IOC) to award Beijing the right to host the 2008 Summer Olympic Games. Jiang Ming, a 7-year-old student at Wu Yi Primary School in Beijing, used to hate learning English. However, he gave his parents a pleasant surprise last week when he grabbed his Olympic English handbook and accompanying cassette tape from his bookshelf and sat down for an evening of hard work. His change of mind was apparently influenced by several boys and girls who recently appeared on Chinese TV saying they wanted to be good English speakers so they could serve as volunteers for the games....

Another reason for the popularity of dubbing is that subtitles divert the audience's attention since they have to read written text while watching the picture. In addition, since subtitles are condensed versions of the actual dialogue, they are not as vivid and entertaining as dubbing.

Then there is the literacy problem. China still has a considerable number of illiterates and semi-literates who cannot read subtitles, in addition to ethnic minorities living in Tibet, Inner Mongolia and the Xinjiang Uighur Autonomous Region, who have their own languages that are completely different from Chinese. The educated members of these minority peoples can now understand oral Chinese, but most of them still have difficulty in reading Chinese.

During the last decade, however, a number of studios and television stations began to provide subtitled Western pictures for those who know English and for English-learners. For example, a few years ago, Shanghai Television (STV) started airing subtitled pictures during its English News Service on STV Channel 2, now known as IBS (International Broadcasting Service).

Screen Translation Before 1978

In early 1949, the Changchun Film Studio in north-east China was the first to start film dubbing. The Changchun Film Studio, the biggest of its kind in north-east China, was actually set up by the Japanese army during its occupation of that area from 1931 to 1945. The reason that Changchun was number one in film dubbing was because north-east China was liberated by the People's Liberation Army in early November 1948 while the rest of China was still in the hands of the Guomindang (Zhang 1993). After 1949, Beijing and Shanghai also began to dub films. In 1950, the Shanghai Film Studio set up a dubbing department and dubbed its first film, which was a Russian film called *The Little Hero*. In 1957, the Dubbing Department was turned into an independent dubbing studio. It was the first and is so far the only independent film dubbing studio in mainland China (Wu 1999). The studio, which has its own translators as well as dubbing actors and actresses, dubs approximately three-quarters of all imported films, which is a quota fixed by a governmental institution called the China Film Distribution Company. The rest are dubbed by other film studios, mainly Changchun, Beijing, Bayi (Army), Emei (Sichuan), and Zhujiang (Guangdong).

However, for reasons known to all, prior to 1978 there was only a limited number of imported films, coming mainly from the former Soviet Union and other Eastern European countries. During the decade of the Cultural Revolution (1966–1976), the only foreign films people were allowed to watch were two Russian films: *Lenin in October* and *Lenin in 1918*. They were shown continuously and repeatedly in all cinemas around China.

Television stations began to appear in China in the 1950s. Beijing Television Station was the first one to come into being, on 1 May 1958, and was the predecessor of the present Central Television Station (CCTV), while Shanghai Television Station (STV) made its appearance on 1 October 1958 (Chen 2000). Later, a few other big cities began to have television stations, but there was no television translation before the 1980s, so television stations occasionally provided the audience with films dubbed by film studios. However, all stations had just two channels, one central and one local. I would like to explain in this connection that, unlike in the United States, where television viewers in every corner of the country can watch ABC, NBC, CBS and CNN, CCTV is the only national television network that enjoys nationwide coverage in China, and all local stations are affiliated to it. Local stations produced few programmes of their own. With most of their programmes coming from CCTV, local stations used to offer only local news and public affairs programmes. The audience was relatively small, as a television set was a big luxury for most families before 1978. For example, when STV came into being in 1958, the entire city of Shanghai had fewer than a hundred television sets (Sheng 1998).

Screen Translation After 1978

Since China opened up to the outside world in 1978, there has been a continuous boom in screen translation as a result of looser controls over the import of foreign films. There are, however, some restrictions. The China Film Distribution Company, which is China's sole film import and distribution institution, generally holds to the following principles in its import of foreign films:

- The company introduces only what it regards as good films.
- An overflow of foreign films is avoided.

- Films that contain violence, pornography or religious propagation are not imported.
- The company makes arrangements so that American films do not exceed 50 per cent of all imported films (Zhao 2000).

Although politics no longer plays such a tremendous role in the choice of foreign films as it did during the Cultural Revolution, it is still an important factor. Here, I would like to translate a passage of what Zhao Huayong, director of CCTV, said at a recent conference on film dubbing:

> American films must not exceed 50 per cent of all imported films. We should try to import more films from other countries to ensure a proper balance. Otherwise, problems may arise. There was a time when Sino-U.S. relations suddenly became strained. We had lots of trouble then. We could immediately stop broadcasting American news, but what could we do with American pictures? At that time our entertainment programmes were filled with American teleplays, and we didn't have enough pictures from other countries to fill the gap. That was a real problem. Finally we had to cancel the American pictures and replace them with poorer ones from other countries or rebroadcast those that had already been shown. Had we controlled the proportion of imported films, the situation would have been better. This is thus a problem of proportion. It is a lesson learned by CCTV. Local stations across the country can also learn from it. (Zhao 2000)

From 1957 to 1999, the Shanghai Film Dubbing Studio dubbed more than 1,000 feature films. At the same time, a large number of documentaries, cartoons and popular science fiction films were also dubbed. With attention being paid to the problem of proportion, films were imported from forty-eight countries. The foreign languages included English, Russian, French, German, Spanish, Italian, Indian, Arabic, Japanese, Korean, Albanian and Vietnamese. As the Studio does not have enough translators for all the above-mentioned languages, it often gets professional help from universities and other institutions. Besides dubbing foreign films into Chinese, the Studio also subtitles Chinese films into foreign languages. In fact, there is difficulty in finding actors and actresses who are able to speak a foreign language fluently enough to do the dubbing.

Nowadays, Chinese films that are exported or entered in international film festivals are always subtitled in English, but never dubbed. Many studios are now doing this subtitling job by themselves, but unfortunately, quite a few of them are actually doing shoddy work. This is one of the factors that affects the box office and sales of Chinese films in international markets (Xu 1998). As is known to all, the standard spoken Chinese language is putonghua, which has always been promoted throughout the country at all levels of government. Nevertheless, a considerable proportion of Chinese people, particularly the inhabitants of the southern provinces of Guangdong and Guangxi, do not have a good grasp of putonghua. So one of the tasks of the Shanghai Film Dubbing Studio is to translate films in putonghua into Cantonese. The population of China is made up of 56 nationalities, some with their own languages. The biggest groups are the Mongolians, Tibetans, Uighurs (of Xinjiang Uighur Autonomous Region) and Koreans. Thus, the Studio has the additional work of translating films in Chinese into Mongolian, Tibetan, Uighur and Korean (Wu 1999).

In 1995, the television coverage of mainland China was 84.8 per cent of its more than 1.2 billion population (Sun 1997), and the proportion has been rising steadily, making a viewing audience of colossal proportions. Most of the country's television dubbing has been done by CCTV 1 and STV. In 1980, not long after China opened up to the outside world, the International Department of CCTV began television dubbing (Zhao 2000). Immediately following CCTV, in 1981, STV also began television dubbing (Sheng 1998). CCTV has its own dubbing directors, dubbing actors, and translators. STV does not have translators of its own, but it gets regular professional help from a number of translators who work at universities or other institutions. The author, for example, is one of them. In the beginning, the number of dubbed pictures was limited, but it went up very quickly. CCTV dubbed only 200 episodes of television plays between 1980 and 1985, averaging less than one episode per week. But from 1985 to 1992 it provided the audience with 200–300 hours of newly dubbed television plays and films each year, reaching an average of 3–5 hours every week. Currently, the figure has risen to around eight hours per week (Zhao 2000). Dubbed teleplays and made-for-television films are broadcasted through five of the eight CCTV channels: namely, CCTV 1, CCTV 2,

CCTV 3, CCTV 6 and CCTV 8 (Sheng 1998). There was a good response to STV's dubbed films, so it was obliged to dub more and more imported movies. To deal with this new situation, STV formed an independent dubbing department in 1987. Over the past decade, it has dubbed 3,500 hours of television plays and films, an average of 6.7 hours per week (Sheng 1998).

Most of the imported films are average ones. Statistics show that in 1997, the Central and provincial television stations in China dubbed and aired some 2,000 hours of television plays and films, of which 66 per cent were soap operas, action films and sitcoms (Zhao 2000). Needless to say, Hollywood films were the mainstay. In that year, CCTV aired 177 newly dubbed television plays and films. (Here, one television series is regarded as one play.) Of these 177 works, 103 were American, comprising 58.75 per cent of the total. In 1998, 78 of the 147 dubbed television plays and films were from Hollywood. The percentage was thus still as high as 53 per cent (Zhao 2000). The rest of the imported pictures came mainly from Japan, South Korea, Russia, France, Germany, Italy, Britain, India, Mexico and Brazil.

In mainland China, the import of films is monopolised by the China Film Distribution Company, and the control over the introduction of television plays is not so strict. Seeing that CCTV and STV were becoming famous as a result of television dubbing, as well as deriving substantial profits from the commercials attached to those programmes, many local television stations began to turn their gaze towards the new realm. Beginning in the early 1990s, local stations, including stations at provincial and city levels, gradually found their own channels for importing television plays, and also started film dubbing. It is impossible for the author to present accurate statistics in this paper, because there are so many local stations and so many different ways of obtaining foreign films. Generally speaking, both the quality and quantity of their products are lower than those of CCTV and STV.

Box Offices and Ratings of Foreign Pictures

When the door of mainland China was suddenly opened to the outside world in 1978, its people, after almost three decades of isolationism and asceticism, were surprised to find such a colourful world outside. Everything they saw in foreign pictures was new and fun. As a result, the box offices and ratings were naturally very high at the beginning.

The box offices of big Hollywood films such as *Jurassic Park, Saving Private Ryan, Titanic* and *Gladiator* were incomparable. Because of the huge costs and highly advanced technology used in shooting these movies, they have always been able to attract large audiences, and their box offices remain very high even now. Take, for example, the latest blockbuster, *Pearl Harbour*. When the film had its premiere at the Shanghai Film Art Centre on 8 August 2001, the theatre enjoyed three consecutive days of a full house and the box office hit the theatre's record high of 600,000 yuan (US$72,000). Its top ticket price was 100 yuan (US$12), which was fairly high for local consumers (Qian 2001).

But the situation with the ratings of foreign television plays is different. Again, I would like to choose as an example the situation in Shanghai with which I am more familiar. Compared with the number of television viewers, that of cinema-goers is very small. All middle-aged and elderly Shanghainese have a vivid memory of what happened in 1981, when Shanghai Television Station showed in prime time the Japanese television series *Sugata Sansilo* (姿三四郎), the first foreign television play aired in Shanghai's history. Although it was a mediocre television series about judo, a Japanese martial art, it created an inconceivable sensation. The entire city nearly went mad. Cinemas and other entertainment centres were almost empty. Shanghai's main shopping street, Nanjing Road, which is usually bustling and packed with shoppers and pedestrians, was all of a sudden silent and deserted. Everybody was watching *Sugata Sansilo*. People either flocked to the houses of those families who owned television sets or swarmed in front of television screens in shop windows. Ironically, the police reported that there were far fewer cases of pick-pocketing and burglary on those days when the play was on. There were no ratings of this television series, simply because China did not know how to calculate ratings at that time. But if there had been ratings, my guess is that they must have been above 90 per cent. A few years later, Hollywood programmes arrived.

American soap operas, sitcoms and action films that began to appear on Shanghai's television screens in the late 1980s also attracted a large audience. Programmes like *Falcon Crest, Hunter, Hotel*

and *Growing Pains* all enjoyed ratings above thirty per cent. However, the ratings of dubbed television plays have been falling since the mid-1990s. At present, very few foreign television plays achieve a rating higher than five per cent. The following factors may account for the fall:

- Chinese audiences have gradually lost their curiosity about foreign pictures, which used to be their only channel to the outside world. Now people read foreign magazines, buy foreign commodities, and travel abroad.
- Foreign pictures are no longer rare. With the rapid increase in the number of imported television plays and made-for-television films, Chinese television viewers now have a much greater variety of shows to choose from. The case is different with foreign motion pictures, the number of imports of which is still limited to around 40 annually.
- There are now many other forms of recreation besides watching television, which used to be almost the only form of entertainment in the past.
- As the Chinese audience develop a greater knowledge of movies, they have become selective about the films they see.
- Generally, there has been a gradual fall in the quality of imported pictures.
- To protect the domestic television industry, the government has ordered that no imported pictures should be shown during prime time (7:00 to 9:30 pm).

A few months ago, Shanghai's governmental administration in charge of film and television decided to merge the Dubbing Department of STV with the Shanghai Film Dubbing Studio. By August 2001, however, this merger had still not taken place.

References

"Bidding spurs English fever." *China Daily.* July 30, 2001.

Chen Zhi'an 陳志昂. 2000.《中國電影藝術通史》(Chinese Film Arts Almanac). Beijing: China Joint Literary Publishing House.

Sheng, Chongqing 盛重慶. 1998.《輝煌與奮進》(Flourishing and Boldly Advancing). Shanghai: Shanghai People's Publishing House.

Staff Reporter. 2001.《《珍珠港》首映三天，影院票房已破紀錄》(*Pearl Harbour*

Breaks Box Office Records in its First Three Days).《上海新聞午報》
   (Shanghai Evening News) August 12.
Sun, Jiazheng 孫家正. 1997.《中國廣播電視電影大事記》(Major Events in
   Chinese Film and Television). Beijing: China Broadcast and Television
   Publishing House.
Wu, Yigong 吳貽弓. 1999.《上海電影志》(Shanghai Film Annals). Shanghai:
   Shanghai Social Sciences Publishing House.
Xu, Zuosheng 徐作生. 1998.〈譯語牛頭不對馬嘴，觀眾如墜雲裏霧中〉.《文匯
   報》(Wenhui Bao), July 7, Shanghai.
Zhang, Junxiang 張駿祥. 1993.《中國電影大辭典》(The Larger Dictionary of
   Chinese Film). Shanghai: Shanghai Dictionary Publishing House.
Zhao, Huayong 趙化勇. 2000.《譯製片探討與研究》(Studies and Research in
   Film Translation). Beijing: China Broadcast and Television Publishing
   House.

3

Subtitling in Japan

Karima Fumitoshi

—⚏—

I am very honoured to have the opportunity to give you a brief history of subtitling in Japan. I teach the history of Chinese cinema and contemporary Chinese culture in Tokyo, and ever since my university days, I have been editing Japanese subtitles for Chinese films.

In the last century, a large number of foreign films that needed translation were imported into Japan every year. These films were mainly from America with only a small portion being from Europe. Chinese movies started to enter Japan at the end of the 1970s with the end of the Cultural Revolution. Since then there has been a Chinese film festival every year, which showed some seven or eight films from China. At that time there was nobody specialising in Chinese films. Although I was just a student at the time, I was called upon to do the subtitles for these films. The first Chinese film I subtitled was *From Slave to General* 《從奴隸到將軍》, and the last film was Jiang Wen's *Devils on the Doorstep* 《鬼子來了》. Over the next two decades, I translated about 50–60 Chinese films.

I did not have the opportunity to study in China, so basically my knowledge of Chinese came from translating Chinese films. Fortunately, when I started my work as a translator and subtitler, the techniques of subtitling in Japanese had been well established. My apprenticeship was with a Japanese subtitler who was an expert in translating French films. At that time over 200 films had to be translated for the Japanese audience, but there were only ten subtitlers, and among them, only five or six could be called experts. Although there were only a few experts, I was fortunate enough to be able to learn from them. Basically, much of what I am talking about comes from my own experience, but I also include the thoughts of expert subtitler Shimizu Shunzi, who published an invaluable memoir called *50 Years of Film Translation* in 1985.

The first foreign film subtitled in Japan was probably *Morocco*, directed by Josef von Sternberg and released in 1931. During the silent era, films shown in Japan would be narrated by a translator, or *benshi*. Most probably, the Japanese were adopting the storyteller tradition, and the Japanese audience relied on the narration of the *benshi* in order to understand the film. Of course, when the talkies arrived in the 1930s, there was a crisis in the *benshi* profession.

In 1932, the manager of Paramount Pictures in Japan decided that films should be subtitled. A few technicians were sent to New York to learn the techniques of subtitling. Already the old controversy had arisen about which was better, subtitling or dubbing. The result was that both were done in New York — they would do a subtitled version as well as a dubbed version. But the people who were employed to do the dubbing were Japanese expatriates living in New York, and as most of these people spoke a dialect of Japanese, the dubbing was a complete failure. As a result, all foreign films shown in the cinema at the time were subtitled. It was very important for the first generation of subtitlers to serve their apprenticeship in New York. People like Shimizu Shunzi, whom I mentioned earlier, had studied all the craft and techniques of subtitling in New York for three years, and he became very familiar with popular culture art forms like operas and musicals.

I do not know what the situation was in Hong Kong or China in the 1930s, but subtitling actually solved the problems of communication between the film and its audience, in addition to making the profession of *benshi* redundant. At that time, the role of subtitler was not as prestigious as it is now because the job came under the jurisdiction of the Promotion and Publicity Department, which was not highly regarded. Shimizu Shunzi, besides being an excellent subtitler, was a key figure in introducing American culture and commercial films to the Japanese audience. The golden age of subtitling in Japan could be said to have been in the 1950s and 60s. But even during that period, there were only five or six subtitlers doing all the subtitling. The total number of films subtitled by Shimizu amounted to over 1,500. Doubtless, he raised the standard of subtitling and translation in Japan and for this, he was given an award by the Japanese government. I mention him in particular because the general public had never appropriately acknowledged the importance of this profession. In Japan, subtitling was regarded as a small part of the distribution process.

Thanks to the hard work and the presence of these experts, by the time I started subtitling in the 1970s, all the groundwork had been laid. I will not go into the technical details owing to time limitations. However, whenever I see foreign films subtitled in China, Hong Kong, or Taiwan, I notice that the subtitling is not well done. There are many problems: for example, those related to timing. I am interested in learning how subtitling and dubbing are done in these places, since Japan has fine-tuned its subtitling techniques and everything is done according to established rules and procedures. Shimizu has a very well known saying: "Film subtitling is not translation." When translating an article or essay, we have to make clear five points: when, where, whom, what and why. With screen translation, everything relies on image and sound, and if the audience does not know the language, the dialogue is simply a part of the overall sound. The chief function of the subtitler, therefore, is to make the dialogue correspond to the intention of the director. In this way, subtitling may be regarded as part of the work of scriptwriting.

There is one advantage in Japanese subtitling: we can make full use of *kanji* or Chinese characters, which enable us to express the maximum amount of meaning in the least amount of space. However, as some Japanese do not know how to pronounce *kanji*, the shape of the character conveys an image rather than a sound. For me, the ideal result of a Japanese audience watching a Chinese film subtitled in Japanese is that they have the same kind of emotional response as their Chinese counterparts. This is the goal I have been striving to achieve.

[The paper was delivered in Chinese with consecutive interpretation by Mr. Shu Kei.]

4

The History of Subtitling in Korea

Lee Young Koo

—〰—

Introduction

In 1903, the first film in Korean history was shown to the Korean Emperor Gojong by Burton Holmes, an American who brought his own video camera and projector with him to Korea. Later, two more Americans began to show movies in the front courtyard of Hansung Electric Corporation near *Tongdaemun*, or the East Gate, charging viewers admission, making movie-going a kind of public entertainment. This was the beginning of the hundred-year-old history of the Korean film industry.

Korean films have gone through several phases of development.

At first, most film-makers were keen to make filmed versions of stage plays. In an attempt to rejuvenate the declining drama industry, Kim Do San produced the first Korean kinodrama[1] , *Uirijok Gutu (The Righteous Revenge)*, in 1919, marking the beginning of the Korean silent film era.

In 1927, a total of 14 silent movies were made and this was the first flowering of the film industry in Korea. *Arirang*, a film depicting nationalistic feelings under Japanese rule, was an important milestone in Korean movie history. In the 1930s, the Korean film industry was in the doldrums owing to strict Japanese censorship. Nevertheless, a number of directors produced some "enlightenment films" to boost national self-esteem and to give a sense of self-strengthening. In 1935, talkies appeared in Korean cinemas. During the silent film era, sound came from film commentators called *benshi* (辯士). Instead of sticking to the original script, the commentators used to amuse viewers with their own wit and humour, and very often became the pivotal factor in the success of a film.

The 1940s marked the height of repressive Japanese colonial rule and film-making was put under strict control. Investigations were conducted into anyone who did not cooperate with the Japanese colonial rule and its policy in Korea, or *nae seon il che* (內鮮一體), as it was called. It was stipulated that prior approval must be obtained for any film production, distribution or even film-related recruitment. Those were the darkest days in Korean movie history.

In 1945, Korea was liberated and the film industry prospered once again. Stories about martyrs and anti-Japanese heroes were a common theme of many films at that time. But the boom was short-lived. With the outbreak of the Korean War in 1950, Korea suffered serious social, economic and cultural setbacks. The film industry was no exception. Although a truce was signed in 1953, film-makers were in no state to produce anything. Hardly any films were made during the next three years owing to the damage to equipment, the deficiency of supplies, and the loss of film stock during wartime. On top of this, films of this period focused principally on military themes, and were more like documentaries than actual movies.

In the 1970s, the focus on youth in Korean films and the new wave of commercialism struck a severe blow at movie standards. Worse still, owing to some problems in the implementation of the laws related to movie-making, film-makers gradually turned their efforts to importing foreign films rather than producing their own. In the late 1980s, Hong Kong films were well received by Korean audiences, resulting in a substantial increase in imported Hong Kong films, which in turn endangered the survival of the home-grown variety.

In the early 1990s, the importation of films directly distributed by foreign motion picture companies met with fierce resistance by the local film industry. These foreign films were boycotted in urban areas and could only be shown in rural areas and small towns. The meagre business was far from profitable. However, with the successes of *Rain Man* 《雨人》 (or 《手足情未了》 in Hong Kong) and *Indiana Jones and the Last Crusade* 《聖戰奇兵》, both with a record high of over 350,000 viewers, films distributed directly by UIP were gradually accepted by the public and attracted stable revenues at the box office.

In December 1990, *Ghost* 《人鬼情未了》 was shown in urban cinemas and the song *Unchained Melody* became a chart hit. This film attracted four million viewers in Korea (1.69 million in Seoul alone) in 1991, easily breaking the box office record of Jackie Chan's *Drunken Master* 《醉拳》 (1979). Foreign films had finally staged a soft landing on the Korean film market. The formula for the success of *Ghost* is a moving love story plus special effects, a classic example of an entertainment film. One can speculate from its brilliance at the box office that local films were not entertaining enough and that local film-makers would now finally be able to grasp the taste of the audiences, who preferred Hollywood films.

From the second half of 1994 onwards, the Korean film industry began to take stock of its future path for survival and development before entering the new millennium.

Film Translation

Korean films with subtitles in foreign languages

Korea started to export films worldwide in 1972, and began participating in foreign film festivals at the beginning of the 1980s. Since then, there has been a growing need for foreign language subtitles. The trade started to boom in the mid-1980s and the export of Korean films to overseas markets gathered momentum from the 1990s onwards.

In 1992, a Korean film festival was held in Pesaro, Italy and 46 films were shown there. In 1993, a foreign film showcase was held at the Pompidou Centre in Paris, at which 80 Korean films were presented with French subtitles. In 1999, a total of 72 Korean films were shown at such film festivals as the Berlin International Film Festival (Germany), Cannes Film Festival (France), San Sebastian International Film Festival (Spain), Venice International Film Festival (Italy), and the Hong Kong International Film Festival. Korean film exports have been growing over the past two or three years.

Foreign films with Korean subtitles

From the 1960s, foreign films started to be shown on television. In the 1970s, Kim Sun Ho (金順浩) became a well known name in the Korean subtitling industry.

There were 74 foreign films imported in 1972, 483 in 1996, and the number has been rising steadily. In 1988, CIC started to distribute films directly, resulting in a new demand for videotape subtitling. The era of cable television commenced in 1990, further boosting the demand for foreign film subtitling.

In the past, the copyright on the cinema and videotape versions of a film belonged to different companies; thus different subtitles had to be used for different versions, but this is no longer the case. Three or four years ago, an amendment was made to the copyright law, giving the copyright on all versions of a film to the same company. Since then, 70 to 80 per cent of all films shown in Korea use the same set of subtitles for both the cinema and video versions.

Other Kinds of Screen Translation

Korean into subtitles in foreign languages

In 1995, Arirang Television Broadcasting Company commenced operations, marking a new era of Korean television programmes being subtitled in foreign languages. Recently, more and more Korean series are being exported to China and the Southeast Asian region. However, dubbing scripts are translated in the region where the film is marketed.

Dubbing foreign languages into Korean

In the 1980s, *Little House on the Prairie* was translated into Korean by Min Byeing Suk (閔丙淑) and was dubbed into Korean before being shown on television. Twenty years ago, Chinese films could not be legally imported, and translation was restricted to those few illegal imports. Once the ban was officially lifted, translation work increased substantially.

Before the economic turmoil, a veteran translator, Lee Deok Ok (李德玉), had to translate three to four series (10 to 20 videotapes) a month. With the development of the Internet and the financial crisis in 1997, the demand for subtitle translation fell drastically.

Problems in Translating Subtitles

Unlike books or other printed materials that are delivered purely through words, films are formed by images (through sight and sound) and story. This special feature makes films unique among other art forms.

To convey messages in sound, language is the most important medium. It not only serves as a bridge between films and the real world, but also brings the audience closer to the characters that inhabit the story. It also enables the audience to "listen" to the story from an objective point of view.

However, the social functions of language also give rise to many limitations. Since every language system used by a particular nation or people has its own special characteristics which express the specific feelings of that nation or people, we cannot always find a one-to-one correspondence between two languages. Sometimes, a word in one language is not translatable into another because the meaning represented will not be perceived in the same way by other nations. As a result, every language has certain areas which others cannot share, and this area becomes a gap that cannot be filled through translation.

It is often said that when Shakespeare's work is translated, 90 per cent of its original flavour is lost. To ensure good subtitle translation, we should first fully understand the personality and image of each figure, and have a comprehensive view of the entire story. Then we should try to find the most natural target-language equivalents that best fit the context.

Now let us look into the issues that arise when translating from and into Korean.

Translating film titles

As most films are made for commercial purposes, their titles somehow need to be attractive to the potential audience. Therefore, the first stage of film title translation is a meaning distortion process. In this stage, most problems occur when translations are done rigidly word for word, or even sound for sound. In Korea, most of the titles of English language films are translated using the latter method. For instance, the title word of the film *Stepmom*《繼母》(《後備媽咪》(港)；

《親親小媽》(台)) (1998) was translated into a meaningless Korean word pronounced *Sta-pu-man*; *Voodoo* 《巫毒娃娃》 (1995) was translated the same way, and became *Fu-du*; *What Lies Beneath*《危機四伏》 (2000) turned into *Wa-lais Be-nis*, while *A Better Way to Die*《獵殺標靶》 (2000) became *Bei-ta wei tu-dai*.[2]

To begin with, *Stepmom* could have been translated into an equivalent Korean kinship term. However, most Korean people tend to hold negative feelings towards stepmothers, and this term would have had a negative connotation. Therefore, it was translated by sound. But in fact, the aim of this film is to tell a story about "another kind of mother," rather than a stereotypical stepmother, and so the title could have been translated into the Korean equivalents of "my other mother" or "my second mother," instead of "stepmother."

Take *Voodoo* as another example. This term, indicating a polytheism originating with the black people of the West Indies, is generally referred to as "black illusions" or "evil power" in Korea. The film title was translated into Korean by sound, and the result sounds very similar to *boodoo*, the same sound as a Korean word for *wharf*. This title may cause Koreans to mistake the film for a story about ships or fishermen. A competent translator should pay attention to both Korean customs and the likelihood of homonyms.

A concise term is more powerful as a title than a long sentence

The Korean titles for *What Lies Beneath* and *A Better Way to Die* are again translations by sound and do not give the audience the slightest hint about the content of the films. They could have been better translated using a meaning-based approach that takes into account the whole story. Of course, a confusing and misleading title may attract some members of the audience, but it may also be a major reason for losing them.

Translations of Chinese film titles can be very confusing. As many Korean words are borrowed from Chinese, certain Chinese characters are not considered "foreign words" and are thus preserved during translation. For example, *Comrades, Almost A Love Story*《甜蜜蜜》 (1996) is about a tender love affair. The Korean title 《陳蜜兒蜜兒》 was a direct adaptation of the Chinese title, since these characters also exist in Korean. However, the meaning of these words in Korean has nothing to do with sweetness or love. The Chinese title of the film

The King of Masks (1997) is 《變臉》, meaning "changing face."[3] The Korean title 《別安哥安姆》 is simply a transliteration of the English title. Since the Chinese character 臉 (meaning *face*) sounds similar to the character 劍 (meaning *sword*) in Korean, many viewers mistook it for a Chinese martial arts movie. This is another example of the negative effect of translating Chinese characters into Korean.

Good film titles are usually translated with various degrees of meaning distortion. Some are chosen with reference to the plot, while other films are named after considering the culture, taste, and customs of the target society.

The Russian film *The Barber of Siberia* (1999) is another good example. The title has three different meanings in the story. First, the term the Barber of Siberia refers to a logging machine invented by Jane's (the main character's) father to cut down Siberian forests. He asks Jane to come to Moscow to provide him with financial support, and while there, Jane falls in love with a military cadet. Second, the pronunciation of Siberia is similar to that of Seville in Mozart's *The Barber of Seville*. This analogy relates the two stories in a subtle way. Third, the phrase "The Barber of Siberia" also refers to Tolstoy, Jane's lover, who was dismissed by the military school and exiled to Siberia and later became a barber. In short, the Barber of Siberia can be interpreted in three different ways, indicating three aspects of the main character's life which can be understood when watching the film in detail. In the Korean version, the word "love" (*The Love of Siberia*) was used instead of the word "barber," in order to convey a more sentimental flavour to the Korean audience. The French film *Le Mari de la Coiffeuse* (*The Hairdresser's Husband*) (1990) is a similar case. If the title had been translated directly into Korean, the audience might have taken it to be an obscene adult movie. It was therefore translated as *Love, Just Like Them*, which is regarded as a successful translation.

With respect to Chinese films, *Lifetimes* 《活著》 (1993) was translated into the Korean equivalent of "life"; *Not One Less* 《一個都不能少》 (1999) was translated as *Fairy Tales in the Bookcase* 《書櫃裡的童話》. Both titles are successful in fully bringing out the content of the film.

Lifetimes describes how a wealthy Chinese landlord becomes an ordinary civilian during the turmoil of the late Qing dynasty. The title succinctly reveals the theme of the story. It is thus appropriate to adopt a meaning-based approach to translate the original title, which means "being alive." However, there is no single word or phrase that corresponds with "being alive" in Korean. A lengthy compound sentence was thus needed. In comparison, a simple word meaning "life" is a better choice because it is concise and clear. *Not One Less* was not translated by meaning either, since it would sound too serious in Korean. Words like "bookcase" and "fairytales" relate to childhood and convey a sense of innocence, and are hence an excellent choice.

Conclusion

Subtitle translation entered its boom period in Korea in the 1960s. The materials being translated varied from films to television programmes, videos, animations, documentaries, corporate training videos, and enterprise campaigns. The emergence of cable television further expanded the scope of this industry.

In addition to other requirements, subtitle translation has to take space and time constraints into consideration. The "six-second principle" is widely followed in subtitle translation in many countries. In Korea, there is no formal rule concerning the number of words. However, translators tend to keep to no more than thirteen words per line (excluding spaces[4]), and to no more than two lines per frame. As Korean scripts are usually longer than those in other languages, translators need to make an extra effort to shorten sentences by eliminating unnecessary words.

Despite efforts to conform to the rules, there are still many mistakes to be found in Korean subtitle translation. These mistakes can be categorised into three patterns: (1) the translator did not fully understand the meaning of the original context; (2) the translator made the mistake deliberately in order to match the customs of the target culture and (3) the translator translated too freely.

Korean culture and lifestyle are different from those of other countries and the things that arouse the emotions of the people are different. Jokes that make foreigners split their sides may not seem at all funny to Koreans. If the translated subtitles are unlikely to arouse any feelings in the target audience, we have to make some adaptations, because the Korean sense of humour can only be understood in the Korean way.

Good subtitle translation requires an in-depth knowledge of the target culture and seasoned skill in using the target language in a natural way. It is therefore of vital importance to have professional translators trained to do such a demanding job.

Notes

1. Kinodrama is a play in which actors perform against a filmed backdrop.
2. A Chinese character indicates meaning, but a Korean or Japanese character represents a sound only. One cannot determine its meaning from its appearance. Therefore, if you use Korean characters to express the English pronunciation of the title, people who do not understand the characters will be completely baffled.
3. The Korean pronunciation of "甜蜜蜜" is "陳蜜兒蜜兒", and that of "變臉" is "別安哥安姆". The pronunciations of "臉" and "劍" are the same in Korean.
4. There should be a space between two words in a Korean sentence.

Theoretical Issues

5

The Two Worlds of Subtitling: The Case of Vulgarisms and Sexually-oriented Language

Gilbert C. F. Fong

—ɯɯ—

Some critics and theorists consider subtitling to be "highly defective translation" (Nedergaard-Larsen 1993: 207). Many insist that subtitles violate the picture on the screen (Gottlieb 1997: 52) to "create a visual static by interfering with the picture," and "intrude upon the film like a boorish uninvited guest" (Lundeen 1999: 3). Others prefer to label subtitling "language transfer," even advocating its banishment from the domain of translation proper (Delabastita 1989: 213–215).

To many cinema-goers who suffer from linguistic insularity, subtitles are a necessary evil. The dislike is especially strong in English-speaking countries such as the U.S. and Britain, where the dominance of the English language and Hollywood films has given birth to a kind of xenophobia that spurns all things unintelligible to a speaker of the English tongue. ("Put simply, American film audiences *hate* subtitles. They loathe them. They would rather not see a four-star motion picture than put up with having to read what people not speaking English are saying" [Berardinelli 1996: 1].) The usual complaints are: "I don't like reading at the movies" or "I spend so much time reading that I never get a chance to look at the visual elements" (Berardinelli 1996: 1). The implication, besides the well known cyber generation's aversion to anything textual, is that films are for "looking," and "reading" just doesn't hit the mark. If some of us are still under the illusion that subtitles are part of a film, then we have a lot of convincing to do to persuade film audiences in the English-speaking world to change their minds.

J. C. Catford asserts that translation between media is impossible: "one cannot 'translate' from the *spoken* to the *written* form of a text or vice-versa."

> The substantial features relevant to a phonological unit or item are sounds produced in a human vocal tract. The substantial features relevant to a graphological unit or item are visible marks on paper, stone ... etc. Phonic and graphic substance are *absolutely different*; therefore there can be no question of a phonological item being relatable to the same substantial features as a graphological item. (Catford 1965: 53)

Taking into consideration Catford's insistence upon "equivalence" and "replacement" between "textual materials" (Catford 1965: 20), all translations tend to be defective in one way or another even under optimal conditions. In the final analysis, any investigation into the possibility or impossibility of translation really hinges on definition. For our purposes, Catford's argument is relevant, as it evidently points to the separateness and even latent incompatibility between dialogue (phonological) and subtitle (graphological), each having its own *modus operandi* and occupying a different communication channel.

In 1984, Raphael Nir (1984: 84) already referred to subtitling as a "double conversion": from one language to another and from one medium to another. A more cogent analysis of the subtitling process is found in Henrik Gottlieb's idea of "diagonal translation." He points out that interlingual subtitling, "being *two-dimensional*, 'jaywalks' (crosses over) from source-language speech to target-language writing" (Gottlieb 1994: 104). And the subtitler has to face both the challenges presented by the switch from one subcode to another and the difficulties of retaining speech characteristics in a written text, especially those in spontaneous speech, such as pauses, false starts, interruptions, ungrammaticalities, and idiolectal, dialectal and sociolectal features (105–106).

Subtitles are graphically extrinsic to the visual track, something that has been tagged on at the bottom of the picture. This extra track activates what linguists describe as "endophony"—internal speech or the soundless mental reading of words (Shocat and Stam 1985: 41). The recalling of the signifier in this process may be exploited, especially for comic effect. In *Annie Hall* (1977), director Woody Allen uses subtitles to reveal the characters' repressed thoughts in an attempt to subvert the spoken dialogue, so that the illocutionary force and the real intentions can be visualised behind the facade of social pleasantries. For instance, when Annie says, "I would like to take a serious photography course," the subtitle reads, "He probably thinks I'm a yo-yo." And when Alfie responds with: "Photography is interesting because, you know, it's a new art form and a set of aesthetic criteria has not emerged yet," the subtitle reveals his hidden desire: "I wonder what she looks like naked" (quoted in Lundeen 1999: 2). This is an extreme case of manipulation, and the subtitles are not even translations per se, but it demonstrates that subtitles *can* be made to deviate from the message communicated by the dialogue. (In representing the suppressed thoughts of the characters, the subtitles are "faithful translations"; in fact, more faithful than what is being heard on the audio track.)

The subtitles in the above examples are supplements, in the sense that they supply information unavailable from the phonetic signifier (dialogue). In poststructuralist logic, supplementarity carries with it the paradoxical qualities of lack and overabundance. Subtitles fill in the information lack, and at the same time supply information already available in the dialogue. In both cases, they point to the underlying insulation between dialogue and subtitle. And if we say that subtitling involves "double conversion" or "diagonal translation" in the encoding process, then the audience would have to be, in a similar fashion, engaged in "double" or "diagonal" decoding in their attempt to comprehend the message in the subtitles. This is a cross-medium endeavour that some may find a strain. It involves not only the behavioural aspects of eye movements and timing, but also conditioning, the acceptance of subtitles as part and parcel of the experience of foreign movie viewing.

With interlingual subtitling, which occurs much more frequently than the intralingual variety, there is the additional issue of cultural construction. Subtitles are linguistic signs, and as such they are capable of generating signifieds as meaning and mental picture. According to Benjamin Whorf,

[E]very language is a vast pattern system, different from others, in which are culturally ordained the forms and categories by which the personality not only communicates, but also analyses nature, notices or neglects types of relationship and phenomena, channels his reasoning, and builds the house of his consciousness. (Whorf 1956: 252)

Thus, by extension, language is culture and culture is language. Contemporary linguists do not entirely agree with Sapir-Whorf's linguistic determinism, which claims that language determines thought, or that reality is but an effect of linguistic convention. There is nonetheless validity in a less ambitious observation, which states that language has some influence on memory recall and perception (Lyons 1981: 305), or on what Whorf refers to as "reasoning" and "consciousness" building. Translation necessarily transforms the source-language signifier so that it portrays a different world through a different signifier, the target language, itself representing another set of discursive relations and another construction of reality that portrays a different world. Gottlieb puts this in a more pragmatic fashion:

All human languages express nothing but their own culture: different languages have different semantic fields and different usage-governed rules for collocation and cohesion between elements. And not only do languages differ in terms of what *can* be said; they also differ in terms of what is *likely* to be said in specific situations. (Gottlieb 1993: 264–265)

Subtitling forces upon the audience an awareness of the coexistence of the original and the translated worlds. As an "overt type of translation" (Gottlieb 1997: 108), it reminds the member of the audience that he is experiencing double—he is seeing a film and reading about it at the same time.

At this point, the question may be asked: Why is it that we are not disturbed by such dualism when watching films? Nor by the schism between the source and target languages? The answer to this question says a lot about the skill of the subtitle translator, but the more important factor is the human mind, which has a predilection towards synthesising, and generating meaning. We all have the desire to find solutions in the face of problems, to seek order out of chaos, and to make sense of what we perceive. The disturbance we feel with our awareness of the differences in a subtitled film, in terms of the verbal and the written modes of presentation, the two languages and what they represent, etc., becomes secondary, weighed down by the desire for meaning and enjoyment, as subtitles are seen as being prerequisite to the foreign film experience.

This is some comfort to the subtitle translator, but he still has to face the problem of negotiating the differences between the two worlds. The decision has to be made as to whether to preserve and transpose the foreign culture in a film or to jettison its exoticism for the sake of creating a feeling of familiarity and intimacy for the local audience. Birgit Nedergaard-Larsen has put forward six strategies for handling culture-bound problems in subtitling: transfer/loan, direct translation, explicitation, paraphrase, adaptation to target language-culture, and omission (Nedgergaard-Larsen 1993: 219). For our purposes, which are less concerned with linguistic translation than with cultural transfer in a holistic sense, we can identify three approaches—foreignisation, neutralisation and naturalisation. Foreignisation is source culture-oriented. It identifies itself with the source language world of the movie, and strives to preserve all the cultural manifestations seen in institutions, personal relations, social customs, etc. At times, even linguistic and extralinguistic features are also represented. Through the subtitles, the audience make an effort to acculturate themselves and to allow themselves to become immersed in the world of the film. Naturalisation, on the other hand, is done for the purpose of localisation. Language is domesticated and familiarised; things and customs that are outlandish are replaced, their places taken by indigenous equivalents. The target-oriented effort is not so much cleansing out the foreign as approximating the local and the familiar for easier consumption. Neutralisation tends to take away any vestige of an identifiable cultural community. In cases of cultural specificity, it resorts to explanation rather than replacement. The language of subtitles may also be indifferent. Neutralisation involves the audience—it becomes self-motivated and voluntary, and plays a more active role in reinforcing the illusion of unity and sameness. In the process, members of an audience may choose to assimilate with the film world, thus temporarily giving up their cultural identity, or identify with their own culture.

For the subtitle translator, the choice is among whether to take the audience to the film, bring the film to the audience, or let the audience go there by themselves. Here, we have to make a few modifications. First, the three approaches may coexist within a film; in fact, more often than not, this is the case. The foreignisation/neutralisation combination is most frequently used; naturalisation emerges in certain situations, such as for comic effect or for characterisation purposes. It would be better to visualise the three approaches as making up a spectrum, with foreignisation and naturalisation occupying the two ends and with neutralisation in the centre. In any film, the pendulum swings back and forth depending on the mood in a particular scene, the preference of the translator, the codability of the linguistic and cultural items, and the availability of local substitutes. Second, the selection of the approach is governed by norms. It varies with the genre, the ascendancy of local culture, censorship, political issues, patronage and marketing concerns. (We will come back to this point later.) Third, naturalisation in subtitles can never be total, and foreignness cannot be fully exorcised. The reason for this is obvious—the film as the embodiment of foreign culture is the focus of attention and is present at all times. Subtitles can never exceed their role as a supplement; even though there may be a tendency towards over-abundance in the form of add-on localising messages, they cannot completely displace the original dialogue and what is represented by the world of the film. In the case of naturalisation, the audience is made aware of the coexistence and contestation between the two worlds.

Let us now take a look at a recent phenomenon in foreign film subtitling in Hong Kong as an example. Hong Kong is a cosmopolitan city and its citizens have long been exposed to Western culture and customs since it became a British colony in 1841. Most people are functionally literate in both Chinese and English. To many of them, subtitles are supplements to the information they already get from listening to the dialogue. (In fact, the favourite game of many audience members is to catch the mistakes made by subtitle translators on the television or cinema screen.) With their Western background, they can easily make the leap over the hurdle of culture shock, and they would not feel alienated in any encounter with foreignised subtitles. The practice of subtitling was first introduced after the war; since then most of the subtitles in Hong Kong have adopted the foreignisation–neutralisation approach. Starting in the late 1980s, local Cantonese words and expressions began to appear in film subtitles. Most of these are a mixture of Cantonese and Standard Chinese, but there are a few that use Cantonese consistently throughout the entire film.

Lo Wai Yan has done an interesting survey on the attitude of the Hong Kong audience towards the use of Cantonese in subtitles (Lo 2001: 126). The survey was done on the Internet with 413 respondents. Predictably, 68 per cent did not object to Cantonese subtitles, but when they were asked to choose between Cantonese and Standard Chinese subtitles, over 50 per cent indicated that the latter gave them more enjoyment, even though the former were more familiar and intimate. (28.1 per cent offered no opinion.) Only 32.1 per cent of the respondents agreed with the statement: "Since movie dialogue is verbal, it is appropriate to translate it into Cantonese, which is also a verbal language." The reason given for this low percentage is that Cantonese subtitles have to be read out loud to be understood:

> As subtitles, I do not like Cantonese. It will block me to understand the movies. I have to read them in my mind so that I can understand them. But for written Chinese, I will understand the meaning just by seeing the words. (Original quotation in English; Lo 2001: 139)

Standard Chinese, which has fewer identifiable regional features, is the national language; it is also the language taught at schools. In comparison, Cantonese occupies a relatively low status, as it has been perceived merely as a spoken language and has never been used consistently in literature or official documents. Some Cantonese sounds have no corresponding written forms. The result of the survey is not surprising, as some people are still not used to seeing Cantonese in a written form, even though its use in newspapers and other print media is becoming more widespread.

As a language, Cantonese is characterised by its liveliness, energy, and tolerance of foreign influences. It is also known for the variety and colour of its repertoire of vulgarisms and swear words (the so-called "three-character classics"). The use of these is widespread, being especially prevalent among the lower classes: one can hear them on public transport and during mobile telephone conversations on the street. (To many people this is a constant reminder that they are in Hong Kong.) Foul language is an outlet for frustration or pent-up emotion; it can also serve the function of identifying a social group and expressing solidarity (Crystal 1978: 61). Many Cantonese vulgarisms are Hong Kong-specific, and the puns and metaphors are only understandable by the locals. With the proliferation of newspaper supplements (many featuring a special men's section) and other media such as VCDs, tabloids, and sleaze magazines, a special lingo of sexually-oriented language has been developed, which is suggestive and humorous, but not offensive enough to be banned or prosecuted under the law. There is no denying that many people find the new sexual expressions perversely delightful while also frowning at their excesses. Many of the vulgarisms and sexual doublespeak have found their way to respectability and into subtitles. In a way, subtitles also reflect language changes in society, and the more topical their usage the more localising they can be, hence the feeling of familiarity they give to the audience.

We can make several observations on the use of Cantonese to translate vulgarisms and sexually-oriented language. First, the majority of the subtitles in Hong Kong are rendered into modern Standard Chinese. In this context, vulgarisms are toned down, neutralised ("neutered"), or omitted. For example, at the beginning of Quentin Tarantino's *Pulp Fiction* (1994), a film containing a great deal of violence and foul language, a young man and a young girl decide to hold up a diner. The young woman shouts out:

Original Dialogue	Chinese Subtitles	Back Translation
Everybody be cool, this is a robbery!	各位，我們打劫	Everybody, this is a robbery.
Any of you fuckin' pricks move and I'll execute every last one of you motherfuckers! Got that?	若有任何人亂動 我會一一殺死你們	If any one of you makes a wrong move … I'll kill you one by one.

The subtitles for the film are terse and not very well done. As the back translation shows (I have attempted to be as literal as possible), they are uninteresting, almost stripped of emotion and belong to a higher register which is closer to written language. Vulgarisms like "fuckin' pricks" and "motherfuckers" have been omitted altogether. The characterisation function and the force of the language in shocking the customers and staff into submission have been reduced. However, this is not to say that the scene's impact has been completely wasted. English f-words are understandable to the Hong Kong audience, and the tone of the voices, the menacing gestures and facial expressions, and the movement of the man climbing up and standing on the tabletop all help to compensate for the loss in the rather lacklustre translation.

Let us take a look at another example from the same film. Here, two killers, played by John Travolta and Samuel L. Jackson, are discussing the fate of a gangster, Antwan Rockamora (known as "Tony Rocky Horror"), who was punished by the gangster boss, Marsellus:

Original Dialogue	Chinese Subtitles	Back Translation
Well, Marsellus fucked his ass up good.	馬沙拉重創他	Marsellus hurt him badly.
And word around the campfire, it was on account of Marsellus Wallace's wife.	謠傳是和馬沙拉的太太有關	Rumour has it that it was related to Marsellus' wife.
What'd he do, fuck her?	他和她上床嗎？	Did he go to bed with her?
No no no no no no no, nothin' that bad.	他沒有	He didn't.
Well what then?	是甚麼事嗎？	What was it?
He gave her a foot massage.	替她按摩足部	He massaged her feet.

Here, the metaphor "fucked his ass up good" has been cleansed with a sense translation—"hurt him badly." And since the word "fuck" cannot be omitted as in the above examples, it has been substituted by "go to bed," a rather harmless expression in any language.

Another example of neutralisation can be found in *The English Patient* (1996). In this scene, Laszlo de Almasy (Ralph Fiennes), a Hungarian mapmaker working in the Sahara Desert, is arrested by British troops, and he is trying desperately to get away so that he can go and rescue his lover, Katherine (Kristin Scott Thomas), who has been wounded in a plane crash.

Original Dialogue		Chinese Subtitles	Back Translation
Almasy	Hey! Hey!	老天	Heavens!
	Stop this jeep! There's a woman dying, there's a woman dying— Hey!	截停那輛車，有個女子快死了	Stop that car. A woman is dying.
Corporal	Listen, Fritz,	德國佬，你聽着	Listen, German dude,
	if I have to listen to another word from you	你再開口	if you open your mouth again,
	I'll give you a fucking good hiding.	我就打到你跪地求饒	I'll hit you until you kneel down and beg for mercy.
Almasy	Fritz? What are you talking about? Who's Fritz?	你居然叫我德國佬？	How dare you call me a German dude?
Corporal	That's your name innit?	不應該這樣稱呼你嗎？	Why shouldn't I call you by that name?
	Count Fucking Arsehole Von Bismarck?	還自稱甚麼伯爵	And you also claim to be a whatchamacallit Count.
	What's that supposed to be then, Irish?	難道叫你做愛爾蘭佬嗎？	Or should I call you an Irish dude?
Almasy	Please—I beg you, I beg you, I beg you, please listen to me,	求求你，你要聽我講啊	I beg you, please listen to me.

Except for the local expression 德國佬 (German dude), which is used as a low-register translation of the derogatory "Fritz," the lines are refined and even literary in tone. The subtitler chooses to neutralise and expurgate the obscenities in the dialogue at the expense of the emotional impact of disgust and intimidation. (The subtitler is Yiu Po Kwong, a very experienced and highly regarded professional who has had years of experience in the business. He is famous for his rhymed rendition of the lyrics in *Evita* (1996). He belongs to the traditional school and is inclined towards finely chosen diction and detailed translation of the dialogue.)

Hong Kong maintains a system of film censorship which is quite liberal compared to other Asian countries. It prohibits extreme violence and explicit sex, but nudity, even in gratuitous display, is allowed. Films are to be considered according to their depiction and treatment of "cruelty, torture, violence, crime, horror, disability, sexuality or indecent or offensive language or behaviour" and other factors such as race and sex discrimination. There are three categories:

I. "Approved for exhibition to persons of any age."
IIa. "Approved for exhibition to persons of any age" but subject to displaying the symbol "Not suitable for Children."
IIb. "Approved for exhibition to persons of any age" but subject to displaying the symbol "Not suitable for young persons and children."
III. "Approved for exhibition only to persons who have attained the age of 18 years."

Special considerations are given for "artistic, education, literary or scientific merit" in relation to "the intended exhibition of the film, the circumstances of such exhibition" (such as film festivals).

Government sources assure us that there are no legal prohibitions regarding the use of vulgarisms in film subtitles. Then what is the reason for the subtitle translators' restraint? Several film distributors I talked to insisted that the box office was their major concern. If only one Cantonese "three-character classic" phrase is found in the dialogue or subtitles, the film will automatically be given a Category III rating by the censor regardless of its content or subject matter. As Category III films are restricted to persons of 18 years and over, and teenagers make up the bulk of the cinema-going public, many of them will not be able to buy tickets even if they want to see the film. A few years ago, the censor's office also requested that subtitles be submitted with the film for examination. Subtitlers and their employers, the distributors, have to be particularly careful with subtitles in order to avoid the risk of losing any possible income on the film. *Pulp Fiction* has been classified as Category III, probably owing to the violence in the film. *The English Patient* belongs to Category IIb, and this probably explains the decision to keep out the f-words. Interestingly, it does not constitute a "sin" (and a Category III rating) when f-words are spoken and heard in English, only when they are written and seen in Chinese. This may be considered a relic of the colonial mentality of the Hong Kong people, but perhaps it has more to do with the fact that English, though widely used and spoken, is not an everyday language and therefore English foul language is not as objectionable. Besides, it is also fashionable to be able to swear in English.

Of course, censorship can be one big leveller. In recent years, there has been a trend towards the increasing use of vulgarisms in Hollywood movies, and locally, we have witnessed the ascendancy of Hong Kong popular culture and local consciousness, including the use of Cantonese in writing. The mood has been for a more open and tolerant society. Under these circumstances, subtitles are also becoming more colloquial and receptive to vulgarisms. The following excerpt from Mike Myers's hilarious film *Austin Powers: The Spy Who Shagged Me* (1999) is a good example. Here, Dr. Evil (Mike Myers) has just launched his phallus-shaped rocket. What follows is a series of wordplays on the male sex organ:

Original Dialogue	Chinese Subtitles	Back Translation
(The Radar Room)		
Colonel, you'd better take a look at the radar.	上校，請你看看雷達	Colonel, please look at the radar.
What is it, son?	甚麼事？小夥子	What is it, son?
I don't know sir, but it looks like a giant ...	我不知道，但看來像巨型的⋯	I don't know, but it looks like a giant ...
(A pilot flying a fighter jet)		
Dick! Yes.	何B仔	Dick!
Take a look at starboard.	看右舷	Take a look at starboard
Oh my God! It looks like a huge ...	天呀！看來像⋯	Heavens! It looks like a ...
(Umpire on a baseball field)		
Two balls!	兩個波！	Two balls!
What is that?	那是甚麼？	What's that?
That looks just like an enormous ...	看起來就像⋯	Looks like ...

Original Dialogue	Chinese Subtitles	Back Translation
(Chinese classroom)		
Wang! Pay attention!	小弟弟！留心聽書	Little brother! Pay attention!
I was just distracted by that enormous flying …	我在看那巨型的飛行	I was looking at the enormous flying …
(Willy Nelson and friend)		
Willy!	細佬	Younger brother,
What's that?	那是甚麼？	What's that?
It looks like a giant …	看起來就像巨型的…	Look like a giant …
(Back to the radar room)		
Johnson!	賓周！	Ben Chow! (male organ)

There are culture-specific items that are untranslatable, such as references to the baseball game and to Willy Nelson, the famous country singer. However, the subtitler is still able to substitute Cantonese euphemisms and puns for their English counterparts (the words in italics), and they fit the context perfectly even when the scene changes. The bilingual audiences have doubled the fun marvelling at the subtitler's ingenuity.

The following, taken from Kevin Smith's *Dogma* (2000), is another example of the deliberate attempt to shy away from obscenities in subtitles. The scene is one in which Bethany, who works for an abortion clinic, is accosted by pro-life protesters:

Original Dialogue	Chinese Subtitles	Back Translation
You're gonna burn in hell, you fucking baby killer!	你這殺人兇手，小心落地獄	You murderer. Be careful or you'll go down to Hell
Holy shit! That's the Pope!	他媽的！那是教宗的問題	His mother's! That's the Pope's problem

All four-letter words have been omitted in the subtitles. "Holy shit" is replaced by the mild "His mother's," a standard Chinese swearing phrase.

A further example is the conversation between Bethany (Linda Florentino) and Jay (Jason Mewes), a habitually stoned suburbanite and a "prophet" sent down by God. Jay sexualises everything and propositions Bethany at every opportunity:

Original Dialogue	Chinese Subtitles	Back Translation
Jersey's pretty far from here. May I ask what brought you here?	為何從新澤西這麼遠來到這裡？	Why did you come all the way from New Jersey?
Some fuck named John Hughes.	有個叫尊曉斯的仆街	There's this son of a bitch called Hughes.
"16 Candles" John Hughes?	拍《16支蠟燭》的——曉斯？	The Hughes who filmed "16 Candles"?
You know that guy too?	你也認識他？	You know him too?
That fucking guy. He made this flick "16 Candles." Not bad.	這仆街拍了《16支蠟燭》，又幾好	That son of a bitch filmed "16 Candles." Not too bad.
There's tits in there, but no bush.	有露兩點，但冇露毛	It shows "points" (nipples) but no hair.
But Ebert here doesn't give a shit about this kind of thing.	但肥佬影評人伊拔有理冇理都讚	But fat Ebert the critic here likes him no matter what.
Cause he's like all in love with this John Hughes guy.	好像他愛上了這傢伙尊曉斯般	It's like he's in love with this guy Hughes.
He rents every one of his movies.	把他每部片都租回家看	He rents every one of his movies and watches them at home.
Fucking "Breakfast Club." All these stupid kids actually show up for detention.	像説幾個學生留堂的《早餐俱樂部》	Like "Breakfast Club." It's about several students,
Fucking "Weird Science," where this babe wants to take her gear off and get down.	《電腦俏紅娘》講條女想扑野	(And) "Weird Science," about this babe who wants to do it …
Oh she don't, cos it's a PG movie …	但礙於不是三級片所以冇扑到	But because it's not a Category III film she doesn't do it.

Sexual references abound in this scene (in fact, in the entire film), but as in the previous example there is a tendency to avoid f-words, even though the register is lower than that used by most subtitlers. The Cantonese expression 扑野 (literally, "pounding on things") is topical and slangy; it is the limit, beyond which would be taboo territory. Many of the lines feature the characteristics of spoken Cantonese, and there are frequent appearances of Hong Kong-style colloquialisms. The result is obvious: it is as if the subtitles are dialogues taken straight from a local film, and through them is constructed a world of Cantonese speakers and Hong Kong ambience. By giving the characters Cantonese traits in their dialogue, the subtitler is also able to portray them with appropriate linguistic traits and comparable register. (The subtitler can be literary and philosophical when called for: for example, when the characters are sermonising or are engaged in discussions on theological issues.)

Shu Kei is one of the new-style subtitlers who does not shy away from a Cantonese milieu or sexual materials. In translating the dialogues in *Being John Malkovich* (1999), he manages to capture the idiosyncrasies of the characters in their comical and fantastic world. The following is part of a dialogue involving the foul-mouthed, sex-obsessed, 150-year-old Dr. Lester (Orson Bean):

Original Dialogue	Chinese Subtitles	Back Translation
I don't want to be your goddamn link. Damn you.	我才不要做你的啥聯繫，收皮啦	I don't want to be your whatchamacallit link. Pipe down!
I want to feel Floris' naked thighs next to mine.	我只想摸住科麗絲的玉腿	I only want to fondle Floris' thigh of jade,
I want my body to inspire lust in that beautiful, complex woman.	用我的身體搞到這位美女慶烙烙	To use my body to make this beautiful girl hot and horny,
I want her to shiver in a spasm of ecstasy, Schwartz, as I penetrate	搞到佢過癮到震	To make her feel so good that she shakes all over,
her wet …	出曬汁，然後長驅直入	and becomes juicy to the core. Then I'll drive all the way in.

The entire piece of dialogue has been translated in the Cantonese vernacular with a distinctive local flavour, fully exploiting the dynamism and colour of the Cantonese language. There is the mandatory avoidance of f-words, but sexual references are handled in ways which are graphic yet not offensive. In his subtitles, Shu Kei pays special attention to characterisation, always taking into account the speaker's social status, educational background and situational needs, and he obviously revels in his own ability to match the style and wordplay of the film dialogue. Shu Kei is a director and a film distributor; he can afford to be more free and daring when he is translating the films his company distributes. He complains, not without a feeling of regret, that local distributors have at times replaced his translations with tamer substitutes. Ironically, the same vulgarisms were retained when the films were shown at film festivals.

Movies are big business in Hong Kong. The local film industry, though not thriving as vigorously as it was a few years ago, is still quite prosperous, taking in high box-office receipts and enjoying increasing recognition overseas. All major Hollywood film-makers are represented in the territory, and many blockbusters frequently premier at the same time as they do in North America. Non-English language foreign films are distributed through smaller companies and shown at various film festivals as well as in regular cinemas. Many of the decisions and strategies, from the selection of films, their venues, translation and promotion, are market-driven. But commercialism is not the monopoly of the Hong Kong media. In a document on the use of slang in subtitling, the BBC (British Broadcasting Corporation) writes:

> We appreciate concerns that the BBC is lowering its standards of written English when this occurs, but with programmes such as dramas and light entertainment series, for example, we must reflect the inevitable changes in language that take place through society in order to portray a realistic atmosphere. If we fail to do this when using subtitles for such programmes, we would create an artificial dialogue to a realistic setting and would probably lose viewers in the process. (BBC 1999: 2)

Obviously, even the BBC is concerned about audience ratings and is willing to accept a lowering of the standard of written English by including slang in their subtitles. Interestingly, it accepts as a matter of course the responsibility to reflect changes in language, claiming that these changes are inevitable. In the Hong Kong situation, film distributors allow or even promote the use of Cantonese in subtitles to reflect linguistic and social changes in order to attract viewers; however, they ensure that the use of the vernacular does not overstep what the censor prescribes (this presumably being the line representing the standards of the community), so that their profits are not compromised.

According to the survey carried out by Lo, more than 50 per cent of the respondents consider that Cantonese is more capable than Standard Chinese of reproducing the spirit of the vulgarisms in the original (Lo 2001: 126). And cinema fans writing in internet chat rooms agree that Cantonese subtitles are "direct," "familiar," and because they can capture the spirit of the original, they increase the audience's sense of involvement and enjoyment. This is despite the feeling that, as a dialect, Cantonese is low in status and considered inartistic by many people, and that Cantonese subtitles may corrupt the Chinese language because "the wordings (*sic*) are so cheap" (Lo 2001: 138–139). Audiences obviously feel more at home when subtitles are localised and translated according to their sociolectal conventions. For this reason, many Chinese subtitling companies routinely employ native dialect speakers to translate different sets of subtitles for regional markets such as the mainland, Hong Kong and Taiwan.

The reasons for the Cantonese phenomenon are many and varied. Subtitling, like language itself, is a site of contestation. One can apply the polysystem theory and find that local cultural manifestations, particularly popular songs (Canto-pop) and films, have been in the ascendant ever since the mid-1970s, when self-confidence derived from the prosperity and wealth of economic development began to emerge. The question of the 1997 handover and the controversies that surrounded it also gave the Hong Kong people a sense of their own identity. Their particular brand of Cantonese dialect, which mixes in English words and phrases in mid-sentence, has become part of the definition of being a Hong Konger. And this vernacular has been widely used in the media and popular writings, essentially breaking the monopoly and hegemony of Standard Chinese in writing.

So far we have been talking about subtitles in terms of their proximity to the original film: that is, whether subtitles can help the audience create a mental picture that is identical or similar to what they see on the screen. The assumption has been that the best subtitles are no subtitles, and that the ideal is for the audience to enjoy direct, unmediated access to the characters and their stories. Abé Mark Nornes recently published an interesting article which offers a different perspective. For him, otherness in foreign movies are to be highlighted through deliberate use of "abuses" in the subtitles, and instead of domesticating and hiding the stamp of mediation, a process Nornes calls "corruption," the subtitler should revel in flaunting the act of translation, re-presenting the "violence" and "polyvalence" already existing in the source language:

> Put more concretely, the abusive subtitler uses textual and graphic abuse—that is, experimentation with language and its grammatical, morphological, and visual qualities—to bring the fact of translation from its position of obscurity, to critique the imperial politics that ground corrupt practices while ultimately leading the viewer to the foreign original being reproduced in the darkness of the theater. This original is not an original threatened by contamination, but a locus of the individual and the international which can potentially turn the film into an experience of translation. (Nornes 1999: 2)

Fidelity is not in question here. Nornes' concerns are the impossibility of translator's invisibility (*à la* Lawrence Venuti) and the perception of the end product (subtitles) as translation, which has to be foregrounded. The issue really hinges on whether one prefers to regard subtitles as supplements that compensate for a lack, or as supplements that add something extra to that which is present in the original. Nornes uses as his example "fansubs," the subtitled videos of Japanese animation (anime) done by "fansubbers," who circulate their subtitles and videos on the Internet. They organise newsgroups and clubs to exchange the latest information, and they even create their own subtitling software for fellow fansubbers to download for free. Footnotes and explanations abound in their subtitles, as well as different fonts, sizes, and colours to indicate the paralinguistic features of the dialogues. And to break even further the illusion of nonexistent subtitles, the fansubbers put them anywhere they like in the picture, more or less at whim (Nornes 1999: 14). Presumably they can afford to be "abusive" because they are non-commercial. (Some big companies are putting out their own fansubs for sale because of their popularity.) Abusive subtitling is thus unapologetically intrusive—it coerces the audience into subverting the source text and the latent target text and puts the audience on the alert, a constant reminder that they are watching something foreign, mediated, even remanufactured with the imprint of translation.

In our scheme of things, abusive subtitling is neither foreignising nor naturalising; it tends to be both at the same time. Its end product is not by any means neutralised. While our attention is focused on how subtitles can transport our imagination into the film world, abusive subtitling insists that the film world on the screen is foreign and exists on its own terms. What it boils down to is the question of functionality: what do we want from subtitles? If our purpose is to understand the film, then the "abuses" are nothing but noise in the communication process, since they simply act as blockages between the two worlds of subtitles and movie. But audiences go to see films for different purposes. Perhaps abusive subtitling can be better considered in terms of transformation, where translation gives the source text a new life, and having been adapted and adopted in the new land, it can live longer and better, but nonetheless differently.

With abusive subtitling, subtitles are to be located "in the place of the other" and "direct spectators back to the original work." They circulate "between the foreign and the familiar," or they try to get to know about the foreign through the familiar (Nornes 1999: 14). That subtitles can be alienating validates our understanding of the two worlds in a subtitled film—its duality is embedded in its very nature and functionality. Even closed captions and intralingual subtitles are capable of constructing a different world. Bad translations and non-synchronisation, too, alert us to the gap between the two worlds of subtitles and film. Conversely, with good subtitling, we can revel in the wonder of two worlds converging seamlessly into one.

There are many factors affecting the subtitler's decision. As we have seen in the case of Hong Kong subtitles, one may identify commercial considerations, censorship and government control, and linguistic and cultural norms, etc. Foreignisation occurs mainly in the areas of personal names, place names, institutions and other cultural items. There are cases when "formal correspondence" is called for, and "people want a direct translation of what is being said, not a complete reconstruction of the dialog in their own language" (Gottlieb 1993: 268). Foreignisation is possible on the syntactic level, but the subtitler does not enjoy the flexibility of a translator of literature, where the luxury of time and space is almost taken for granted. However, foreignised subtitles can become alienating, as the member of the audience has to acculturate himself to the otherness before he can begin to appreciate the characters and their stories. For instance, Bruce Lee's early films, such as *Fist of Fury* (1971) and *The Chinese Connection* (1972), were dubbed into English with a combination of British, American and cockney accents. The dubbers try to imitate the tone, pitch and intonation of "Chinglish," a deliberate attempt to sinicise the English dialogue. This, coupled with blatant mistranslations and non-synchronicities, makes the dubbed version involuntarily funny. The films are interesting cases of foreignisation through naturalisation, or vice versa. It would be interesting to conduct a survey on audience reactions to the dubbing. Another example is the obligatory bilingual subtitles in Hong Kong films. The Chinese subtitles are often an exercise in futility, as the Cantonese dialogues are reproduced verbatim with Cantonese vocabulary, usages and syntax. Cantonese speakers have no need for the subtitles, and non-Cantonese speakers are hard put to understand them. The English subtitles, too, are usually literal translations, and they unwittingly become a source of entertainment themselves.

Naturalisation, in rubbing out the cultural edges, produces easily absorbed, and in commercial terms, consumable doses of the foreign. Excessive naturalisation, however, might have the opposite effect of maximising the loss which occurs in the process of translation. With the 1996 French movie *Hate*, which was full of slang and hard-hitting language, the translators decided to use a street, hip-hop lingua franca for the subtitles, hoping that everyone would understand it, but many admitted that much was lost in the translation (Riding 1996: 20). Then there is also the question of authenticity. In an article entitled "The Translation of Films: Sub-Titling Versus Dubbing," Hans Vöge claims that "the film illusion is always based on a generally recognizable, concrete situation, specific in time and place." He therefore makes his case against dubbing because it tends to distort "the reality of time and place" (Vöge 1997: 123). Again, this is a matter of assimilating or matching up the two worlds, and the relevance to subtitling is obvious: dubbing is the ultimate form of naturalisation. As Gottlieb puts it, there is danger when two or more semiotic channels collide, or when the distance between them becomes too great:

> The feedback-effect from the original—whether that consists of recognizable words, prosodic features, gestures, or background visuals—may be so strong that a more idiomatic, "functional" rendering will be counterproductive ... This means that a consistently target-language oriented, "idiomatic" translation may backfire. (Gottlieb 1993: 268)

In the hands of an overzealous translator, the naturalised subtitles will produce a world very different from that in the movie proper. Thus the audience is liable to see double and become disoriented. As we have seen in our discussion on Hong Kong subtitles, some genres are more suited to naturalisation than others. It is fair to say that the more the subtitles are naturalised, the more the audience will be made aware of the two "solitudes" in a subtitled film.

It has been reported that there are problems with the extreme local tone used for dubbing and subtitling foreign films in Argentina, and audiences in other Spanish-speaking countries find the translations unintelligible. Argentines are urged to adopt a more neutral variety of Spanish, as this would better preserve the films' contexts without distortion (Pardal 1989: 64). Neutrality, seen from this perspective, does have its virtues. In fact, the mode shift in the subtitling process often has a "levelling effect" (Hatim and Mason 1990: 79), and neutralisation is the anticipated and natural outcome. Raphael Nir also asserts in his article on television and film translations in Israel: "In many cases the translator will have no choice but to use a 'neutral' unmarked style. The inevitable result is that the translation of mimetic dialogue will be more homogeneous than the original speech." (Nir 1984: 87) Neutralisation can only be relative—after all, subtitles are but words in a language, which of necessity constructs its own world. Neutralised subtitles reduce cultural specificities and are unintrusive by design. Compared to the foreignised or naturalised varieties, they may tend to be basic, unadorned and perhaps even unexciting. But films are multi-channel forms of communication; besides the dialogue, there are other equally important verbal, visual and aesthetic channels that are capable of generating messages in compensation. And since neutralised subtitles shy away from defining specificities, they leave more space for the audience to imagine for themselves and become more actively involved in the decoding process.

References

Berardinelli, James. 1996. "No talking in the theater—To dub or not to dub?" http://movie-reviews.colossus.net/comment/121896.html

British Broadcasting Corporation. 1999. "Subtitling—Provision and how to obtain them." http://www.bbc.co.uk

Catford, John. C. 1965. *A Linguistic Theory of Translation.* London: Oxford University Press.

Crystal, David. 1978. *The Cambridge Encyclopedia of Language.* Cambridge: Cambridge University Press.

Delabastita, Dirk. 1989. "Translation and mass-communication: Film and TV translation as evidence of cultural dynamics." *Babel,* Vol. 3, No. 4: 193–218.

Gottlieb, Henrik. 1993. "Subtitling: People translating people." In Cay Dollerup and Annete Lindegaard (eds.), *Teaching Translation and Interpreting 2: Insights, Aims, Visions.* Amsterdam: John Benjamins, pp. 260–274.

———. 1994. "Subtitling: Diagonal translation." In Cay Dollorup (ed.) *Perspectives: Studies in Translatology.* Copenhagen: University of Copenhagen, pp. 101–121.

———. 1997. *Subtitles, Translation & Idioms.* Ph.D. thesis, Main Volume. Copenhagen: Centre for Translation Studies and Lexicography, Department of English, University of Copenhagen.

Hatim, Basil and Ian Mason. 1990. "Politeness in screen translating." In Basil Hatim and Ian Mason, *The Translator as Communicator.* London and New York: Routledge, pp. 78–96.

Lo, Wai Yan. 2001. "Film translation in Hong Kong: Cantonese subtitles and transparency." M.Phil. thesis, Hong Kong: The Chinese University of Hong Kong.

Lundeen, Kathleen. 1999. "Pumping up the world with cinematic supplements." *Film Criticism,* Vol. 24, No. 1, Fall 1999: 60–72.

Lyons, John. 1981. *Language and Linguistics: An Introduction.* Cambridge: Cambridge University Press, reprinted 1983.

Nedergaard-Larsen, Birgit. 1993. "Culture-bound problems in subtitling." *Perspectives: Studies in Translatology,* No. 2: 207–241.

Nir, Raphael. 1984. "Linguistic and sociolinguistic problems in the translation of imported TV films in Israel." *International Journal of the Sociology of Language,* No. 48: 81–97.

Nornes, Abé Mark. 1999. "For an abusive subtitling." *Film Quarterly*, Spring, 1999.

Pardal, Ines. 1989. "The rub in the dubbing." *Americas*, Vol. 41, No. 2: 64.

Shochat, Ella and Robert Stam. 1985. "The cinema after Babel: Language, difference, power." *Screen*, No. 26: 35–58.

Vöge, Hans. 1997. "The translation of films: Sub-titling versus dubbing." *Babel*, Vol. 23, No. 3: 120–125.

Whorf, Benjamin Lee. 1956. *Language, Thought and Reality. Selected Writings of Benjamin Lee Whorf*, ed. John B. Carroll. Cambridge, MA: MIT Press, 11th printing, 1974.

6

A Functional Gap between Dubbing and Subtitling

He Yuanjian

—ᴠᴠ—

Introduction

It has long been observed that linguistic contrasts exist between translations from the same source. For instance, while film subtitles may display an over-representation of source language features, this is not found in dubbing scripts rendered from the same source. A culturally receptive approach to such contrasts is to attribute them to contextually determined functional factors. Subtitles, for instance, switch the mode of communication from audio to visual, but dubbing scripts are designed to maintain audio communication in new cultural settings. Studies that espouse this approach are well documented in the literature. Nida (1964) and Bassnett-McGuire (1990) both cited cultural differences as causes of the oppositions between centralism and vernacularism in Bible translations in history and in modern times, and other authors (Snell-Hornby 1988; Hatim and Mason 1990; Toury 1995; Nord 1997a, b) sought functional explanations for translation diversities. For Chinese dramatic translations in particular, a dichotomy of foreignisation versus localisation has been put forward to explain linguistically diverse translations from the same source in a cultural dimension (Fong and Tsoi 1992; Chan 1992), or it has been suggested that translations should be viewed as forming a continuum from foreignisation through neutralisation to naturalisation on a cultural platform (Fong 2001; see also Venuti 1995, 1998).

A cultural or contextual approach is one that is based mainly on the product. However, the contrasts in question have received much less attention from the perspective of the translation process. In this paper, I therefore attempt to account for the contrasts from a text processing perspective. The case I shall discuss involves Chinese subtitles and dubbing scripts rendered from the same English source. As has been observed, subtitles tend to over-represent source language features, but dubbing scripts do not do this, and they consequently possess more target-language-specific features. The key to our explanation for the contrast is the notion that source texts may act as stimuli in the translation process (Eskola 2001). The question is why the source text acts as a stimulus in one case, but fails to do so in the other, given that it is the source for both translations. In order to answer the question, we incorporate the stimuli theory into the text processing model for translation developed by Holmes (1978). In this model, text processing for translation takes place on two planes: serial and structural. The serial plane is responsible for sentence translations, and the structural plane oversees a mapping processing where the discourse structure of the source text as a "mental map" is projected onto the target text.

According to Holmes, the processing that takes place on the structural plane is the core of text processing for translation, and it governs the way individual sentences are ultimately translated. We thus assume that, firstly, source language features (phonological, lexical and syntactical) may stimulate the serial processing, and secondly, the discourse structure, or the "map," as Holmes calls it, of the source text may act as a stimulus to the structural processing, or "mapping." Because the degree of stimulus is dependent on or varies with contextual factors, its interactions with the processing respectively as well as jointly on the serial and structural planes will thus yield predictable results. For instance, a high stimulus (i.e. inert processing) at the serial level in conjunction with a low stimulus (i.e. active processing) at the structural level means that we will have a target text with many source language features, but the distribution of these features will not be the same as in the source text. In contrast, a low stimulus (i.e. active processing) at the serial level in conjunction with a high stimulus (i.e. inert processing) at the structural level means that we will have a target text with appropriate target language features, and the distribution of these features will be similar to that of their source language counterparts.

If high stimuli operate on both the serial and structural planes, inert processing at these levels will produce a target text that is almost source-text-bound: i.e. not only are the source language features over-represented, but also their distribution is as they appear in the source text. In other words, the translation is word for word. In contrast, low stimuli, and hence active processing, on both planes will produce a target text with appropriate target language features as well as a target-text-specific distribution of these features. This is a semantics-based translation, so to speak.

A text-processing model set up in this way will therefore provide just the right explanation we seek for the contrastive target texts in question: i.e. Chinese subtitles and dubbing scripts rendered from the same source. Also, we have answered the question of why the stimuli theory works for some translations but seemingly fails for others. As a matter of fact, since contrastive target texts rendered from the same source are constrained by the same set of conditions and variables, they serve as evidence which will help with the setting up of such a processing model.

The following section demonstrates the contrast between Chinese subtitles and dubbing scripts which have been translated from the same English source. In the subsequent section—"A Text Processing Account"—we present a detailed explanation for this contrast based on Holmes' (1978) text-processing model for translation, as well as on an extension of Eskola's (2001) stimuli theory to the current study.

A Pair of Contrastive Discourses

Traditionally, (Chinese) translators are encouraged to do away with, and hence leave as few traces as possible in their translations of the discourse structure of the source text. A counter-argument that is increasingly heard these days is that each author has his or her unique way of composing a text, hence a unique discourse of his or her writing. If the translator, who supposedly has his or her own way of composing a text as well, treats every author in the same way by effectively struggling to break free from the original discourse structure, then what is offered to the target reader is very much a textual embodiment of the translator himself or herself. In the case of Chinese scripts of the dubbed and the subtitled versions of the same English film, we have observed, through an examination of a substantial collection of films dubbed and subtitled in mainland China and Taiwan, that subtitles appear to contain significantly more source language features than dubbing scripts, which are consequently more target-language-oriented. Such over-representation may be seen as an instance of the target text coming under the strong influence of the original, since such influence is generally assumed to be possible (e.g. Nida 1964; Baker 1993; Eskola 2001).

The questions are why a target text seems always, one way or another, to come under the influence of the source text, why this influence is much stronger in some cases than in others, and particularly why a disparity occurs between texts rendered from the same source. Studies have shown that such influence has certain universal tendencies that may characterise the translation process (Baker 1997, 2001; Laviosa-Braithwaite 1997; He 1999; Chesterman 2001; Jones 2001). A recent study by Eskola (2001) on how source language features are cross-represented in the target text seems to be a breakthrough. She claims that source language features that have *translation equivalents* in the target language may cognitively stimulate the translator and thus result in an over-representation of them in the target text. Naturally, when this occurs, a complementary under-representation of target-language-specific features in the target text is inevitable. Let us call Eskola's theory "the stimuli theory," and assume with her that the stimuli theory applies universally to all translations.

While the stimuli theory certainly offers an explanation for why the source text would always find its way into the target text, it fails at the same time to explain why the source text features are represented more in one translation than in another, when in fact the source text serves as the original for both translations. Such disparity calls for still further investigation. In the case of Chinese subtitles and dubbing scripts translated from the same English source, while we see an over-representation of source language features as well as an under-representation of target-language-specific features in the subtitles, we find neither in the dubbing scripts. To illustrate, consider the following Chinese subtitles and (transcribed) dubbing scripts taken from the same sections of two English films—*Gone With The Wind*

(Selznick International Pictures, the 1989 edition of the original 1939 film) and *Titanic* (a James Cameron film, 1997):

Gone With the Wind:

English Original:	Subtitles:	Dubbed Scripts:
1. Thank Heaven you are here.	#感謝上天你來了。	你來得正好。
1a. I need everything I have.	#我需要你的幫助。	幫幫忙吧。
1b. Wake up.	來，	Ø
1c. We've got work to do.	#這裡有好多工作要做。	我馬上要給他做手術，
2. But Melanie's having a baby.	#但美蘭要生寶寶，	美蘭要生孩子啦，
2a. You've got to come with me.	#你一定要來。	你跟我去一趟。
3. Are you crazy?	Ø	你瘋了嗎？
3a. I can't leave these men for a baby.	#我不能為了一個嬰兒丟下他們。	我會拋下這些傷員嗎？
3b. They are dying.	#他們快死了。	Ø
3c. Hundreds of them.	#上百人。	Ø
3d. Get some woman to help you.	#找些女人去幫忙。	你找個女人幫忙吧。
4. But there isn't anybody.	#但沒有別人了。	Ø
4a. Doctor Mi,	Ø	Ø
4b. she might die.	她可能會死掉。	可是你不去她會死的。
5. Die?	死掉？	#死？
5a. Look at them.	Ø	看看這些人。
5b. Bleeding to death in front of my eyes.	#在我眼前他們都快要失血而死。	他們都要死的。
5c. No morphine,	#沒有麻藥，	#現在沒有藥，
5d. no bandage,	#沒有紗布，	#沒有紗布，
5e. nothing.	甚麼都沒有。	甚麼都沒有。
5f. Nothing to ease their pain.	#沒有東西可以減緩他們的痛苦。	只有我這個醫生，

| 5g. | Now, | Ø | Ø |
| 5h. | leave me alone. | 別煩我。 | 我都忙不過來了。 |

Titanic:

English Original:		Subtitles:	Dubbed Scripts:
6.	Give to me.	#孩子交給我。	上船。
7.	Take up.	沒關係，	#給你這孩子，
7a.	Look out.	別怕。	別擔心。
8.	Daddy.	爸爸上船。	爸爸、爸爸快上船。
9.	It's goodbye for a little while.	#只是分開一下而已。	爸爸只是和你暫時分別。
9a.	Only for a little while.	#一下子而已。	Ø
9b.	The other boat is for Daddy.	#爸爸要坐另一艘船。	#爸爸要坐另一條船。
9c.	This boat is for Mummy and the children.	Ø	#這船隻坐媽媽和孩子。
9d.	You hold Mummy's hand	#抓緊媽媽的手，	聽話，孩子，
9e.	and be a good little girl.	要乖。	聽媽媽的話。
…			
10.	I'm not going without you.	你不走，我也不走。	你不走我也不走。
11.	No,	Ø	Ø
11a.	you have to.	#你非走不可，	#你必須走。
11b.	Now.	現在。	Ø
11b.	Get on the boat.	#快上船。	快。
12.	No,	#不要，	#不，
12a.	Jack.	傑克。	傑克。
13.	Yes.	上船！	快上船，蘿絲。
14.	Yes,	#對，	是時候了，
14a.	get on the boat,	上船吧，	#快點上船，
14b.	Rose.	蘿絲。	蘿絲。
14c.	My God,	Ø	瞧，
14d.	look at you.	看看你，	蘿絲，瞧你。

14e.	You look so frightened.	#樣子好可怕。	#這麼憔悴。
14f.	Here,	#來，	#來，
14g.	put this on.	把這穿上，	#換上這件，
14h.	Come.	快。	快。
15.	Go on,	去吧，	#你先走，
15a.	I'll get the next one.	#我搭下一艘船。	我坐下一趟。
16.	Not without you.	#不，我要跟你。	不，要走一起走。
17.	I'll be all right.	Ø	我沒事的，
17a.	Listen,	#聽我說，	真的，
17b.	I'll be fine.	我沒問題。	沒事。
17c.	I'm a survivor,	#我很能生存。	我的命很大。
17d.	right?	Ø	Ø
17e.	Don't worry about me.	Ø	你快走吧。
17f.	Go on,	#快去。	上船。
17g.	get on.	Ø	#快走。
18.	I have an arrangement with the last one on the other side of the ship.	#我已經安排妥當，	剛才我已經和一個當官兒的說好了，
18a.	Jack and I can get on safely.	#傑克可以跟我走。	傑克和我不會有事。
18b.	Both of us.	#兩個一起。	都能坐。
19.	See,	看吧，	#瞧，
19a.	I have my own boat to catch.	#我有別的船好搭。	我也能走了。
...			
20.	You're a good liar.	#你很能說謊。	還挺會裝。
21.	Almost as good as you.	還差你一點。	彼此彼此。
21a.	There's no ... no arrangement, is there?	沒有安排好吧？	沒有說好，是吧？
22.	There is,	#有，	說好了，
22a.	Not much of a benefit for you.	#但對你沒好處。	可是沒你的份。
22b.	I always win.	#我總是贏家。	#我贏了，
22c.	Jack.	Ø	Ø
22c.	One way or another.	#不管用甚麼辦法。	你輸了。

The hatch mark "#" in the Chinese sections indicates a "translation equivalent," and the symbol Ø an omission or compression of message, which we consider to be a non-equivalent.[1] We define a "translation equivalent" as containing the whole or a fragment or a variant of the original syntactic structure, and containing no target-language-specific features (lexical or syntactic). Under the stimuli theory, if the source acts as a factor of stimulus, it has to be traceable in the target text, either in a lexical item or in a syntactic construction.[2]

In the above, target-language-specific features are, for instance, Chinese end-of-clause propositional markers (e.g. 吧、啦、嗎、的 in renditions in Lines 1b, 2, 3 and 4b), measure particles being the head of a nominal expression used either as an adverbial complement (e.g. 趟 and 點 in renditions in Lines 2a and 21) or as an argument (e.g. 份 in rendition in Line 22a), idiomatic expressions (e.g. 彼此彼此 for "almost as good as you" in Line 21), distinctive lexical and syntactic structures like verb reduplications (e.g. 看看 for "Look" in rendition Line 14e), V-V resultative compounds (e.g. 死掉 in renditions in Lines 4b and 5), indefinite use of question words (e.g. 甚麼都沒有 for "nothing" in Line 5e), covert conditionals (e.g. 你不走我也不走 for "I'm not going without you" in Line 10), V-de resultative constructions (e.g. 來得正好 for "Thank Heaven you are here" in Line 1), and ba-constructions (e.g. 把這穿上 for "put this on" in Line 14g).

The number of "translation equivalents" (defined as *per se*) in the subtitle section for both films amounts to 39 (out of a total of 74 renditions, including omissions), and the number of "translation equivalents" in the dubbed scripts section is 15. The percentage of "translation equivalents" in each case is 52.7 per cent and 20.2 per cent respectively. As a result, the subtitles seem significantly more source-language-bound than the dubbed scripts, which in contrast appear to be more target-language-oriented. Lastly, it is worth noting that the contrast we have seen in the above examples is persistent not only throughout the films from which these excerpts are taken, but also in fact exists between Chinese subtitles and dubbing scripts rendered from the same English sources in general, as far as the data at our disposal have shown.

A Text Processing Account

Theoretically, the contrasts we have seen above pose a challenge to the stimuli theory. Assuming that the theory holds for the subtitles, we have to wonder what has blocked it in the process of translating for the dubbing scripts. One solution, which has both theoretical as well as empirical implications, is to assume that the stimuli theory works at both the serial level of processing (i.e. sentence to sentence) and at the level of structural mapping (i.e. projecting the discourse structure of the source text onto the target text). Both levels appear in Holmes' (1978) model of text processing for translation.

The model, also known as the structural mapping theory, rejects Nida's (1969) linear processing theory and argues for a three-dimensional translating process: a process that operates on the text plane, the textual processing plane and the rules plane. On the textual processing plane, which we are concerned with here, two sub-planes are further identified: the serial and structural planes, as illustrated below (Holmes, 1978/1988: 84):

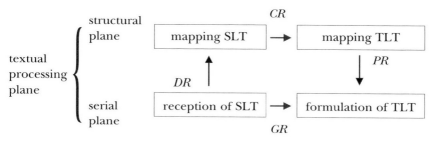

CR = correspondence rules   DR = derivation rules
GR = grammatical rules   PR = projection rules

Individual sentences are translated one by one on the serial plane, and rules that apply here are grammatical rules. For Holmes, the structural plane is the core of textual processing for translation and deserves the attention of researchers. It is a mental mapping processing where the translator "abstracts a 'mental conception' of the original text, and then uses that mental conception as a kind of general criterion against which to test each sentence during the formulation of the new, translated text" (Holmes 1978/1988: 82–83).

Holmes assumes the translator to be a skilled and experienced reader able to process a conglomerate of highly disparate pieces of information. Although the translator shares certain phases of the mapping process with every reader or writer of any literary texts, the mental abstraction of the source text and the mapping of it onto the target text are uniquely a translational operation: i.e. a specific kind of meta-textual operation. As the diagram shows, the translator abstracts his map from the source text first (i.e. the derivation), and then develops his map of the prospective target text from his source text map (i.e. the corresponding or matching phase). Finally, he makes use of his map of the prospective target text in order to formulate the text itself (i.e. the projection). Note that the derivation and the projection are phases that constitute the common experience of every skilled and experienced reader and writer. It is in the phase in between, i.e. the corresponding or matching phase, where the translator develops a prospective map of the target text, which is essential to the translation process.

The key question here is how we should determine the properties of this "map" of a text. For the current study, I equate this map to the discourse structure of a text. By discourse structure, we mean the unique distribution pattern of linguistic features (phonological, morphological and syntactic) inherent in each text. One possible way to map the distribution is to examine the proportions of linguistic features of different categories in the text—categories such as language-specific phonological and morpho-syntactic structures, propositional markers, logical-grammatical connectors, discourse or utterance markers, and so on.

Assuming that the stimuli theory works on the serial plane as well as on the structural plane of Holmes' model, a further question we ask is what this means to the processing process as a whole. Presumably, the degree of stimulus is inherent in contextually determined factors, and is therefore dependent on or varies with these factors. As the degree of stimulus fluctuates, the interactions between the stimuli and the processing process will thus produce certain salient results. Two of these are as follows:

(1) *There is a high degree of stimulus at both the serial level and the structural level.*

This would mean that the processing effort at these levels is inert, suggesting that the translator would render the original as far as possible into so-called "translation equivalents," while at the same time preserving the distribution pattern of the original (now in the form of "translation equivalents") in the target text. As a result, the target text will contain neither many target-language-specific features nor much of a formulation of a new discourse structure in the target language setting. It will be rather source-text-bound, like the Chinese subtitles we saw earlier.

(2) *There is a low degree of stimulus at both the serial level and the structural level.*

In contrast, a low degree of stimulus at both levels would mean that there is very active processing there, suggesting that translators would do away with the "translation equivalents" and with the distribution pattern of the original. In addition, they would render the original into target-language-specific constructions, and distribute the renditions in a new pattern they deem appropriate for the target text. The outcome is likely to be a target text with few source language features, and at the same time many target-language-specific features. The Chinese dubbing scripts we saw earlier may serve as a good example here. Another example would be translations from a classical language into its modern counterpart, or into another modern language. Here, the source text performs little stimulus function from the point of view of either linguistic traits or discourse pattern. Instead, very active processing is expected, producing a fresh discourse with linguistic features compatible with the target language. The so-called "creative factor" in literary translation (Jin and Nida 1984) may thus also be understood along these lines: that is, the more creative a translation is deemed to be, the more active must have been the processing that produced it.

These results have thus accounted for the apparent contrasts between the Chinese subtitles and dubbing scripts that we are seeking to explain. As already stated, which type of processing has been selected is determined by the degree of stimulus available, which is in turn determined by the decisions made by the translator in accordance with the contexts in which the target text is to be used. For instance, subtitles are used to switch the mode of communication from audio to visual, but dubbing scripts are to be uttered in an interpreting fashion. This difference in function between the target texts may have guided the translator in his decisions on how to approach the source texts in the translation process, and hence decided the processing approach. However, we are not concerned here with how the translator may make his decisions on how to approach the source text. Rather, we are interested in identifying theoretically well-defined processing options that are consistent with the resulting target texts. In other words, we presume that once the translator has made his decisions on how to approach the source text, what happens afterwards in the translation process could conceivably be along the lines we have formulated in our description of the above processing options. These options are conceivable because, again, they are consistent with the resulting target texts, and because we would otherwise be unable to explain the linguistic contrasts between them when they are from the same source.

Other processing options are also available. One is when stimuli and processing each play an equal or balanced role, neither overriding the other. Resulting translations are neither source-text-bound nor particularly target-language-oriented in respect of either individual language features or the discourse structure of the target text as a whole. They possess a "neutral, unmarked variety of language or style," as Nir (1984), Pardal (1989), and Hatim and Mason (1990) have commented from their own perspectives.

Another option would be when asymmetrical processing is at work: i.e. with active processing at one level and high stimuli at the other, or vice versa. On the one hand, active processing on the serial plane and high stimuli on the structural plane will produce texts with lexical and syntactical features of the target language, but which still preserve the distribution pattern of the source text to a significant extent. For instance, while in English adverbial clauses (i.e. those marked by "though/because/if/when/where" etc.) tend to follow the main clause, in Chinese it is always preferable to place this type of clauses before the main clause. However, it is found in many Chinese translations from English that although the adverbial clauses themselves contain sufficient Chinese language-specific features, such as verb-reduplication, object-dislocation, and extra-complementation, they are, despite the salient Chinese discourse pattern, most often placed after the main clause just as the English originals are. On the other hand, high stimuli on the serial plane and active processing on the structural plane will produce texts with many so-called "translation equivalents," but which have a new distribution pattern different from that of the source text. News passages translated from foreign sources are often of this style.

Finally, to sum up the new model of textual processing for translation with a stimulus component based on Eskola (2001), we have:

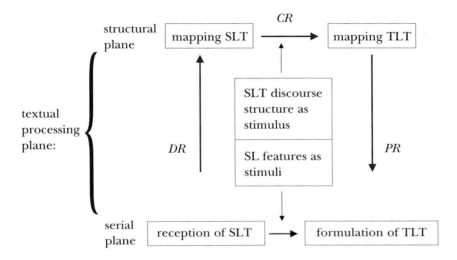

The new model is, as we see, a small and specific development of Holmes' (1978) model. It can, as we have demonstrated above, help us describe and interpret how the translation process operates in more specific terms than we could before.

Conclusion

The fact that translations from the same source may display contrastive linguistic features, as shown by Chinese subtitles and dubbing scripts rendered from the same English films, has raised certain interesting theoretical questions. One of these is how to explain such representational disparity in relation to the translation process. Eskola's (2001) stimuli theory offers a good starting point, but is not adequate to explain the contrast in question. We therefore propose to incorporate this theory into the textual processing model of Holmes (1978). In this way, we have not only accounted for the contrast we seek to explain, but have also shed some light on the theoretical issue of how the source text may act as a stimulus both at sentence and text level in the translation process.

As a concluding remark, it may be appropriate to mention that although more than two decades old, Holmes' (1978) model has stood the test of time for its theoretical insights and analytical technicality. One of the reasons for its endurance is its call for an empirical study of possible translational universals that govern the translation process irrespective of the language pairs. The cognitive aspect of the translation process that involves the mental abstracting of the source text, as Holmes suggested, is one of the areas where universals are likely to be identified. The stimuli theory and the operational options we have proposed under it in this paper are potentially relevant universal elements. For instance, we may view stimuli, processing, and the interactions between them each as a continuum and treat all three as elements of a processing system that thus yields a wide range of target texts. It is not yet clear how the system might be developed further. Questions such as this can only be answered by further studies on translated texts of a contrastive nature in association with a further investigation into the properties of the translation process in general.

Acknowledgements

I wish to thank the two anonymous reviewers for their critical but valuable views and comments. Any remaining error is mine.

Notes

1. It is unclear at this stage how to interpret an omission under the stimuli theory, and I leave it for future studies.
2. The definition of "translation equivalent" here is of a linguistic nature, as in Popovič (1976), and refers mainly to code replacement or substitution, as in Catford (1965), hence different from other definitions such as in Nida (1964).

References

Baker, Mona. 1993. "Corpus linguistics and translation studies: Implications and applications." In Mona Baker et al. (eds.), *Text and Technology: In Honour of John Sinclair.* Amsterdam: John Benjamins, pp. 233–250.

Baker, Mona. 1997. "Corpus-based translation studies—The challenges that lie ahead." In H. L. Somers (ed.), *Terminology, LSP and Translation.* Amsterdam: John Benjamins, pp. 175–186.

———. 2001. "Universals? Norms? Idiosyncrasies? On the danger of terms, categories and comparisons." Paper presented at *The International Conference on Translation Universals—Do They Exist?* October 19–20, 2001, Savonlinna School of Translation Studies, University of Joensuu, Finland.

Bassnett-McGuire, Susan. 1990. *Translation Studies.* London: Routledge.

Catford, J. C. 1965. *A Linguistic Theory of Translation.* London: Oxford University Press.

Chan, Sin-wai. 1992. "Drama translation in Hong Kong (1980–1990)." In G. C. F. Fong and H. S. C. Tsoi (eds.), *Studies on Hong Kong Drama.* Hong Kong: High Noon Production, pp. 167–192 (in Chinese).

Chesterman, Andrew. 2001. "Beyond the particular." Paper presented at *The International Conference on Translation Universals—Do They Exist?* October 19–20, 2001, Savonlinna School of Translation Studies, University of Joensuu, Finland.

Eskola, Sari. 2001. "Untypical syntactic frequencies in translations: A study on a comparable corpus of literary texts." Paper presented at *The International Conference on Translation Universals—Do They Exist?* October 19–20, 2001, Savonlinna School of Translation Studies, University of Joensuu, Finland.

Fong, G. C. F. 2001. "The two worlds of subtitling: The case of vulgarisms and sexually oriented language." Paper presented at *The International Conference on Dubbing and Subtitling in a World Context.* October 18–20, 2001, The Chinese University of Hong Kong.

Fong, G. C. F. and H. S. C. Tsoi. 1992. "Preface—The characteristics of Hong Kong plays." In G. C. F. Fong and H. S. C. Tsoi (eds.), *Studies on Hong Kong Drama.* Hong Kong: High Noon Production, pp. 3–22 (in Chinese).

Hatim, Basil and Ian Mason. 1990. *Discourse and the Translator.* London: Longman.

He, Yuanjian. 2000. "Translating: Towards a principles-and-parameters theory." *Journal of Translation Studies,* No. 3, pp. 97–113.

Holmes, James S. 1978. "Describing literary translations: Models and methods." In James S. Holmes (1988), *Translated!—Papers on Literary Translation and Translation Studies.* Amsterdam: Rodopi, pp. 82–92.

Jin, Di and Eugene Nida. 1984. *On Translation—With Special Reference to*

Chinese and English. Beijing: China Translation and Publishing Corporation.

Jones, F. R. 2001. "In search of strategic universals: Principles, parameters and poetry professionals." Paper presented at *The International Conference on Translation Universals—Do They Exist?* October 19–20, 2001, Savonlinna School of Translation Studies, University of Joensuu, Finland.

Laviosa-Braithwaite, Sara. 1997. *The English Comparable Corpus (ECC): A Resource and a Methodology for the Empirical Study of Translation*. PhD thesis, the University of Manchester Institute of Science and Technology.

Nida, Eugene. 1964. *Towards a Science of Translating*. Leiden: E. J. Brill.

———. 1969. "Science of translation." *Language*, No. 45, pp. 483–498.

Nir, Raphael. 1984. "Linguistic and sociolinguistic problems in the translation of imported TV films in Israel." *International Journal of the Sociology of Language*, No. 48, pp. 81–97.

Nord, Christiane. 1997a. *Translating as a Purposeful Activity*. Manchester: St. Jerome.

———. 1997b. "A functional typology of translations." In A. Trosborg (ed.), *Text Typology and Translation*. Amsterdam: John Benjamins.

Pardal, I. 1989. "The rub in dubbing." *Americas*, Vol. 41, No. 2, p. 64.

Popovič, Anton. 1976. *A Dictionary for the Analysis of Literary Translation*. Edmonton, Alberta: Department of Comparative Literature, University of Alberta.

Shuttleworth, Mark and Moira Cowie 1997. *Dictionary of Translation Studies*. Manchester: St. Jerome, pp. 161–162.

Snell-Hornby, Mary. 1988. *Translation Studies: An Integrated Approach*. Amsterdam: John Benjamins.

Toury, Gideon. 1995. *Descriptive Translation Studies and Beyond*. Amsterdam: John Benjamins.

Venuti, Lawrence. 1995. *The Translator's Invisibility: A History of Translation*. London: Routledge.

Venuti, Lawrence. 1998. *The Scandals of Translation: Towards an Ethics of Difference*. London: Routledge.

7

Subtitling as a Multi-modal Translation

Chuang Ying-ting

—ɯ—

A New Environment for Subtitling

The focus of this paper is on investigating representation in subtitle translation. With the changing social, technological and economic contexts, subtitling practice, like other translation practice, is evolving, as more modes, forms, media and channels are available and used for creating meaning. The technology of the new information and communication media has made more and more semiotic modes available and easy to use and has analysed and stored them in the form of digital codes.

Given the information technology around us, the working environment for subtitling is shifting from paper-based to electronic-based. To be more specific, the subtitle translator used to watch a videotape, write on the transcript of the film or programme, and then translate the transcript into subtitles. Nowadays, the translator can watch a film or programme, mark the transcript and do subtitling on the same computer screen simultaneously, which allows him or her to work on more than one semiotic mode at the same time, and to pay attention to how the modes of moving images, music, sound effects, etc. are related to dialogues in order to integrate the subtitles into the film or programme. Around a decade ago, these things could not be easily or cheaply dealt with.

This is the present reality, which is leading to changes and new challenges, reshaping subtitling practice and moving the study of subtitling in a new direction. In the previous era, scholars were concerned with technical problems that can only be found in subtitle translation, such as the maximum length of a subtitle, the location of subtitles in the film, the speed of switching subtitles and the synchronicity between subtitle and dialogue or subtitle and image (de Linde and Kay 1999). Some were concerned with the specific features that distinguish subtitle translation from other translation practices (Gottlieb 1994, 1998; Zabalbeascoa 1997; Chaume Varela 1997), emphasising the fact that subtitle translation involves not only two languages but also two modes. Within this point of view, instead of considering subtitling as a kind of 'horizontal' translation, Gottlieb defines subtitling as "diagonal translation" (1994: 104–105), since it deals with 'diagonal' translation from the spoken to the written mode, rather than from written to written or from spoken to spoken. He also suggests that the translator should take into account other visual and audio elements (such as music and sound effects) which contribute to the verbal elements, because non-verbal modes form the context in which the speech or writing is embedded. Thus, this view of subtitling shows an attempt to consider non-verbal semiotic modes, a move which is supported by other scholars of subtitle translation (Delabastita 1989, 1990).

Later, the focus was expanded from two modes to multi-modes and multimedia (Gambier and Gottlieb 2001; Remael 2001; Taylor 2003). Remael's and Taylor's approaches are both based on Halliday's functional-systemic tradition, and partly on Kress and van Leeuwen's semiotic concepts. Remael looks at the semiotic and pragmatic specificities of multimedia translation, pointing out that the role of language changes according to the multi-modal text in which it is embedded. Taylor proposes a multi-modal methodology, adapted from Thibault's model for television advertisement texts, to analyse different screen genres by breaking subtitles into single frames/shots/phases to show how semiotic modalities operate in each frame/shot/phase and to formulate subtitling strategies. He discusses the effects of 'maximum subtitling' (expressing as much of the original message as possible) and 'minimum subtitling', and suggests that reduced-version subtitles may receive greater appreciation than elaborated ones, in particular from audiences looking to be entertained, because they could learn from "the contextualization created by the other semiotic modalities" (Taylor 2003: 204).

Remael and Taylo both recognise the importance of multi-modality in studying subtitles, which is a significant move in this field. This paper will go a step further, on the basis of the view that subtitle translation involves a multiplicity of semiotic modes which give shape to the text of film and of subtitled film, to look into how this multiplicity of modes actually works in the subtitling process, and to discuss both how the modes interact with each other and generate meanings and how this kind of translation is transformed to meet cultural and communicational demands.

The Interplay of Multi-modality

The use of technology, in particular computers and the Internet, facilitates, supports and modifies the process of subtitling, so that "multimodality is made easy, usual, 'natural' by these technologies" (Kress 2003: 5). The co-presence of other modes in subtitles raises the question of their functions: how do they contribute meanings to the subtitled film? And if they do contribute meanings, do they represent the same meanings in the original film as in the subtitled film? Is the spoken mode, represented principally as 'dialogues' in the original film, always the main source of meaning, while others remain marginal?

To discuss subtitle translation from a multi-modal perspective, the concept of semiotic mode should be clarified. In this paper, the concept of semiotic mode is based upon the theories of certain social semiotic scholars (O'Sullivan et al. 1994; Nöth 1995; Lemke 1998; Kress and van Leeuwen 1996, 2001; Kress, Jewitt, Ogborn and Tsatsarelis 2001; van Leeuwen 1999), in particular, Gunther Kress (1997, 2003), who notice the close link between materiality and making and interpreting signs and meanings. For them, mode bears material aspects that are culturally and socially fashioned resources for making meanings. Since the potentials and limitations of modes are absolutely related to materials, language should be classified into two modes: i.e., written and spoken.

Because mode is developed from materials, each mode has its materiality, affordance, functional specialisation and functional load. "Cultures work with these material affordances in ways which arise from and reflect their concerns, values and meanings" (Kress 2003: 45), so that the **materiality** of the mode (e.g., the material of 'sound' in music or speech) determines its **affordance** in certain contexts (e.g., sound cannot be afforded in writing, painting, or photography). However, the affordance is not fixed, but is constantly changing (e.g., sound could not be afforded in emailing ten years ago, but after it became possible to digitalise sounds, they could be used in emails). "The distinct representational and communicational affordances of modes lead to their **functional specialization**, either by time or by repeated uses" (ibid.: 46), which means that the functions or the represented meanings of a mode are closely related to its affordances; for instance, an image is better for representing things in space, and sound is better for representing things in time. The functional specialisation and affordances of modes determine the **functional load** which each mode carries in a text. For instance, in Kress's observation (ibid.), the functional load in school textbooks of thirty years ago was for the most part carried by writing, but nowadays it is carried by images of all kinds.

New technologies of information and communication improve the affordances of modes, support the multiplicity of modes and redistribute the functional load of multi-modal texts. In a multi-modal text, modes work individually and collectively at the same time. This means that "modes produce meaning in themselves and through their intersection or interaction with each other" (Kress, Jewitt, Ogborn and Tsatsarelis 2001: 14). In the case of subtitle translation, semiotic modes, such as the spoken mode, the written mode, the mode of music, the mode of sound effects and the mode of moving images, become affordable with the aid of technology, and they operate in the subtitling process individually and collectively. As a result, to interpret the text of a film, or to be more specific, to decode the meanings of the text of a film, the subtitler has to deal with the meaning potentials generated from the multi-modality of the text.

Multi-modal Translation Practice

Up to this point, it is clear that subtitle translation does not involve translating from dialogues to subtitles, but translating from the text of a film to the text of a subtitled film. It is worth noting that, if one takes subtitling as a multi-modal practice, the source text is the film and the target text is the subtitled film. To be more specific, the subtitler has to consider the source or target text as a whole, rather than taking verbal modes as the major object to deal with and other visual and audio modes as merely the context (see, for instance, Taylor 2003). If the source or target text acts as a whole, the context should be the social and cultural environment in which the text is embedded, rather than other audio and visual modes.

In the multi-modal approach, the text of a film is perceived as a meaningful whole that integrates meanings from all the semiotic modes represented in the text (Chuang 2007). Although the translator can make meanings only by the written mode, it does not mean that he/she cannot distribute meanings to other semiotic modes. To be more specific, in cases where the translator chooses not to render some meanings of the dialogues in the subtitles, he/she may distribute certain meanings in the visual modes (such as the moving images), or in the audio modes (music or sound effects). In other words, if the translator perceives the representation of a subtitled film as an integrated entity, then he/she could distribute meanings in all modes involved in the text of a film.

Hence, the equivalence relationship between the source text and the target text in subtitle translation is very complex, because it does not deal with one-to-one modal translation, i.e., from dialogues into subtitles, but with multi-modal translation, i.e., from all the involved modes in the source text into all the involved modes in the target text.

The meaning potentials of these modes are redistributed according to their functional specialisation. That is, the realisation of a particular mode may not be achieved in an equivalent mode in the subtitling process; the meaning potential of a particular source mode may be realised in more than one mode, possibly including the equivalent mode, in the target text. For instance, the meanings of the dialogues in the source text may be redistributed and realised in the subtitles as well as in the sound effects in the target text.

While redistributing, interpreting and representing the meaning potentials of the modes from the source text into the target text, certain meanings may be lost or gained in different aspects, so the totality of the meaning, sense, function and representation will be different between the source text and the target text. In fact, even if the translator tries to render everything in the dialogues into subtitles without redistributing meanings into other modes, the functional loads and the totality of the meanings will be changed in the process of subtitling, because other semiotic modes involved in the text of a film (such as moving images and music) may be interpreted differently by the source and target audiences.

To make the idea of the multi-modal approach more concrete, in the next two sections I shall give some examples to show how the concept of mode works in the process of subtitle translation and how the translator represents the meanings of the source through the target modes.

The Concept of Modes in Subtitling

To discuss how the concept of mode, or the materiality of mode, influences the process of subtitling, I will consider how in the subtitles of the film *Crouching Tiger, Hidden Dragon[1]*, the translator deliberately omits certain oral expressions, such as "Hey," "Yo," tag questions (e.g. "isn't it") and repetitions, because they are more often used in the spoken than in the written mode. Hence, when the translator produces the written subtitles, he/she tends to choose not to represent the features of the spoken mode. Examples of these are shown underlined in Figure 7.1.

Figure 7.1   Examples from *Crouching Tiger, Hidden Dragon*

Dialogues	Subtitles
嘿，你這個老太太，怎麼張口就罵人哪？ Hey, you old witch! Why do you shout at me, Hah?	That's what you think, old witch!
只怪那位孟大俠福薄，愛就愛了唄 Too bad for Meng, but love is love, isn't it?	Too bad for Meng, but it's not your fault, or Li Mu Bai's.
千里迢迢啊！千里迢迢 A long journey. A long journey.	What a godforsaken place!
呦！頭兒回來啦 大姐這一去怎麼那麼久？ Yo, the boss is back. Why are you away for so long?	It's you! You've been gone a while.

The differences between the spoken and written modes are much discussed with regard to the issue of linguistic transference. Next, I would like to show that subtitles are not the only mode that can be handled by the translator; he or she may choose to distribute meanings among other modes, in particular when they deliver stronger and clearer messages than the spoken mode. As illustrated in Figure 7.2, the first image shows a girl holding a sword and pointing it at a person's neck. In the film the girl says, "Don't move." The message of the image is strong and clear, and can be comprehended through experiences common to most people. The girl's utterance in this case serves to repeat or to emphasise what is represented in the moving images. The translator chooses not to render the meanings conveyed by the spoken mode (dialogues) into any written mode (subtitles), such as "Don't move" or "Freeze."

Figure 7.2   Examples from *Crouching Tiger, Hidden Dragon*

Moving Images	Dialogues	Subtitles
	別動！ (Don't move!)	(None)
	他手裡有寶劍！ (He has a sharp sword!)	(None)

Instead, the translator makes the visual mode (moving images) carry a more functional load.

In the second image, a swordsman holds a sword in his hand, which is a clear visual message to the audience. Although someone in the film shouts out, "He has a sharp sword," the translator chooses not to render the meanings conveyed by the spoken mode (dialogues) into any written mode (subtitles). Again, the translator makes the visual mode (moving images) carry a more functional load. The spoken mode (dialogue) is turned into an audio mode rather than a verbal mode when the translator decides not to produce any subtitle. It may be said that the functional load of the spoken mode is reduced and redistributed not to the written mode (subtitles) but to the visual mode (moving images).

The translator's decision in the process of subtitling is, without doubt, influenced by the materiality of the semiotic modes of the film. Therefore, to approach subtitle translation from the perspective of mode helps the translator to understand the way meanings are transferred across the modes represented in the text of a film.

The Representation of Modes in Subtitling

Having illustrated the operation of materiality, I shall now examine how the concept of totality works in subtitling. By looking at the distribution and integration of the meaning potentials in the semiotic modes, I shall attempt to show how the target text, or the subtitled film, works as a whole in response to the expectations of the target audience and to the demands of the social and cultural context.

In considering the wholeness of equivalent relationships between the source and target texts, I shall first discuss how the semiotic modes in the source text working as a whole contribute meanings in the subtitles. I shall then examine how the meanings embedded in the source text are redistributed and realised in the semiotic modes of the target text, which also presents itself as a whole to the target audience.

Figure 7.3 shows that the spoken mode is not the only resource for contributing meanings in the subtitles. This instance illustrates how other semiotic modes (i.e., moving images and sound effects in this example) contribute their specific meanings to the process of subtitling. The translator integrates the meanings of certain sections of dialogues, moving images and music to create the meanings that make the same sense to the target audience as presented to the audience of the source text.

Figure 7.3   An example from *Crouching Tiger, Hidden Dragon*

Dialogues	Subtitles	Moving Images	Sound Effects
有本事就別用寶劍！ If you have real stuff, don't use the sword.	Without the Green Destiny, you are nothing.	Two women are fighting. One of them changes many weapons.	Various weapons rattling and clanking.
哼！打不贏怪兵器不好 Ha! Don't blame it on your weapons.	Don't be a sore loser.		

In Figure 7.3, the moving images and the sound effects show that two women are fighting fiercely while one of them uses many weapons against the Green Destiny sword. The transformation from "Don't blame it on your weapons" to "Don't be a sore loser" suggests that, apart from the meanings of the source dialogues, the translator selects meanings from the modes of moving images and of sound effects, showing that the Green Destiny is used against the other weapons.

If the translator did not integrate the meanings from the modes of moving images and sound effects, it is very likely that the target audience would miss the significance of why the utterance is expressed at that particular time and on that particular social occasion. That is, in the source text, the utterance "Don't blame it on your weapons" is a metaphor, implying that the woman with the Green Destiny thinks she defeats the other not because of weapons on that social occasion, but because of her better martial arts. Without the moving images and sound effects, even the source audience would find it difficult to understand the meanings embedded in this specific section of the source text. Consequently, when the translator integrates the meanings of the sound effects and the moving images, the subtitle certainly loses the meaning of the metaphor in the utterance, but it signifies the wholeness of the meanings represented in the source text.

Figure 7.4   An example from *Crouching Tiger, Hidden Dragon*

Moving Images	Dialogue	Subtitles
	你沒摸過兵器 就覺得它沈 (沉) You've never touched a <u>weapon</u> before, so you think it is heavy.	You're just not used to handling <u>it</u>.

Figure 7.4 illustrates how the translator uses certain semiotic modes in the target text to represent the wholeness of the equivalence of the source text. The image shows two girls appreciating a famous sword, while one of them tells the other that the weapon is heavy for one who has no experience with swords. The dialogue integrates meanings from the moving images in the source text, implying that the weapon is the sword. In the target text, words like "weapon" and "sword" are not used in the subtitles; the translator uses the pronoun 'it' to draw the audience's attention to the moving images. By choosing to use the pronoun 'it' in the subtitle, the translator actually integrates the meanings of the spoken word with the meanings of the moving images, and represents the integrated meanings in the written mode and the moving images. In doing so, the functional load of the moving images in the target text is heavier than that in the source text.

This shows that the written mode (subtitles) is not the only mode handled by the translator, and all the modes represented in the target text are available to him or her. Although the translator cannot change the representation of these modes (apart from the subtitles), he/she can change, i.e., reduce or increase, the functional load of any of them, and to make them operate as a whole to represent the meanings of the source text.

Conclusion

This paper has investigated the concept of multi-modality in the process of subtitle translation, in which equivalence relationships range from a one-to-one to a many-to-many relationship, in terms of the concept of semiotic mode. That is, the translator has to create a kind of equivalent wholeness between the source and target texts by engaging in multi-modal translation. All the semiotic modes used in a film are the resources and representational tools of meaning potentials. The translator can redistribute the functional loads according to the functional specialisation of each mode. As the mode of images has now become dominant, it can work more efficiently nowadays than ever before. What's more, it is likely that other semiotic modes, such as sound effects and music, could become more active in a multi-modal text with the changes in communication needs and functions, in contrast to the declining importance of the verbal mode. In this situation, the translation of multi-modal texts, as in subtitling, requires not only a one-way decoding and encoding process, but multiple ways of translating. Subtitling could be the best area to study the newly-developed and growing multi-modal type of translation.

Note

1. The film *Crouching Tiger, Hidden Dragon* was directed by Ang Lee and released in 2000. It was nominated for numerous awards and won 4 Academy Awards in 2001.

References

Chaume Varela, Frederic. 1997. "Translating non-verbal information in dubbing." In Poyatos, Fernando (ed.), *New Perspectives and Challenges in Literature, Interpretation and the Media.* Amersterdam: John Benjamins, pp. 315–325.

Chuang, Ying-ting. 2007. "Studying Translation from a Multi-modal Approach." *Babel,* 52/4: 372–383.

de Linde, Zoé and Neil Kay. 1999. *The Semiotics of Subtitling.* Manchester: St. Jerome.

Delabastita, Dirk. 1989. "Translation and mass communication: Film and TV translation as evidence of cultural dynamics." *Babel,* 35/4: 193–218.

———. 1990. "Translation and mass communication." In Bassnett, S. and A. Lefevere (eds.), *Translation, History and Culture.* London: Pinter Publishers, pp. 97–109.

Fairclough, Norman. 1992. *Discourse and Social Change.* Cambridge: Polity Press.
———. 1995. *Critical Discourse Analysis: The Critical Study of Language.* London: Longman.
Gambier, Yves and Henrik Gottlieb (eds.). 2001. *(Multi) Media Translation.* Amsterdam: John Benjamins.
Gottlieb, Henrik. 1994. "Subtitling: Diagonal Translation" *Perspectives: Studies in Translatology* 2/1: 101–121.
———. 1998. "Subtitling." In Mona Baker (ed.), *Routledge Encyclopedia of Translation Studies.* London: Routledge, pp. 244–248.
Kress, Gunther. 1997. *Before Writing: Rethinking the Paths to Literacy.* London: Routledge.
———. 2003. *Literacy in the New Media Age.* London: Routledge.
——— and Theo van Leeuwen. 1996. *Reading Images: The Grammar of Visual Design.* London: Routledge.
——— and Theo van Leeuwen. 2001. *Multimodal Discourse.* London: Edward Arnold.
———, Carey Jewitt, Jon Ogborn, and Charalampos Tsatsarelis. 2001. *Multimodal Teaching and Learning: The Rhetorics of the Science Classroom.* London: Continuum.
Lemke, Jay L. 1998. "Multiplying meaning: Visual and verbal semiotics in scientific text." In J. R. Martin and R. Veel (eds.), *Reading Science.* London: Routledge, pp. 87–113.
Nöth, Winfried. 1990. *Handbook of Semiotics.* Bloomington: Indiana University Press.
O'Sullivan, T., J. Hartley, D. Saunders, M. Montgomery, and J. Fiske. 1994. *Key Concepts in Communication and Cultural Studies.* London: Routledge.
Remael, Aline. 2001. "Some thoughts on the study of multimodal and multimedia translation." In Yves Gambier and Henrik Gottlieb (eds.), *(Multi) Media Translation.* Amsterdam: John Benjamins, pp. 13–22.
Taylor, Christopher J. 2003. "Multimodal Transcription in the Analysis, Translation and Subtitling of Italian Films." *The Translator*, 9/2: 191–205.
Zabalbeascoa, Patrick. 1997. "Dubbing and the nonverbal dimension." In Fernando Poyatos (ed.), *New Perspectives and Challenges in Literature, Interpretation and the Media.* Amsterdam: John Benjamins, pp. 327–342.

8

Let the Words Do the Talking:
The Nature and Art of Subtitling

Gilbert C. F. Fong

—⚏—

Subtitling is the most common among all translation activities. Outside English-speaking countries, subtitles are encountered almost daily—whenever people turn on their television or go to a Hollywood cinema, they are sure to see subtitles coming at them from the screen. If we say that watching television has become an everyday ritual not without pious followers, then subtitles have acquired an almost religious status: we look for them and become psychologically dependent on them, and their absence can be the cause of discomfort. To the film-maker, subtitles are just as necessary and important, as they can make or break a film when it enters a foreign market. Ang Lee, the famous director, once admitted that it was fortunate that he had decided to use subtitles instead of dubbing for his film *Crouching Tiger, Hidden Dragon* (2000); otherwise, it would not have won the Academy Award for Best Foreign Language Film.

Cross-media Transference

Subtitles represent and re-present dialogue, which is speech, as writing; in this sense, subtitling is a cross-media transference of meaning and message: the process involves a double conversion, traversing from one language to another and from one medium to another. In 1984, Raphael Nir (1984: 84) already referred to subtitling as a "double conversion" from one language to another and from one medium to another. A more cogent analysis of the subtitling process is found in Henrik Gottlieb's idea of "diagonal translation":

Figure 8.1   Henrik Gottlieb's idea of "diagonal translation" (1994:104; modified)

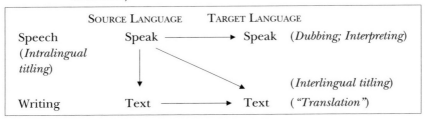

Gottlieb points out that interlingual subtitling, "being *two-dimensional*, 'jaywalks' [crosses over] from source-language speech to target-language writing" (Gottlieb 1994: 104). And the subtitler has to face both the challenges presented by the switch from one sub-code to another and the difficulties of retaining speech characteristics in a written text, especially those in spontaneous speech, such as pauses, false starts, interruptions, ungrammaticalities, as well as idiolectal, dialectal and sociolectal features (105–106).

What does this mean for the subtitle translator? First, he has to pay attention to the incompatibility between the oral and written codes, which can interfere with the intended correspondence between dialogue and subtitle. Spontaneous speech is characterised by "normal non-fluency" features, including voiced fillers, short, silent pauses, mispronunciations, unnecessary repetitions, grammatical structures which are abandoned, attempts at taking turns that are lost, and the competition to take the conversation off onto a topic of choice (Short 1996: 176). The dialogues in a film or television programme, like those in drama, are written to be spoken, while everyday conversation is unprepared and unrehearsed. The normal non-fluency features do not occur as frequently in a film, but when they do, they are usually intended to serve a purpose. So subtitles have to "transfer the dialog from one subcode (the seemingly unruly spoken language) to another (the more rigid written language)" (Gottlieb 1994: 106). The dichotomy has its drawbacks, for the written text often cannot fully reproduce the mannerisms of speech, and is liable to neutralise their impact. For instance, in the case of vulgarisms, subtitles tend to replace them with milder expressions, thus mitigating their offensiveness (Fong 2009: 39–61). The fact that the transference is between two languages also increases the difficulty, especially when phonetic features such as pronunciation, accents and dialectal features are involved.

System of Interacting Signs

Unlike other kinds of translation that operate in one semiotic mode (usually words), subtitling is sited in a system of interacting signs. There are sights and sounds in the movie, and all of them possess iconic, indexical, and symbolic values. Chuang Ying-ting (2009) proposes in her paper entitled "Subtitling as a Multi-modal Translation" that there are five semiotic modes most frequently represented in the text of a film: the spoken mode, the written mode, the mode of music, the mode of sound effects and the mode of moving images. Taking issue with Gottlieb, she argues that subtitling is not just conversion from the spoken to the written mode, for subtitles can be made to represent the signifieds coming from all the semiotic modes in a film.

> [I]n the process of subtitle translation, … equivalence relationships range from a one-to-one to a many-to-many relationship, in terms of the concept of semiotic mode. That is, the translator has to create a kind of equivalent wholeness between the source and target texts by engaging in multi-modal translation. All the semiotic modes used in a film are the resources and representational tools of meaning potentials.
>
> (Chuang 2009: 88–89)

In her opinion, subtitles should be a semiotic catch-all which may be used to translate not only dialogues, but also images coming from sound effects, visual images and others. Even if we find her assessment overly optimistic, we have to admit that in a subtitled film the written text does not operate by itself, but is accompanied and compensated for by other signs. And if the words do not fully convey the effect of the dialogue: for instance, its emotive value, they can be compensated by the tone, pitch and volume of the actor's voice, and by the actions, gestures and body movements, i.e., the body language. That is why some subtitlers tend to focus on information transfer and dispense with the dramatic quality of the dialogue, obviously thinking that it will be picked up by the audience during the course of the film. Needless to say, such an approach will usually result in the loss of colour and specificity. Subtitles are symbolic signs, and as such they should be fully utilised to contribute to the signification value. As they are already there at our disposal, it would be a waste not to put them to good use, to facilitate the communication process and to make the film-viewing experience more interesting and entertaining.

Space and Time Constraints

Subtitling operates within constraints of both space and time. The norm is to put 35–40 characters on one line of subtitle and to have a maximum of two lines on screen at any given time. Lengthiness should be avoided to give the audience sufficient time to read the words. (With Chinese subtitles, the maximum is 15 characters, and the norm is for only one line. This is probably owing to the fact that Chinese characters take up less space and are capable of carrying more semantic load than English words.) When bilingual subtitles appear together, normally two one-liners (one from each language) are used to avoid overcrowding the picture.

Taking the place of the sound of speech, subtitles are almost like silent dubbing, the dubber being the audience members themselves, who read the subtitles and put the words into the characters' mouths. Because of this, subtitles have to be synchronous with the dialogues they are translating. In a film, subtitles normally appear 0.25 second after the utterance starts (the brain needs time to prepare the eyes to move to the bottom of the screen in anticipation of the subtitles), stay on the screen for 3–6 seconds, and are removed no more than 2 seconds after the utterance finishes (lagging-out time). With single-word subtitles, the minimum is 1.5 seconds—if the time were shorter, the subtitles could easily be missed by the audience as they would only be flashes on the screen. According to Fotios Karamitroglou, a literate person aged 14–65 can normally read 150–180 words per minute, i.e., between 2.5 and 3 words per second (Karamitroglou 1998). As mentioned above, films operate by means of a system of interacting signs, so the audience has to attend to both the sight and the sound on the screen in order to get the complete picture: that is to say, they cannot give the subtitles their undivided attention at all times. Subtitles cannot, therefore, just flash by on the screen for a short time, since the audience would not have enough time to read them; nor can they stay on the screen for too long, as the audience would automatically reread the words and become confused.

Condensation and Ellipsis

Working under space and time constraints, the translator has to resort to condensation and ellipsis techniques in order to accommodate the need to include all the information required to understand the movie. Information units in the dialogue are ranked according to their "relevance," when deciding whether to retain or omit them. In order to optimise relevance—to convey the maximum amount of information using the minimum number of words—expansion, explication, vocatives, appellatives, proper names, circumstantials and modifiers are usually the first to be discarded if space is limited (Kovačič 1994). Subtitling is thus "defective translation," in the sense that subtitles often cannot fully reproduce the content of the source text (the dialogue). For example, with lyrics in Chinese operas, which are essentially lines of verse densely packed with emotions, connotations and metaphorical devices, the reduction in subtitles is drastic. The following are two lines of lyrics from the Cantonese opera *The Purple Hairpin* [紫釵記 *Zichai ji*] (1975):

1. 願折蟾宮桂，
2. 來伴玉瓶花　　I'm willing to accompany a beauty

A literal translation of the lines goes like this:

1. I wish to pluck osmanthus flowers from the toad palace (51 characters)
2. As company for the flower in the vase of jade (41 characters)

The "ground" of these two lines, which include many metaphors specific to Chinese culture, is that the speaker is willing to go to any lengths to please his beloved, even to the point to travelling to the moon to pluck osmanthus flowers to be company for his beautiful lover, who is as beautiful as a flower. Here, the subtitler combines the two lines into one. He also dispenses with the metaphors and tries to translate the sense, which is quite acceptable, except that in this case, his interpretation is unfortunately misleading. One may adopt a compromise approach, and using the "relevance" principle, come up with the following:

1. I wish to gather flowers from the moon (38 characters)
2. As company for my beloved (25 characters)

The name of the flowers (osmanthus) is omitted, and the culture-specific metaphor "toad palace" is replaced by "the moon," in which the image of the "moon" is universal. The change is necessary for easy comprehension even though it takes up more space. In line 2, the ground (my beloved) of the metaphor (flower in a jade vase) is used, again for easy comprehension. "Flower" as a metaphor for the female sex signifies beauty, which is omitted, as this quality may be assumed and can be seen by the audience. The two lines are short enough to be written out as one-liners, which are tidier and easier to read.

Linguistic and Stylistic Features

Linguistic features, especially when they are motivated and foregrounded, are an essential element of a text and they should not be passed over in translation. The properties of speech and those of the written word are different. The former makes use of phonic features such as pitch, tone, voice and rhythm to convey extralexical messages, and these are not easily reproduced in words. But there are sufficient overlaps in function between the two forms of language to enable subtitles at least to approximate what is said in terms of cognitive content and emotive value.

The space and time constraints put a limit on how much the translator can do in his or her attempt to reproduce stylistic features. This is not to say that we should just throw in the towel and tell ourselves that nothing can be accomplished. Translation, like most things, involves compromise and has to operate within limits. The translator has to try to recreate the same vocabulary, register and manner of speaking of the dialogues, even if only as reinforcement, rather than relying indirectly on the sights and sounds on the screen to compensate for the characterisation void that exists in the subtitles. Otherwise, colour and details will be lost, and the subtitles will become so bland that the audience will lose interest in reading them.

For example, in the Mike Myers's movie *Austin Powers: International Man of Mystery* (1997), we encounter the villain, Dr. Evil, and his son Scott. The son is a rebellious, good-for-nothing teenager and he speaks in a style typical of a street-smart kid of the 1990s:

> Well, me and a buddy went to the video arcade in town and, like, they don't speak English right, and so my buddy gets into a fight, and he goes "hey quit hassling me cause I don't speak French or whatever," and the other guy goes something in Paris talk, and I go "um, just back off" and he goes "get out" and I go "make me."

The simple vocabulary, halting rhythm, and ungrammaticalities are indications of slackness and a dearth of intellect. These character traits as expressed in the dialogue should be incorporated in the subtitles. Scott's father, Dr. Evil, still lives in the 1960s (he was frozen in the 1960s and was defrosted after 30 years). His speech, characterised by conceitedness, is a farcical showcase of his pedantry. It is packed with multisyllabic words and complicated sentence structures. The following are two examples:

> I'm going to put him in an easily-escapable situation involving an overly-elaborate and exotic death.
> All right, guard, begin the unnecessarily Slow-Moving Dipping Mechanism.

Besides linguistic features, interpersonal relationships in the film are also important. Many plot lines are built on the changing of power positions between the characters, and these changes invariably have an impact on the manner in which they speak, their choice of vocabulary, syntax and timing. These have to be adequately reflected in the subtitles. Here, the techniques of discourse analysis can be helpful, as they identify the deviations from the expectations of normal conversation, such as relevance, appropriate economy, honesty and clarity (Grice 1975); and if these deviations occur, then we have to be careful in our interpretation of the dialogue to convey the inferences and hidden meanings. In other words, the translator has to translate not only what the character says but also what lies behind the words.

Power relations among characters can also be gauged through politeness or impoliteness as they are revealed in dialogues. Impoliteness makes dramatic situations interesting, and there are many such cases in every film. In the dialogue we can find threats, politeness and its reciprocity (or lack of), together with other forms of social interaction, as indicators of power and change. Another revealing device is to examine turn-taking in the dialogue. Powerful speakers usually have the most frequent and the longest turns, initiate conversations, control the subject, decide who talks when, and interrupt others (Short 1996: 205–217). Conventions governing politeness and turn-taking vary among cultures, but many are universal and their implications are translatable into the target language through linguistic means.

Translating Song Lyrics

The graphical arrangement of subtitles has an impact on the translation of lyrics. Some years ago, a famous Hong Kong subtitler took great pains to translate the lyrics of the film musical *Evita* (1996) into subtitles that rhymed.

1.	Don't cry for me, Argentina!	阿根廷，別為我淚盈盈！
2.	The truth is I never left you	說句心底話，我從未離開過大家
3.	All through my wild days ... my mad existence	儘管當年任性墮落
4.	I kept my promise	我仍遵守承諾
5.	Don't keep your distance	請勿和我隔膜
6.	And as for fortune ... and as for fame ... I never invited them in	名名利利，我從不希冀
7.	Though it seemed to the world ... they were all I desired	世人以為我熱衷名與利
8.	They are illusions	名利如水中月
9.	They are not the solutions they promise to be	難把問題解決
10.	The answer was here all the time	解決之道，早在這裏為你鋪好
11.	I love you and hope you love me	我對你們好，也希望得到回報

In order to accomplish this, he had to resort to padding and altering meanings to accommodate the rhymes. However, this proved to be a futile exercise, because Chinese subtitles usually appear one line at a time and the audience could not see the rhymed lines coupled together. With English subtitles, unless the rhymed lines are couplets shown at the same time, the rhymes would not be noticed. Intricate rhyming schemes are particularly difficult to follow. As the audience can hear the songs along with the rhymes in them, there is no need for rhymed subtitles having the same rhyming scheme as the songs in the film. A group of students in one of my subtitling classes once translated and subtitled the lyrics of a song from the musical *A Chorus Line* (1985). They took great pains and succeeded in retaining the original rhyming scheme. Afterwards, they conducted a survey and to their disappointment found that the audience had not actually noticed the rhymes they had laboriously put into the subtitles. On the other hand, the audience did appreciate the effort in timing the subtitle breaks to coincide with the rhythm of the songs. A song's tempo can have a bearing on the timing of subtitles. If the tempo is fast, then the subtitle breaks may be fast and frequent. In that case, it is better to have short subtitles, so that the audience will have enough time to read the translated lyrics.

Translating Puns

Puns are the use of one word or words of the same or a similar sound to suggest different meanings, usually for humorous effect. As wordplay, they occur in many text types, especially in drama and other literary writings. There are two distinguishable but inseparable elements in a pun: meaning (homonymy) and sound (homophony). We find several meanings of one word, or the difference in meaning between two words pronounced the same and/or spelled somewhat similarly. In order to accomplish a translation of a pun, a correspondence has to occur between sound and meaning and between the languages. There are contextual and noncontextual puns; the former features a meaning (usually the primary meaning) related or bound to the linguistic environment (the context), and which has to be retained in the translation. The latter of course can be flexible, and the choice of the pun is left to the imagination of the translator. The challenge of translating puns in films is that the meaning or meanings in question often appear as images on the screen and cannot be substituted at random. With some situation comedies on television, the laughter of the studio audience is heard on cue (sometimes canned laughter is used) and the subtitler has no choice but to translate the humorous pun, otherwise the audience would feel themselves cheated and lose confidence in the subtitles. Let us take a look at another scene from *Austin Powers: International Man of Mystery* as an illustration. In this scene, a confrontation arises between Austin Powers and the guard at Dr. Evil's headquarters, and the latter's head dissolves in some kind of acidic poisonous liquid. Austin Powers, who never misses a chance for wisecracks, just cannot resist the temptation:

	Dialogue	Chinese subtitles	My translation
1. Austin	Hang on!	捉緊	扶好
2. Austin	Judo trip!	空手絆	空手道
3. Austin	Not a good time to lose one's **head**	不是當甩**頭**蝦的時候	沒頭沒腦
4. Vanessa	Indeed.	對	對
5. Austin	That's not the way to get **ahead** in life	也不是出**頭**的好方法	要出人**頭**地也 不要這樣
6. Vanessa	No		
7. Austin	It's a shame he wasn't more **headstrong**	如他硬着**頭**皮就不會 這樣	硬着**頭**皮就不會 這樣
8.	He'll never be the **head** of a major corporation	他永遠都做不成頂 **頭**上司	要當頂**頭**上司， 永遠當不成
9. Vanessa	Okay. That'll do.	好了，夠了吧	好了，不要再鬧了

The wordplay is on *head,* and the pun is contextualised, or bound, because *head* is the base or stem from which all the other meanings are derived. Fortunately, the Chinese language also offers many *head* phrases and thus the subtitles are able to sustain the joke. For those of you who know Chinese, you can see that the subtitles, except for line 7, largely retain the original pun and the expanded meanings. This is a happy coincidence, for in most cases the meanings represented by the punning word are not the same as those represented by its counterpart in the target language (hence the difficulty of translating puns). Perhaps the frequent use of *head* in idioms, as in this case, is universal among languages.

The Two Worlds of Subtitling and *Skopos* Theory

A subtitled film is characterised by the contemporaneous existence of both the source and target texts, i.e., the audience hears the dialogues and sees the subtitles at the same time. There is no hiding the translation act in subtitling, which in fact flaunts its "translatedness." As languages are symbolic of their respective cultures and realities, the source language in the film and the target language of the subtitles naturally lead to dual conceptual worlds. The challenge is to bridge the gap between the languages and the two worlds, so that the audience can comprehend the dialogue and gain access to the characters and their stories. There are three approaches that we can identify: foreignisation, neutralisation, and naturalisation. **Foreignisation** is source-oriented; it transports the audience to the film world. Through subtitles, members of the audience make an effort to acculturate themselves and to become immersed in the film world. **Naturalisation**, on the other hand, is for the purpose of localisation and it takes the film world to the audience. The language is domesticated and familiarised: the target-oriented effort involves not so much cleansing out the foreign as approximating the local and the familiar for easier consumption. And **neutralisation** attempts to take away local colour and references, emphasising the universality of characters, setting and situation. In cases of cultural specificity, it resorts to explanation rather than replacement. The audience play a more active role in reinforcing the illusion of unity and sameness. They may choose to assimilate with the movie world, thus temporarily giving up their cultural identity, or identify with their own culture. (Fong 2009)

Contemporary translation theory favours the foreignisation approach, with its retention of the source text culture and linguistic features. Lawrence Venuti (1995) advocates "visibility" in the target text, which highlights the linguistic character of the source language even to the point of sacrificing fluency and readability in the target text. With subtitling, the audience does not have the luxury of slow and leisurely reading as does the reader of written texts, thus comprehensibility is imperative. The challenge then is how to balance target language fluency and readability with the language-specific and stylistic features of the source text. This is where *skopos* theory, which focuses on the purpose of the translation act as the major factor influencing methods and strategies, comes in. While *skopos* theory does not preclude coherence between the target and the source texts, it demands that the target text be internally coherent. The target text is in fact accentuated and given a higher priority, for the aim is to produce a functionally adequate result (Reiss and Vermeer 1984: 119; quoted in Munday 2001: 79). Although *skopos* theory has been criticised for its inapplicability to literary texts, which are considered to have no specific purpose and are stylistically too complex, it is quite apposite to our discussion of subtitles, whose *skopos* is unmistakable and clearly defined—they are to serve the needs of the audience who are the end-users. In this connection, target text transparency is highly desirable, being the yardstick by which to measure the functional adequacy of the subtitles.

The Trend towards Domestication

The recent trend in Hong Kong film subtitles is towards domestication in language and cultural specificity. Instead of using the conventional modern Standard Chinese, which is a neutral language by comparison with the regional dialects, Hong Kong subtitlers increasingly adopt Cantonese, the local dialect, as the language of translation. This is more prevalent in comedies and action films, as Cantonese is not a literary language and it connotes a lower status. But even in drama or adaptations of literary classics, Cantonese expressions and syntax also crop up occasionally, and local references are frequently adopted to displace foreign people and things.

An interesting example is the Cantonese film *The Flirting Scholar* [唐伯虎點秋香 *Tang Bohu dian Qiuxiang*] (1993), a story about the famous Ming Dynasty scholar Tang Bohu (Stephen Chow) and his courtship of a beautiful maiden (Gong Li). In an impromptu poetry contest between the hero scholar-painter and his rival, the subtitles read:

Do a deer a female deer,
Re a drop of golden sun;
Me a name I call myself,
Fa a long long way to run ...

Obviously these lines are not translations of the dialogue. The appropriation of lyrics from the American musical *The Sound of Music* was likely to have been prompted as much by the difficulty of translating classical Chinese poetry into English as it was by the lack of sufficient space for a full translation. From the point of view of the English-speaking audience, they are of course aware of the inconsistency (or heterogeneity), but the subtitles and the world they construct are at least familiar to them, more so than if there were a literal translation of Chinese poetic lines. The incongruity, which is absurd and is blatant to the point of being self-conscious, also adds to the fun and humour of the action (which the audience can also see on the screen). (In some films, the subtitles are unintentionally funnier than the film itself.) If we move away from the traditional demands for fidelity and accuracy for a moment, the subtitles do manage to produce a functionally adequate result. Interestingly, if we can assume that the English subtitles in *The Flirting Scholar* were done by a local translator, then they were the product of an act of foreignisation for the sake of domestication for a foreign audience.

According to *skopos* theory, a target text does not have to be clearly reversible in relation to the source text (Munday 2001: 79). However, domestication cannot be an end in itself. There is a limit to how much a subtitler can domesticate before the subtitles overwhelm the movie world. At some point and to a large extent the subtitles have to be compatible and homogeneous with what the audience sees on the screen. Adaptation and rewriting are out of the question in subtitling, for unlike other types of translation, subtitles are not for independent reading. Thus the deconstructionist idea of translation as transformation does not apply. In other words, subtitling is parasitic, depending totally on the movie, which is the mother body, for the justification of its existence. It serves no other purpose than to help the audience understand the dialogue and enjoy the film.

The power dialectics between dialogue and subtitle remain fluid in a film. Kathleen Lundeen (1999) has argued interestingly for the ascendancy of subtitles over images and words (dialogue):

Nevertheless, titles act upon the original film in ways that exceed translation. Along with supplying an alternative to speech for those who are not fluent in the language of the film ... they also take on the character of a latent text. Even though they appear simultaneously with speech, they have retained the belated nature of the printed titles in silent movies. Detached from the visual montage and foregrounded on the screen, subtitles emerge as a subliminal voice in the art. They occupy the lower part of the frame, are usually positioned below the speaker's mouth, and are silent, as if they were indeed a repressed discourse.

Because of their editorial nature, Lundeen continues, subtitles can usually assert their authority and are more persuasive as a "truth-teller" than dialogue or images in a movie. In this, she appears to favour the subversive capability of subtitles. However, as a kind of meta-text, subtitles can just as easily reinforce the dialogue as they can subvert it, and one has to admit that subversion is for the most part confined to intralingual subtitling. It would not make sense for interlingual subtitles to subvert something that does not exist. And the audience's confidence can be shaken by the incompetence of a subtitler, thus depriving the subtitles of their truth-telling authority. As many bilingual cinema-goers can tell us, this unfortunately happens quite frequently. Perhaps the importance of subtitles hinges not on media hierarchy, i.e., the power positions occupied by dialogue, image and subtitles, but on the need to assist the audience to overcome their linguistic deficiency. Subtitles are supplements—they supply information that is already there (even though in another language), and paradoxically they are also indexical of a lack on the part of the audience. To them, subtitles are the indispensable channel of access to a film.

References

Chuang, Ying-ting. 2009. "Subtitling as a multi-modal translation." In this volume, pp. 79–90. Paper presented at *The International Conference on Dubbing and Subtitling in a World Context*. October 18–20, 2001, The Chinese University of Hong Kong.

Fong, Gilbert C. F. 2009. "The two worlds of subtitling: The case of vulgarisms and sexually-oriented language." In this volume, pp. 39–61. Paper presented at *The International Conference on Dubbing and Subtitling in a World Context.* October 18–20, 2001, The Chinese University of Hong Kong.

Gottlieb, Henrik. 1994. "Subtitling: Diagonal translation." In Cay Dollerup (ed.), *Perspectives: Studies in Translatology.* Copenhagen: University of Copenhagen, pp. 101–121.

Grice, H. Paul. 1975. "Logic and Conversion." In P. Cole and J. L. Morgain (eds.), *Syntax and Semantics,* Vol. 3: *Speech Acts.* New York: Academic Press, pp. 41–58.

Karamitroglou, Fotios. 1998. "A proposed set of subtitling standards in Europe." *Translation Journal* [Online serial]. Vol. 2, No. 2, http://www.accurapid.com/journal/04stndrd.htm.

Kovačič, Irena. 1994. "Relevance as a factor in subtitling reductions". In Cay Dollerup and Annette Lingegaard (eds.), *Teaching Translation and Interpreting 2: Training, Talent and Experience.* Amsterdam: John Benjamins, pp. 245–251.

Lundeen, Kathleen. 1999. "Pumping up the world with cinematic supplements." *Film Criticism,* 24, No. 1 (Fall 1999): 60–72.

Munday, Jeremy. 2001. *Introducing Translation Studies: Theories and Applications.* London: Routledge.

Nir, Raphael. 1984. "Linguistic and sociolinguistic problems in the translation of imported TV films in Israel." *International Journal of the Sociology of Language,* 48: 81–97.

Reiss, Katherina and Hans J. Vermeer. 1984. *Grundlegung einer Allgemeinen Translationstheorie.* Tubingen: Niemeyer.

Short, Mick. 1996. *Exploring the Language of Poems, Plays and Prose.* London: Longman.

Venuti, Lawrence. 1995. *The Translator's Invisibility: A History of Translation.* London: Routledge.

9

A Critical Evaluation of a Chinese Subtitled Version of Hitchcock's *Spellbound*

Chapman Chen

—ɯ—

Introduction

Categorisation

The mainland Chinese subtitled version[1] (1999) of the famous Hitchcock film *Spellbound* is a counter-example of good subtitling, in that it breaches without good reason almost all of the constraints of subtitling—technical, textual, intra-linguistic, and extra-linguistic, as proposed by Paola Guardini (1998).[2]

For our discussion, technical constraints are sub-divided into spatial and temporal ones (involving captions and dialogue). Textual constraints are sub-divided into the presentation of visual components and the reduction of the original according to relevance theory. Intra-linguistic constraints are sub-divided into "translationese," or undesirable linguistic Westernisation, common English expressions/idioms, proper use of Chinese idioms, segmentation, punctuation, and the choice of the correct equivalents of words. This article will also discuss issues related to extra-linguistic constraints including culture-specific items (personal names and jargon, psychoanalytical terms in our case), ideology (political, legal, gender, age, racial and filial), and poetics as revealed by the misinterpretation of culture-specific items.

The conditions of subtitling in China

The appalling quality of the subtitled version in question can probably be explained by three factors. First, mainland Chinese in general do not speak English and are not acquainted with Anglo-American culture. Most Chinese were forbidden to learn or to speak English during the Cultural Revolution (1966–1976). Secondly, the social status of subtitlers in China is very low. Poor working conditions compel them to translate very quickly with almost no time for revision. Thirdly, there is little specialised training in translation in mainland China, let alone specialised training in subtitling. Few universities in China provide a translation degree programme. (By contrast, there are seven universities in Hong Kong offering a translation degree programme.) The situation is even worse than that in Spain (Aixela 1996: 66–67).

Before examining the counter-example provided by the mainland Chinese subtitled version of *Spellbound*, let us first quickly go through the plot of the story.

Plot Summary

Dr. Anthony Edwardes (played by Gregory Peck) comes to Green Manors Psychiatric Hospital to replace the senile Dr. Murchison as head of the hospital. Dr. Constance Peterson, a beautiful but cold member of the hospital staff, falls in love with Edwardes at first sight. Edwardes is soon exposed as an amnesiac impostor, J. B. (tentatively called John Brown), who has possibly killed the real Edwardes. Peterson, firmly convinced that J. B. is innocent, helps him to escape from the police and seek refuge at the home of Dr. Alex Brulov, who is her former teacher. Peterson and Brulov then psychoanalytically interpret a recurring dream of J. B. Using the clues obtained from this interpretation, Peterson and J.B. find the spot where the death of Edwardes took place. At a critical moment, J. B. finally remembers that he ran into the real Edwardes when he was in the Cumberland Mountains trying to recover from a nervous breakdown he had had as a result of a plane crash. Edwardes had invited J. B. to go skiing with him in Gabriel Valley as a therapeutic procedure, and while they were out skiing, he plunged over a cliff to his death. This triggered J. B.'s old guilt complex regarding his younger brother, for whose accidental death during childhood he holds himself responsible. In an attempt to escape from his feelings of guilt, J. B. pretends to himself and to others that he is Dr. Edwardes.

Just when J. B., whose real name is now known to be John Ballyntine, and Peterson are congratulating themselves on their discovery, the police find them and arrest Ballyntine because a bullet has been found in the corpse of Edwardes. Peterson continues to trust Ballyntine and fight for his freedom. In a final encounter with Dr. Murchison, Peterson notices a Freudian slip made by Murchison and discovers that he is the real murderer, who committed the crime out of jealousy. Dr. Murchison then commits suicide.

Technical Constraints

To borrow the words of Guardini, technical constraints refer to the "time and space of presentation, (both) imposed by the original" (1998: 97).

Spatial constraints

According to Kenneth K. L. Au (1991), a maximum of two lines of subtitles in the case of English subtitling, and one line in the case of Chinese, should be presented at a time so that not too much of the screen image is covered. Moreover, the number of characters per line should not exceed 13 (1991: 337). Actually, in films subtitled in Hong Kong, the subtitles are usually single-lined; the maximum number of characters per line of subtitles varies from 13 to 16.

However, in the mainland Chinese subtitled version of *Spellbound*, although the subtitles are single-lined, many lines are between 16 and 19 characters long. The following example is not atypical.

Peterson:

When I made fork marks on the tablecloth they agitated you.
上次我用餐叉在白桌布上劃線條符號 (16 characters) (Last time when I drew lines and signs on the white tablecloth with the fork)
Then—that night you—you kissed me—you pushed me away. Because of my robe.

也使你緊張我吻你時期 (10 characters) (It also made you nervous when I kissed you)

It was white—

你的目光落在我的帶暗線條的白色長袍上時 (19 characters) (When you caught sight of my dark-lined long white robe)

it had dark lines on it.

你也非常恐懼 (6 characters) (You also became very frightened)

Time constraints

As pointed out by Guardini, "the time of presentation of the translation and the original coincide and the subtitles are presented at a pace that the receptor cannot control" (1998: 97).

Captioning

The following caption appears at the very beginning of the film. The first line of subtitles does not appear until the first paragraph of the caption has been on the screen for three seconds. And the last paragraph remains on the screen eight seconds after the last line of subtitles has disappeared. This gross temporal discrepancy between the verbal-visual element and the subtitles, to borrow the words of Karamitroglou, "would generate feelings of distrust toward the (quality of the) subtitles, since the viewers would start reflecting that what they have read might not have actually corresponded to what had been (captioned), at the time it had been (captioned)" (1998: 5).

> Our story deals with psychoanalysis,
> the method by which modern science
> treats the emotional problems of
> the sane.
> The analyst seeks only to induce
> the patient to talk about his hidden
> problems, to open the locked doors
> of his mind.
> Once the complexes that have been
> disturbing the patient are uncovered
> and interpreted, the illness and

confusion disappear ... and the
devils of unreason are driven from
the human soul.

Dialogue

According to Karamitroglou, the ideal duration of a full single-line subtitle is 3 1/2 seconds and "about 1/4 of a second needs to be inserted between two consecutive subtitles in order to avoid the effect of subtitles overlay" (1998: 4–5). If the time is too short, the reader will not be able to digest the subtitle fully; if the time is too long, automatic rereading of the subtitle will result (Karamitroglou 1998: 4; Au 1991: 338).

Consider the following dialogue, which is uttered urgently. The first subtitle (12 characters) and the second subtitle (13 characters) each last only 1.5 seconds, while the third (only 5 characters), disproportionately, lasts 2 seconds. No time is inserted between consecutive subtitles.

The fourth to the seventh subtitles, each 14 to 17 characters long, are no better. They occupy only 8.25 seconds together, i.e., 2.1 seconds each on average. And the last subtitle lasts 1.25 seconds. The overall effect is like that of machine gun fire (cf. Au 1991: 338).

Peterson's voice (urgently):

(1) No, No! You mustn't say you killed him darling!
    不，你沒有必要説是你殺了他 (12 characters) (No, you don't have to say you killed him)

(2) Try to remember what happened before Edwardes
    努力回想愛德華醫生翻下去前 (13 characters) (Try hard to remember before Dr. Edwardes fell over)

(3) went over.
    發生的情況 (5 characters) (what happened.)

Peterson's voice (desperately):

(4) But when he said he killed him, he wasn't himself!
    你説當時是他自己翻下去的時候 (14 characters) (When you said he fell over of his own accord)

(5) He was in a state of great mental distress.
    你的頭腦很正常沒有任何精神障礙 (15 characters) (Your mind is very normal, without any mental disturbance)

(6) [void]

你得保持頭腦清醒，你的供詞至關重要 (16 characters) (You have to remain sober, your statement is most important)

Peterson's voice (more frantic):

(7) But you can't put him away! You can't! It'll destroy his mind!

我要救你，証明你無罪，都要依據你的供詞 (17 characters) (I will save you, prove that you are innocent, it has to depend on your statement)

(8) Don't you understand?

你懂不懂！ (4 characters) (Don't you understand!)

Textual Constraints

As pointed out by Guardini, textual constraints refer to "the presence of the visual and verbal elements of the original, the spatial constraints implying the reduction of the original" (1998: 7).

Presence of visual components

According to Gottlieb, the visual components of the source text are composed of the verbal visual (captions and written signs) and the non-verbal visual (the images on the action screen) (1994: 265).

Graphic representations of linguistic signs

Graphic representations of linguistic signs, i.e., captions and written signs, must be translated for the benefit of the viewer. However, in the mainland Chinese version of *Spellbound*, a written note by J.B. and a written police order, both of a considerable length, are not subtitled at all, leaving viewers who do not read English in the dark. The police order is as follows:

DR CONSTANCE PETERSEN AND SUSPECT
FILE # 14298 NOW AT GABRIEL LAKE
LODGE. NEW EVIDENCE UNCOVERED
MAKES SURVEILLANCE ESSENTIAL
UNTIL ARRIVAL OF OFFICERS IN CHARGE =
                              LT J R HUNGATE
                              BY SGT DOAN.

Constraints Imposed by the Action Screen

Subtitles are supposed to match what is visibly happening on the screen. As pointed out by Guardini, "In subtitling, the significant content of the verbal-acoustic channel (the dialogue) is shifted to the verbal-visual … this shift must be executed without impairing the balance of the pre-existing visual and verbal channels. The subtitler must therefore pay heed to the visual information provided by the film" (1988: 99). In addition, Ian Mason (1994) says, "Subtitles are intended to be only a semi-verbatim rendering, which viewers match with their visual perception of the action screen, including gesture, body language, etc." (1998: 1068). However, in the mainland Chinese version of *Spellbound*, the subtitles often contradict the action shown on the screen.

> Example:
> J. B.:   How does it feel
>   現在你覺得做個精神分析家 (Now about being a psychoanalyst)
>   to be a great analyst?
>   有何感受？(What do you feel?)
> Peterson: Not so bad.
>   挺不錯的 (Not bad)
> J. B.:   And a great detective?
>   你還是一個大偵探 (You are also a great detective)
> Peterson: Wonderful.
>   挺好的 (Great)
> J. B.:   And **madly adored**?
>   想想你做的事，讓人佩服 (Think of what you have done: it's admirable)
> Peterson: Very wonderful.
>   很美妙！(Very wonderful)

Here, given the adoring expression in Gregory Peck's eyes on the screen, "madly adored" should be subtitled "令人愛慕 (profoundly adored)" instead of "Think of what you have done: it's admirable."

Reduction of the original

According to Delabastita, "[as] the film dialogues are usually delivered at a faster speed than a translation that is rendered graphically on the screen can keep up with...a certain compression or reduction of the text seems to be unavoidable" (1989: 203). As pointed out by Helene Reid, in many cases the reduction merely involves "deciding what is padding and what is vital information" (quoted in Gottlieb 1994: 264). Kovačič applies the relevance theory of Sperber and Wilson to subtitling reductions. Borrowing the words of Guardini, Kovačič relates the theory "to a 'cost-benefit' view of the subtitling process, whereby the viewer may get the maximum contextual effect with the minimum processing effort" (1998: 102). Kovačič identifies three types of contextual effect: (a) addition of contextual implications, (b) strengthening of old assumptions, and (c) elimination of false contextual assumptions (1994: 246).

Partial reduction

A film dialogue/monologue is delivered unusually fast when the speaker is in a desperate situation or a frantic mood, in which case reduction of the original in line with Kovačič's concept of relevance is especially necessary. Consider the example given in the section on time constraints above. It is rendered as eight lines of subtitles in the mainland Chinese version, but I believe we can condense the monologue to five lines of subtitles, as shown below:

Petersons voice (urgently):

No, No! You mustn't say you killed him darling!

不！你不可説自己是兇手 (No, you mustn't say you're the murderer)

Try to remember what happened before Edwardes went over.

試回想當時情況 (Try to remember the situation at that time)

Peterson's voice (desperately):

But when he said he killed him, he wasn't himself!

他説自己殺了人時 (When he said he killed him)

He was in a state of great mental distress.

不知自己在説甚麼 (he didn't know what he was saying)

Peterson's voice (more frantic):

But you can't put him away! You can't! It'll destroy his mind! Don't you understand?

不可囚禁他！那會毀了他的神經 (Don't lock him up! It will destroy his psyche)

In the first subtitle, the vocative "darling" may be omitted as the identity is clear. The emotive effect is already conveyed by the tone of the speaker. In the second subtitle, the decision to omit the reference to Edwardes' fall (cf. its retention in the mainland Chinese version) is based on the assumption that the viewers will be able to retrieve that piece of information from the previous context, in which the characters have been discussing whether or not the male protagonist had killed Dr. Edwardes. The fourth subtitle, "he didn't know what he was saying," carries a functional resemblance to the two expressions "he wasn't himself" and "he was in a state of great mental distress," which in turn bear a semantic resemblance to each other. In contrast, in the mainland Chinese version, the two expressions are translated in a very lengthy manner, and in a semantically incorrect way. In the last subtitle, "you can't" and "don't you understand" are omitted (cf. their retention in the mainland version) as they are double constructions designed to reinforce the emotive effect, which, however, is already being conveyed by the desperate tone of the speaker on the screen.

Total reductions

In subtitling, total deletion of lines of dialogue which are other than interjections or simple "yes" and "no" responses may result in the reduction of the subtitler's credibility in the eyes of the viewer. Consider the following dialogue. In the mainland Chinese version, the last two lines of dialogue were not translated at all.

Peterson: But that's not the point. The point
             詩也反映出詩人的內心世界 (Poetry can also reflect the inner world of the poet)
             is that people read about love as one thing—and experience it as another.
             人們讀關於愛情的詩。實際上 (People read poetry about love. In effect)
             They expect kisses to be like lyrical poems

相當於體驗別人的感情經歷 (it is equivalent to experiencing other people's emotional experience)
and—and embraces to be like Shakespearean dramas.
我讀莎士比亞的詩經常受感動 (When I read Shakespeare's poetry I am often moved)
愛情能拯救一個人的靈魂 (Love can save a person's soul)
使人從病患中康復 (It makes people recover from their illness)
Edwardes: And when they find out differently—
我有時卻發現有的人為了愛情 (Sometimes, however, I find that some people, for the sake of love)
Then they get sick and have to be analysed, eh?
把自己搞得病兮兮的 (make themselves quite ill)
Peterson: Yes—very often.
對，經常有這種情況 (True, this kind of situation happens very often)
Edwardes: Professor, you are **suffering from mogo on the gogo.**
Peterson: **I beg your pardon?**

The last two lines were not subtitled. The reason why the second last line was not translated is probably because the subtitler did not know what it meant. The line is likely to be psychoanalytical gibberish, which may be translated as "你患了分析症" (you have caught psychoanalysis mania).

The omission of information highly relevant to the plot is even more unforgivable. For example:

Hanish: He **has only brought one suitcase**. [not subtitled]
Perhaps he doesn't intend to remain very long.
他不會在這裏呆很久 (He won't stay here very long)

Here, the first untranslated English line provides the basis for the inference in the second line.

Linguistic Constraints

Linguistic constraints consist of intra-linguistic constraints, which are a consequence of syntactical and grammatical discrepancies between the two languages; and extra-linguistic constraints, which are largely imposed by culture-specific items (cf. Guardini, 1998:97).

Intra-linguistic constraints

The mainland version defies intra-linguistic constraints in its undesirable Westernisation, apparent ignorance of common English expressions, abandoning of good Chinese idioms, improper segmentation, problematic punctuation and failure to choose the correct equivalents of words.

Undesirable Westernisation

Under the influence of the poor English-Chinese translation carried out after the May Fourth Movement in 1919, an incongruous and clumsy "translationese" style of writing became popular in China. The mainland Chinese subtitled version of *Spellbound* is no exception. Quite a few of the lexical items used are redundant, including Chinese articles/measure words like *yige* 一個, *yizhong* 一種; the plural suffix *men* 們; third person pronouns, especially the inanimate pronoun, etc. (cf. Si Guo 1972; Laurence Wong 1996). These redundancies not only waste the precious word-space available for subtitling but also affect its flow.

On the other hand, according to Au (1991), the subtitles should read like Chinese (1991: 340) and according to Delabastita, syntax and style should not have a "foreign ring" (1989: 208).

Common English expressions/idioms

In order to do subtitling correctly, one has to be familiar with idiomatic expressions in the source language. The mainland Chinese subtitled version of *Spellbound*, however, often shows that the subtitler does not know the meaning of many common English expressions or idioms. In the following example, the phrase "take me in" is ridiculously misinterpreted as "take part in":

Miss Carmichael:

That smug, frozen face of yours **doesn't take me in**!

你不要參與我的事 (**Don't you take part in my affairs**)

In the following example, "in the first place" is misinterpreted as "in that place":

Peterson:

Because I'm convinced you didn't kill

因為我要你確信在那個地方 (Because I want you to believe firmly that **in that place**)

in the first place.

你沒有殺過人 (You didn't kill a person)

Proper use of Chinese idioms

According to Au (1991), the summarising power of Chinese idioms is so strong that when used properly, they will make subtitles concise and vivid (1991: 343). But the mainland Chinese subtitled version of *Spellbound* rarely, if ever, uses good Chinese idioms. In the following example, for the English expression "used to such surprises in my work," the four-character Chinese idiom, 見怪不怪 (become inured to the weird), is clearly much more succinct and appropriate than 我經常遇到驚訝的事情，我已經習慣了 (In my work I frequently come across surprising matters, I have got used to them). The contrast in length is 4 as opposed to 16 characters.

Mainland Chinese Version

Peterson:

I—I am used to such surprises in my work.

在我的工作中我經常遇到 (In my work I often come across)

驚訝的事情 我已經習慣了 (**Surprising matters I have got used to them**)

My Suggestion

Peterson:

I—I am used to such surprises in my work.

我…是醫生，見怪不怪 (I … am a doctor, **got used to strange things**)

Segmentation

Concerning segmentation, Karamitroglou has the following to say:

Subtitled text should appear segmented at the highest syntactic nodes possible. This means that each subtitle should ideally contain one complete sentence. In cases where the sentence cannot fit in a single-line subtitle and has to continue over a second line or even over a new subtitle flash, the segmentation on each of the lines should be arranged to coincide with the highest syntactic node possible... where the semantic load has already managed to convey a satisfactorily complete piece of information. (1998: 8–9)

The mainland Chinese subtitled text, however, more often than not, appears segmented at the lowest syntactic nodes possible:

Example:

Dr. Murchison:

I am sorry, Constance,
真抱歉，彼特森醫生，我覺得你有 (So sorry, Dr. Pi-te-sen. I think you **some**-)
That our staff still retains the manners of
時候不像個醫學院的學生，很 (**times** do not resemble a medical student very much **very**)
Medical students.
容易開小差 (easily slinking away)

Punctuation

Ideally, no more than two sentences should occupy the same line (cf. Karamitroglou 1998: 9). But, if necessary, the two sentences should be separated either by some punctuation mark, e.g., comma, semi-colon, full-stop, or by the space of a character (Karamitroglou 1998: 7).

Peterson:

When I made fork marks on the tablecloth they agitated you.
上次我用餐叉在白桌布上劃線條符號 (Last time when I drew lines and signs on the white tablecloth with the fork)
Then—that night you—you kissed me—you pushed me away. Because of my robe.
也使你緊張我吻你時期 (It also made you nervous when I kissed you)
It was white—
你的目光落在我的帶暗線條的白色長袍上時 (When you caught sight of my dark-lined long white robe)
it had dark lines on it.
你也非常恐懼 (You also became very frightened)

Peterson:

I intend to learn a great deal from Dr. Edwardes.

我覺得愛德華醫生應該是一個治學 (I think Dr. Edwardes should be a serious)

I think we all can learn from a man of such obvious talents.

嚴謹的學者，起碼他在心理研究分析上卓有成效 (scholar, at least he is very accomplished in psychoanalysis)

Choice of the correct equivalent

To borrow the words of Dollerup (1974: 201), "the failure to choose the correct equivalent when one word in the source language covers (or splits up into) two or more in the target language" occurs not infrequently in the mainland Chinese subtitled version of *Spellbound*. For example, "case" has at least two meanings: namely, "a situation requiring investigation or action" and "a box or receptacle for holding something" (*Webster's Ninth New Collegiate Dictionary*). In the following dialogue, the word "case" obviously has the former meaning, but is misinterpreted to be referring to a suitcase, probably because the subtitler does not know the word "amnesia."

Garff:

I say the fellow expected to get away with it—like any criminal

跟其他罪犯一樣 (Like other criminals)

這傢伙目前肯定急於逃走 (This fellow must be eager to run away now)

Fleurot:

Nonsense. Obviously a **case** of amnesia.

廢物。他來的時候只帶了一隻手提箱 (Useless thing. He only brought a suitcase when he came)

Extra-linguistic Constraints

Now we will examine extra-linguistic issues involving culture-specific items (personal names and jargon; psychoanalytical terms in our case), ideology (political, legal, gender, age, racial and filial), and poetics.

Personal names

The usual practice when translating personal names in mainland China is transliterating according to the *Hanyu Pinyin* system (Chen Dingan 1990: 158). As pointed out by Tao Jie, in China, "th" is invariably transliterated as 兹, "r" as 爾, "d" as 德, "t" as 特, as a result of which translated names are often lengthy and difficult to pronounce. For example, "Albright," the name of the former Secretary of State of the USA, obviously may be translated as *Ou Bu-lai* 歐布萊, but the translation used by Beijing is "*Au Er Bu Lai Te* 奧爾布賴特" (1999: 186).

Translation circles in mainland China also object to translating the surnames of Westerners as Chinese surnames, as well as translating names with either positive or negative connotations (Zhang Peiji 1980: 198).

On the other hand, the usual practice of personal name translation in Hong Kong is to try to be as concise as possible and also to sinicise as far as possible, taking into account both sound and meaning. As pointed out by Tao Jie, from the point of view of broadcasting psychology, the translation of a Western proper name must not contain more than four Chinese characters; otherwise, the receiver will not be able to assimilate it (1999: 186). For example, "MacDonald" is translated as *Maidanglao* 麥當勞, instead of *Maikeduonuoerte* 麥克多諾爾特, which would result if the strict transliteration practice were adopted, and which would probably repel many potential customers, and even mainland China has followed suit.

According to Gilbert C. F. Fong (1998: 423–426), during the colonial period, the Hong Kong government, when translating the names of Hong Kong governors and senior British politicians, tried to sinicise as much as possible. Since even the names of important Western politicians can be sinicised, it should only be more appropriate to sinicise names of characters in imaginative fiction and films, to render the translation easy to pronounce, empathetic to the audience, and compatible with the personality, background and status of the character concerned.

This practice, however, is not adopted by the mainland Chinese subtitler of *Spellbound*. In the table below, the two ways of translating personal names found in *Spellbound* are juxtaposed.

Original Names	Mainland Chinese Subtitled Version	Suggestion by the Author
John Brown	John Brown	包約翰 (Bao John)
John Ballyntine	*Yuehan Beilanteyin* 約翰・貝蘭特因	白逸鴻 (Bai Easy Swangoose)
Constance Peterson	*Bitesen* 彼特森	彭冠仙 (Peng Top Fairy)
Alex Brulov	*Ailikesi* 艾禮克斯	布樂夫 (Bu Happy Guy)
Fleurot	*Fularuo* 福拉若	傅樂天 (Fu Optimistic)
Dr. Graff	Pogodu	郭立夫 (Guo Upright Guy)
Murchison	*Mo qingsheng* 莫慶生	梅志森 (Mei Ambition Gruesome)
Miss Carmichael	*Mali Xiaojie* 瑪麗小姐	金小姐 (Miss Jin)

Here, it can be seen that the subtitler's translated names are lengthy, clumsy and difficult to pronounce. The names have no intelligible meaning so the audience cannot associate the names with the characters. In some cases, the subtitler even retains the original without doing any translation at all: e.g., "John Brown." Sometimes, an English name is orthographically adapted rather than transliterated: e.g., "Dr. Graff" is rendered as "Pogodu." By contrast, my versions are concise, sinicised and meaningful. For instance, my translation of the name of the graceful heroine, Constance Peterson, as Peng Guanxian 彭冠仙, implies a high-ranking goddess. The name of the bad guy, Murchison, on the other hand, is translated as Mei Zhisen 梅志森, implying gruesome ambition.

Psychiatric/Psychoanalytic jargon

When faced with a technical term, a subtitler should conduct research into it in order to find out its correct meaning, instead of ignoring it or improvising the rendition, especially when the jargon concerned is of great importance to the plot. As *Spellbound* is a story about psychoanalysis, there is quite a lot of psychiatric or psychoanalytic jargon which is crucial to be understood in order to appreciate the plot. The practice of psychoanalysis was briefly introduced into China during the early Republican years (1910s), but was interrupted by Japan's invasion of China. It was practically banned by the Communist Party until the end of the Cultural Revolution. In the 1980s, many works by Sigmund Freud and his followers were translated into Chinese.[3] However, almost all of the psychoanalytic jargon in *Spellbound* is either bluntly transliterated, ignored or grossly distorted by the mainland Chinese subtitler.

For example, *kleptomaniac,* which means a person who has a persistent neurotic impulse to steal, is transliterated in Chinese as the three-character term 梅尼亞 (*Mei-ni-ya*) without giving the viewer a clue as to what on earth the term means. For example:

Peterson:

I was going to lunch with Dr. Hanish.
我要與黑米基醫生共進晚餐 (I have to go to dinner with Dr. Hei Mi-ji)
He has an interesting new patient—a **kleptomaniac** who—
因為他對**梅尼亞**的病例很感興趣 (Because he is very interested in the case history of Mei-ni-ya)

Edwardes:

Kleptomaniacs for lunch!
談論梅尼亞的時候，小心嘴裏面 (When discussing Mei-ni-ya, beware lest)
They'll steal this food out of your mouth.
的東西會掉出來啊！ (the food in the mouth falls out!)

Often, a psychiatric or psychoanalytic term simply gets lost in the subtitles. Another example:

Dr. Murchison:

In order to conceal his crime—
取代了他的位置來掩蓋自己的罪行 (taken his place to conceal his own crime)
By pretending the victim was still alive.
一個罪犯就這樣成了大名鼎鼎 (In this way, a criminal has become a renowned)
This sort of unrealistic act is typical of the short-sighted cunning that goes with **paranoid** behaviour.
的心理分析醫生，真讓人意想不到 (Psychoanalyst. What a surprise)

Often, psychoanalytic concepts are grossly distorted: for example,

Peterson:

He was my analyst. He psychoanalysed me.
他是我的師父，精神分析專家和我一樣 (He is my master, a psychoanalyst like me)

J. B.:

Really! What—what was wrong with you?
真好！你有精神病要治嗎？(Wonderful! You have mental illness that needs to be cured?)

Peterson:

All analysts have to be psychoanalysed by other analysts
到他那兒可以請他幫忙解決你 (Go there and you may request him to help solve your)
before they start practising.
的問題 (problem)

Here, the professional role of classical psychoanalysts is totally misinterpreted in the mainland Chinese version and the mistranslation is textually not cohesive with the previous subtitle.

At other times, a psychoanalytic term is given a translation which deviates from the standard translation. For instance, according to *Zhongyi Xinlixue Cihui* (A Glossary of Psychological Terms), edited by the Editorial Committee of the Glossary and Social Research Centre, the standard translation of "resistance"[4] is *kang-ju* 抗拒 (1982: 172), but the mainland Chinese subtitler translates it as *di-zhi* 抵制 (boycott):

Peterson:

This room reminds you of something.
這個房間使你想起了什麼事情 (This room reminds you of something)

J. B.:

No.
不 (No)

Peterson:

You are **resist**ing a memory. What is in your mind?
你在自己的思想中**抵制**自己的記憶 (You are boycotting your own memory in your own mind)

Ideology and poetics as revealed by mistranslation resulting from mishearing

Mistranslation resulting from mishearing, in the mainland subtitled version of *Spellbound*, often reveals the ideology[5] and poetics of the subtitler and even that of the target language culture. This version is so full of mistranslations that we can only infer that the subtitler did not have access to the film script when doing the subtitling. As noted by Dollerup, "when there is no script … words may be misheard … translation does function as a kind of control of our understanding of what is being said, and mishearings will thus be revealed in the target language" (1974: 199). Many of the mistranslations are apparently the result of mishearing. For instance, the word "lieutenant" is mistranslated as *zuo-shou* 左手 (left hand), probably owing to the similarity in sound between "lieutenant" and "left hand."

Mistranslation as a result of mishearing reflects not only the linguistic incompetence of the subtitler but also the ideology and poetics of the target language side.[6] According to Freud, seemingly unintentional faulty actions or parapraxes are actually full-blown psychical phenomena that invariably have a meaning and a motive unknown to the conscious mind (1975: 300). Lefevere thinks that translation is always under the control of the ideology and poetics of the translator or of those in power, so much so that it will never truthfully reflect the original. Lefevere therefore calls all translation and edition (of literature, anthology, literary history and dictionaries) "rewriting," by which he means manipulation, or an effective means of serving the authorities (1992: 4–9).

Here, for the sake of discussion, we will divide the ideology revealed by the mainland Chinese subtitler's mistranslations into the categories of politics, law, sexism and filial culture. "Poetics" here refers to the concept of the function and the creation of literature.

Politics

The following mistranslation reveals the "old-people" politics of mainland China.

Brulov:

Do you know who makes the most trouble in the world—

你知道在屋子裡什麼人最能製造麻煩嗎？ (Do you know who creates the most trouble in the house?)
Old people. They are always worrying what is going to be
老年人。他們總是擔心他們謝世之後 (Old people. They are always worrying after they leave this world)
in the world tomorrow—after they are gone.
世界會變成什麼樣子 (what it will become)
That's why we have **wars**—
這對老年人**最有價值** (**This is of the greatest worth to the old people**)
Because old people got nothing else
因為現實世界中沒有什麼新奇的東西 (for there is nothing novel in the real world)
they can get excited about.
能夠再引起他們的激情 (that can arouse their fervour again)

Here, the misinterpretation of "wars" as "worth" reflects the fact that mainland China has been ruled for ages by old people who have been over-esteemed. It was Chairman Mao in his old age who started the catastrophic Cultural Revolution in the 1960s. So the mainland subtitler may unconsciously still think that elderly people have "the greatest worth," and would not be prepared to admit that it is old people who cause wars.

Law

The mainland Chinese subtitled version reflects the fact that there is still a great deal of room for improvement in China's legal system. For example:

Hickson:

We shall have to detain you, sir
我們得讓你明白，先生 (We have to make you understand Sir)
—and it's my duty **to inform you**
在事情還沒有徹底查清之前 (Before the matter is thoroughly investigated and clarified)
that **anything you say may be used**
你是最大的疑犯，所有的証據都對你不利 (You are the biggest suspect, all the evidence is against you)
against you.

我們要履行職責，必須把你帶走 (We have to do our duty, must take you away)

Here, in the original, the policeman, Hickson, is administering a caution to the suspect, J.B. In Britain and in Hong Kong, the police have to remind suspects of their right to remain silent immediately before arresting or taking any statement from them. This is known as a "caution," the full version of which reads, "You are not obliged to say anything. Whatever you say may be written down and may be used as evidence against you in court." It is based on the spirit of Common Law, which assumes every suspect to be innocent before proven guilty beyond all reasonable doubt by the court. This is, however, not the case in mainland China, where those suspected of a crime are assumed to be guilty by the police, who will not allow them to remain silent, but will coerce them into confessing by various means, including threats and torture. This is probably the unconscious ideological reason why the mainland subtitler misinterprets[7] the caution as a warning that J. B. is "the biggest suspect" "before the case is thoroughly investigated" and cleared up.

Sexism

Some mistranslations in fact reflect sexual discrimination. In the following example, the subtitler assumes that a beautiful woman like Constance Peterson can only be a sex symbol, instead of a fighter for truth. (Sexism is also reflected in the example cited in the later section on poetics.)

Fleurot:

You know, if you were anybody but Constance Peterson—
你們知道 沒有幾個人能抵擋得住人間尤物 (You know very few people can withstand the sexiest being in the world)
The human glacier and the custodian of truth—I'd say—
下凡仙女一樣的彼特森的魅力，我是說 (an angel on earth, Pi-te-sen's charm I mean to say)

Peterson:

Yes. You'd say what?
你要說什麼？(What do you want to say?)

Fleurot:

My dear, forgive me my scurvy thoughts.

我的感覺告訴我 (My feelings tell me)

You are not telling the truth,

有些事情你可能沒講真話 (About some matters you may not have told the truth)

Ageism, national prejudice and filial culture

Apart from sexism, the mainland version is also inclined towards ageism, national prejudice and filial culture. In the following example, the subtitles, which have little to do with the English dialogue, reflect biased assumptions on the part of the subtitler. First, "rheumatism" having been misheard as "romanticism"; it is assumed that young and middle-aged Westerners are all "romantic," which mainland Chinese understand to mean promiscuous. Secondly, "starting from childhood I have been following her/and suffering with her. Now she still has to count on my support" seems to be an unconscious derivative of the phenomenon of the symbiotic mother-son relationship[8] which is prevalent in China.

Gillespie:

How's your mother **lately**?

你的媽媽後來又去**晚**了吧 (Did your mother then arrive there **late** again?)

Cooley:

Oh, she's still complaining about **rheumatism.**

她一直在抱怨**浪漫主義** (She's been complaining about **romanticism**)

She figures I ought to get myself transferred down to **Florida.**

她老人家對沒有**實際用處**的東西不以為然 (She as an elder doesn't approve of **impractical** things)

I said, "do you expect me to

他讓我轉告你 (She asked me to tell you)

sacrifice **all chance of promotion** just

以後生活方面**不要過於浪漫** (that you should **avoid being too romantic** in your way of life henceforth)

because you've got rheumatism?"

多考慮點實際 (should be more practical)

Gillespie:

Did you take the subject up with Hennessy?

你把這種建議當耳邊風嗎？ (Do you regard this kind of advice as a puff of wind passing the ear?)

Cooley:

Yes. He says a transfer could be arranged,

對，她老人家這樣要求我未免 (Yes, for her the elder to make demands on me in this way)

But I'd probably have to start

有點太不公平了，我從小就跟 (Is somewhat too unfair. Starting from childhood, I have been following her)

all over again as a sergeant.

著他受苦受難，現在她還得靠我供養 **(and suffering with her. Now she still has to count on my support)**

I said, "Personally, I think that's unfair,

我沒有上過大學 (I have never received a college education)

After all the work I did on that **narcotics case.**"

但一些**現代思想**我還是能夠接受的 (But some modern thoughts I can still accept)

Gillespie:

What did **Hennessy** say to that?

她老人家也是一片用心良苦 (Anyway she the elder has expended much care and thought)

Poetics

The following example of misinterpretation reveals mainland Chinese assumptions about poetry—especially love poetry, and love itself. First, the phrase, "poetry is just tricks played by big kids to cheat small kids," condemns poetry more seriously than Dr. Constance Peterson, who simply says that poets are dull boys and that poetry fills people's minds with delusions about love. Secondly, the extract indicates that poems are all composed by single persons of high status, and love affairs fill people with the inspiration to compose poetry. Thirdly, the Chinese version implies that all women, including Dr. Constance Peterson, must like love poetry and must be convinced that love can save a person's soul. This must be the result of sexist assumptions about women on the part of the subtitler, who would not expect a woman to say something like "the greatest harm done by the human race has been done by the poets," and would not expect Peterson to be a rational woman who wants to demythologise love poetry and romanticism.

> Peterson:
>
> I think the greatest **harm** done by the human race has been done by the poets.
> 我覺得這一帶的風景比某些 (I think the scenery here is more)
> 詩歌裏描寫的還要**迷人** (charming than that described in certain poems)

> Edwardes:
>
> Poets are **dull boys**, most of them—but not especially fiendish.
> 詩歌不過是**大孩子騙小孩子的把戲** (Poetry is just tricks played by big kids to cheat small kids)

> Peterson:
>
> They keep filling people's heads with **delusions** about—about love.
> 但我對那些歌頌愛情的優美 (But those love-praising, elegant)
> Writing about it as if it were a
> 詩歌一直很欣賞，有的人說愛情 (poems I always appreciate very much, some people say love)
> symphony orchestra and **a flight of angels.**
> 詩都是一些**單身貴族**寫出來的 (poems are all composed by single persons of high status)

> Edwardes:
>
> Which it isn't—eh ?
> 難道不是這樣嗎？(Isn't it true?)

> Peterson:
>
> Of course it isn't.
> 當然不是 (Of course it isn't)
> People fall in love—as they put it—
> 墮入愛河的人，往往是在一刹 (People who fall in love usually in an instant)
> because they respond to certain **hair colouring**,
> 那間兩人心中同時產生愛意的 (begin to experience love for each other at the same time)

or vocal tones, or mannerisms that remind them of their **parents.**
這之後的一段時間是**人們靈感** (The period immediately afterwards is the time)
最豐富的時候，感情這東西真奇妙 (when people's inspiration is richest. The love thing is really curious!)

Edwardes:

Sometimes for no reason at all.
有時候毫無緣由產生了 (sometimes it occurs without any reason)

Peterson:

But that's not the point. The point
詩也反映出詩人的內心世界 (Poetry can also reflect the inner world of the poet)
is that people read about love as one thing—and **experience it as another.**
人們讀關於愛情的詩，實際上 (People read poetry about love. In effect)
they expect kisses to be like lyrical poems
相當於體驗別人的感情經歷 (It is equivalent to experiencing other people's emotional experience)
and—and embraces to be like Shakespearean dramas.
我讀莎士比亞的詩經常受感動 (When I read Shakespeare's poetry I am often moved)
愛情能拯救一個人的靈魂 (love can save a person's soul)
使人從病患中康復 (It makes people recover from their illness)

Conclusion

In order to be a good English-Chinese subtitler, one must learn from the failures of some bad subtitles, like the mainland Chinese subtitled version of *Spellbound*, and observe the technical, textual, intra-linguistic and extra-linguistic constraints on subtitling. Furthermore, in order to produce good subtitles, certain things have to be done.

Technically, the subtitler should observe the temporal constraint of around three and a half seconds for a full-line subtitle, and the spatial limit of 13 to 16 characters per single-line subtitle. Regarding textual constraints, the visual components must match the subtitles and the original has to be compressed and condensed according to the relevance theory.

Regarding intra-linguistic constraints, "translationese," i.e., the abuse of articles, pronouns, the passive marker, *bei*, and the plural suffix, *men*, has to be avoided. Subtitlers must familiarise themselves with common English expressions and idioms. Appropriate Chinese idioms may also be used to make the subtitles concise and vivid. Moreover, segmentation should occur at the highest syntactic node possible. If two sentences are placed on the same single-line subtitle, they should be separated by either a comma, or a semi-colon, or a full-stop, or by the space of one character. Care must also be taken to choose the correct meaning in relation to the context from the various meanings of a word.

In terms of extra-linguistic constraints, it is better for names of characters to be sinicised in order to render the translation easy to pronounce, capable of arousing empathy in the receiver, and compatible with the personality, background and status of the character concerned. Instead of translating the surface meaning, the subtitler must carry out research into technical jargon. Moreover, although conscious naturalisation is acceptable when it does not entail gross distortion of the original, unconscious misinterpretation of culture-specific items triggered by linguistic incompetence is to be avoided in subtitling. The misinterpretations in the mainland subtitled version of *Spellbound* represent a snapshot of China at a particular point in its history. In order to raise the standard of its subtitling service, a city or country should try its best to provide a bilingual and bicultural environment, improve the working conditions, salary and social status of subtitlers, and provide related training at university—translation training, in general, and subtitling training, in particular.

Notes

1. Produced and distributed by Fujian Sheng Yinxiang Chubanshe.
2. The classification of constraints on subtitling into these four categories was first made by Paola Guardini (1998) in his article, "Decision-making in subtitling."
3. For a comprehensive survey or review of the introduction of Freudianism to China, please refer to Zhang Jingyuan (1992) and Sun Naixiu (1995).
4. Resistance is a famous manifestation of defense discovered by Freud (Freud 1984: 355). To borrow the words of Rycroft, it refers to "the

opposition encountered during psychoanalytical treatment to the process of making unconscious processes conscious (Rycroft, 1995: 158; Freud 1989: 355–356).

5. Ideology is defined by Lefevere as "a certain concept of what the world should be like" and poetics as "a certain concept of what literature should be like" (1985: 217).

6. Given the linguistic incompetence of the subtitler as seen above, we think the mistranslations are mostly unconscious misinterpretation rather than conscious naturalization. Whether ideology and poetics are involved or not, unconscious misinterpretation triggered off by linguistic incompetence is to be avoided in subtitling though conscious naturalization is acceptable when it does not entail gross distortion of the original.

7. Given the linguistic incompetence of the subtitler as seen above, we think it is unconscious misinterpretation rather than conscious naturalization.

8. According to Sun Longji, the Chinese people, more than any other people in the world, have always been strongly attached to and immaturely dependent upon the mother and have always tended to identify the mother with the mother country (1992: 184–185). As Margery Wolf points out in *Revolution Postponed: Women in Contemporary China*, in the patriarchal society of China, Chinese women, in order to establish their range of power, can only use their reproductive capacity to create a "uterine family"—to render a patriarchal family into a mother-centred family in which the children are all biased for the mother (see Sun Longji 1995: 21). During the May-Fourth period in 1920s, Chinese intellectuals advocated "Down with the Shop of Confucius," i.e. the overthrow of patriarchy. One of the results was an even more comprehensive infantilization of Chinese males—unduly strong attachment to the mother and to the mother country (Sun Longji 1995: 119, 150, 160–161, 185).

References

Aixelia, Javier Franco. 1996. "Culture-specific items in translation." In Roman Alvarez and M. Carmen-Africa Vidal (eds.), *Translation, Power, Subversion*. Clevdon: Multilingual Matters, pp. 52–78.

Au, Kenneth K. L. 1991. "Xianggang dianshi zimu fanyi chutan" (A Preliminary Study of Television Subtitling in Hong Kong). In Liu Ching-chih (ed.), *Fanyi Xinlun Ji* (New Theories in Translation). Hong Kong: Commercial Press, pp. 335–346.

Chen, Dingan. 1990. *Fanyi Jingyao* (The Essence of Translation). Hong
    Kong: Commercial Press.
Delabastita, Dirk. 1989. "Translation and mass-communication: Film and TV
    translation as evidence of cultural dynamics." *Babel*, Vol. 35, No. 4, pp.
    193–218.
Dollerup, Cay. 1974. "On subtitles in television programmes." *Babel*, Vol. 20,
    pp. 197–202.
—— and Annette Lingegaard, eds. 1992. *Teaching Translation and Interpret-
    ing 2: Training, Talent and Experience*. Amsterdam: John Benjamins.
Fawcett, Peter. 1983. *Translation Modes and Constraints*. Inaugural Meeting of
    Yorkshire Regional Society of the Institute of Linguistics. Yorkshire,
    England, March 1983, pp. 186–190.
Fong, Gilbert C. F. 1998. *Gangdu yu Ma ji Qita—Yiming yu Yishi Xingtai*
    (Governors of Hong Kong, Horses and Others–Translated Names and
    Ideology). In Jin Shenghua (ed.), *Fanyi Xuehui Huiyi–Waiwen Zhongyi
    Yanjiu yu Tantao* (Translation Academic Conference–Research an
    Conference–Research and Studies of English-Chinese Translation).
    Hong Kong: Department of Translation, The Chinese University of
    Hong Kong, pp. 420–444.
Freud, Sigmund. 1984. *Pelican Freud Library. Vol. 11. On Metapsychology*, ed.
    Angela Richards, trans. James Strachey. Harmondsworth: Penguin.
——. 1975. *Pelican Freud Library. Vol. 5. The Psychopathology of Everyday Life*,
    ed. Angela Richards, trans. Alan Tyson. Harmondsworth: Penguin.
Fujian Sheng Yinxiang Chubanshe, subtitles. 1999. *Ai De Hua Yisheng*
    (Spellbound). Directed by Alfred Hitchcock, starring Ingrid Bergman
    and Gregory Peck. Xiamen: Fujian Sheng Yinxiang Chubanshe.
    (Original film produced by Fox, USA, 1945.)
Gottlieb, Henrik. 1995. "Subtitling." In Chan Sin-wai and David E. Pollard,
    An Encyclopaedia of Translation. Hong Kong: The Chinese University
    Press, pp. 1004–1015.
——. 1994. "Subtitling: People translating people." In Cay Dollerup and
    Annette Lingegaard (eds.), *Teaching Translation and Interpreting 2:
    Training, Talent and Experience*. Amsterdam: John Benjamins, pp. 261–
    274.
Guardini, Paola. 1998. "Decision-making in subtitling." *Perspectives: Studies in
    Translatology*, Vol. 6, No. 1, pp. 91–113.
Karamitroglou, Fotios. 1998. "A proposed set of subtitling standards in
    Europe." *Translation Journal* [Online serial], Vol. 2, No. 2, http://www.
    accurapid.com/journal/04stndrd.htm.
Kilborn, Richard. 1993. "'Speak my language': Current attitudes to television
    subtitling and dubbing." *Media Culture and Society*, Vol. 15, No. 4, pp.
    641–660.

Kovačič, Irena. 1994. "Relevance as a factor in subtitling reductions." In Cay Dollerup and Annette Lingegaard (eds.), *Teaching Translation and Interpreting 2: Training, Talent and Experience.* Amsterdam: John Benjamins, pp. 245–251.

Lefevere, André. 1985. "Why waste our time on rewrites?" In Theo Hermans (ed.). *The Manipulation of Literature—Studies in Literary Translation.* London: Croom Helm, pp. 216–247.

————. 1992. *Translation, Rewriting, and the Manipulation of Literary Fame.* London: Routledge.

Lung, Rachel. 1998. "On mis-translating sexually suggestive elements in English-Chinese screen subtitling." *Babel,* Vol. 44, No. 2, pp. 97–109.

Ma, Yueren. 2000. *Fanyi de Yishu* (The Art of Translation), trans. Chen Maiping. *Ming Bao Monthly,* July 2000, pp. 56–61.

Mason, Ian. 1994. "Dubbing and subtitles, film and television." In R. E. Asher (ed.), *Encyclopedia of Language and Linguistics* (10 vols). Oxford: Pergamon Press Ltd., pp. 1066–1069.

Rycroft, Charles. 1995. *A Critical Dictionary of Psychoanalysis.* 2nd ed. London: Penguin.

Si, Guo. 1972. *Fanyi Yanjiu* (Translation Studies). Taipei: Dadi Chubanshe.

Sun, Longji. 1995. *Wei Duannai de Minzu* (The Unweaned Race). Taipei: Juliu Tushu.

————. 1992. *Zhongguo Wenhua de Shenceng Jiegou* (The Deep Structure of Chinese Culture). Hong Kong: Jixian She.

Sun, Naixiu. 1995. *Fuluoyide yu Zhongguo Zuojia* (Freud and Chinese Writers). Taipei: Yejiang.

Tao, Jie. 1999. "Lieyi quzhu liangyi" (Bad Translation Chases Away Good Translation). In Tao Jie, *Zaijian Susi Huang* (Goodbye Suzie Wong). Hong Kong: Huangguan Congshu, pp. 186–187.

Wong, Laurence. 1996. *Fanyi Tujing* (Ways of Translation). Taipei: Shulin Chubanshe.

Zhang, Jingyuan. 1992. *Psychoanalysis in China: Literary Transformation 1919–1949.* Ithaca: East Asia Program, Cornell Univeristy.

Zhang, Peiji. 1980. *Yinghan Fanyi Jiaocheng* (A Teaching Programme of English-Chinese Translation). Shanghai: Shanghai Waiyu Jiaoyu Chubanshe.

Zhongyi Xinlixue Cihui Bianyi Zu yu Shehui Yanjiu Zhongxin (Editorial Committee of the Glossary and Social Research Centre), ed. 1982. *Zhongyi Xinlixue Cihui* (A Glossary of Psychological Terms). Hong Kong: The Chinese University Press.

SECTION THREE

The Profession

10

I Translate, You Adapt, They Dub

Sergio Patou-Patucchi

—🌣—

It is universally accepted that fiction and drama represent a privileged medium of communication through which it is possible to pass basic cultural elements: i.e. the universe of values and the way of life of every ethnic group. For thousands of years, poetry, fables, travellers' tales and parables have served as effective narrative media to get certain messages across to different audiences. Today, these techniques are also used for less noble things, such as soft drinks, alcohol, cigarettes, or washing-up liquid, albeit through high-tech means.

Of course, the diffusion may be even more effective when the tale is decorated with sparkling garments, as seductive and full of fascination as are those put at our disposal by the various forms of media that are out there.

I am sure that every one of us remembers the feeling of going on their first virtual journey into an encyclopaedia via CD-ROM. A few clicks had us ready to throw our reference works in the rubbish bin. What were once our greatest friends now looked clumsy, cumbersome and obsolete as a short and scattered row of gas streetlamps would look after a trip to Las Vegas; luckily, most of us changed our minds and gave them another chance.

Let the scholars, who are surely more cultured and better prepared, talk on the psycho-sociological framework of this topic and let me more modestly dedicate this paper to the complexities of my everyday work.

It is possible to split dubbing into two main fields: writing (translation and adaptation) and acting, with a director taking care of the performances of the dubbing actors. On this special occasion, we will devote particular attention to the literary side of the work: that is, the strict relationship between the activities of translation and adaptation of dialogue, as it is our opinion that this could be an ideal meeting point for academia and the business community.

It is rather obvious that if we have the same professional translating and adapting a multimedia work, we simply do not have any kind of problem—Briusov wrote: "It is impossible to transmit the creation of a poet from one language to another; but it is also impossible to give up such a dream." (My translation)

The problem also does not exist if we remain in a pure translation scope, because literary translation and film translation share so many similarities.

So, when and why do we speak of a problem? And, *what exactly is the problem we are talking about?*

Most adaptors are self-taught people. At best, and only for the luckiest of them—as is the case with me, for example—they learnt their craft through the benevolence and disposability of some experienced colleagues. In any case, this apprenticeship-type system is essentially based on the empirical method of "fail and learn."

In my country, it may happen that dubbing and subtitling are done by professionals who do not know the original language of the multimedia works they are commissioned to adapt. Sometimes they do not know *any* foreign language at all. So it would not be too hasty to consider their work as a mere adaptation from their *own* language into their *own* language. They use a translation someone else has done for them, about which they cannot even say whether it is good or bad.

This explains the odd interpretations of some expressions of other cultures, including the use of expressive moves (you sometimes notice this in an Italian-dubbed audio-visual work, even when the dubbing can be objectively considered well done, if judged by some other standards). It is also evident that fidelity to the original text cannot but be accidental and fortuitous, as every departure from it will never be intentional, unless the adapter asked for a very good translation in the first place. In this case, you might think that we are back to the case of the translator-adaptor. But we are not.

The problem remains because those who do not know that particular *method* cannot have nurtured a problem-solving attitude that can only be acquired after years of application and study in translation. It also does not imbue them with that particular sense that stops the translator in their thinking at a particular moment, causing them to run to consult their dictionaries, encyclopaedias, CD-ROMS or whatever materials are at their disposal until every morsel of meaning, not only about a particular word, but also about *that* particular sentence structure, or about the strange style of a sentence, or an unusual use of the adjective or preposition that makes that line *different,* has been obtained. Afterwards, you realise that you may have over-reacted, that the author was only being lazy, and that the sentence you have devoted so much attention to is only an absolutely banal "computer error."

But would you honestly consider that this kind of research work constitutes "a useless waste of time," even if that particular doubt turns out to be groundless? We are convinced that translators consider this kind of "failed research" as one of the activities which is most effective in widening their knowledge of the language from which they translate.

All this, however, simply does not exist for non-translator-adaptors, because to them, the entire process of translation is nothing but "a technical support to adaptation."

Moreover, the non-translator-adaptor usually relies on "hypo translation," which is very poorly paid (statistically no more than 10% of their fee), to understand the *general meaning* of the speech only.

I agree with those who consider "hypo translation" a phenomenon that makes translators:

(a) Unable to understand the real message of the source language and therefore limit their work to an act of simple lexical transfer, without paying any attention to the intelligibility of the text or the non-concordance of the semantic fields in the source and target languages;
(b) Ignore the rules of the target language (i.e., their own language) and the grammatical structure of the source language.

A common response to this critique is that a telefilm remains understandable even if you simply look at it. The truth is that this happens not only to a series of telefilms, or soap-operas, but also to important works (and in fact this has happened) when, unfortunately, they do not benefit from the consideration of distributors and therefore there is no elevated commercial value to protect them. In other words, they are not considered to be audio-visual products within which Mr. Seller-of-Boiled-Ham would be keen to insert his commercial spot. It is then easy to predict for them a miserable future of sporadic or lonely midnight showings.

Some years ago in Italy, somebody attempted to insert the translator's name into the credit titles, with a dignity equal to that of the adaptor, in addition to splitting the fee fifty-fifty. However, almost in compliance with the acknowledgement to the Rights of Repetition, the practice was abandoned. We are not able to identify the judge who sentenced it, nor the name of the executioner of this sentence. But, in every case, it seems that Justice has NOT been done.

If the translation of a multimedia audio-visual programme involves a commitment identical to that of any other translation, the same yardstick must simply apply to every other possible specialisation. Moreover, if we really want to respect the law and authorial rights, we have to pay attention to all translation practices that are "authorial," particularly when they require the *interpretation of the cinematographic language* into a critical vision of the product, leaving out only the technical requirement of adapting the text to lip synchronisation.

Obviously, a script translated—let's say badly—and adapted in accordance with the strict commercial requirements of the customer will suffer all kinds of mayhem and rewriting. In the recording studio, the tight schedule turns some dubbing actors—usually polite people—into Jekyll and Hyde types with wild and ravenous attitudes. In these cases, we assist in the summary elimination of those words which should be articulated in a slightly more demanding tone than usual, as well as lynching those terms whose only crime is a degree of affectation. All these are from people who have never seen the particular sequence they are dubbing, let alone the actual telefilm.

Of course, these are extreme situations, intentionally exaggerated, just to make my point even clearer.

Peter Newmark instead notes that "... the translator must be an expert in textual criticism, literary and non-literary, in order to evaluate the qualities of a script before deciding how to interpret it and therefore how to translate it." (My translation from Italian) He then says further:

> Only seldom, and above all if the original text is translated by a poet, may the work maintain the colour and taste it has from the beginning. However it is important that the translator should have a thorough knowledge of the foreign language from which he translates, in order to be able to determine at which point the text departs from the linguistic norm usually adopted for a given argument in that situation. He must determine the degree of grammatical and semantic originality of the text. These must be maintained in the case of well written, "expressive" texts, but it is possible to decide to normalise in a badly written "informative" or "vocative" text. He needs, besides, a wide creative vision going from fantasy to common sense. The translator must acquire the technique of moving easily among the fundamental processes: comprehension—which may require an interpretation—and formulation—which may require a recreation. (My translation)

On interpretation, G. C. Marchesini, in *Il traduttore e il suo occhio (per una semeiotica della traduzione)* (The Translator and His Eye— Towards a Semeiotics of Translation), notes:

> I would like, here, to plead the cause of the much execrated free translation. Any translation (when not incorrect) is, in its own, an interpretation, more or less fortunate, just as any other reading is an interpretation. It is impossible to read again without bringing again what we are "making ours" to a series of personal categories (our way of looking at reality, the quantity of synapses that transmit the formation of thoughts, the experiences based on which are based connections and associations that gush from our literature); yet the expression "making ours" indicates the subjectivity of the reading process and, even more, of translation. To find this courage, obliging the text to unfurl all its production of sense (or even better, to understand all the possible sense potentialities of the text intentions) signifies to give, at last, a semiotic fundamental to the translation activity.

I find it opportune now, to quote verbatim an official document published by the AIDAC (the Italian Association of Dialogue Adaptors for Cinema and Television), on 29 April 2001:

The script that the actor has on the reading desk is exclusively the fruit of the work of the dialogue adaptor, who has sole responsibility for it.... The mere translator is not directly connected with the "operation generically defined dubbing." The translator, in this productive cycle, is simply—and in most cases—an advisor to the dialogist. (My translation)

But let us give a little attention also to subtitling; more particularly, to some of the possible reasons on why subtitling is not so considered in Italy.

Until some years ago, the possibility—even in the University—of a linguistic formation within the framework of a more general scientific formation was considered just as an *optional.*

The story of the cinema also teaches us that in Italy the so-called hybrid *voice/face* (i.e.: two actors , a *voice* and a *face,* for the same character) was born with the introduction of a 1933 Fascist law that, taking as a pretext the high percentage of illiterates among the Italian population at the time, privileged dubbing against subtitling.

According to this argument, it may be useful to remember one of the most recent articles by a well known Italian columnist, Indro Montanelli; it is the answer he gave to one of his readers asking for some information about journalism (*Corriere della Sera.* 3 June 2001):

I think I can explain approximately why Italian print journalism was born and developed so late as compared to that of Great Britain, France, the Netherlands, etc. and why so many difficulties accompanied its development.

Reason number one was the Counter-Reformation, which prevented the formation of a readers' public. I do not know whether the Protestant Reformation did a good service to the cause of the Lord. However, it is certain that, in obliging the "devotee" to read the Holy Scripture and making him responsible for the interpretation and the application of the dictates, he was taught how to read and write.

The Counter-Reformation followed the opposite direction. Being distrustful of the interpretations he could give, it took away from the devotee the freedom of reading and interpreting the Scriptures, leaving Italy at the mercy of the depositories of the so-called "revealed truth." Revealed by whom? By the priest of course, who follows the dictates of the Church which, monopolising the culture, and together with the individualistic layman, was fully interested in excluding the so-called "common people" to grant their subjection. The effects on the culture were catastrophic. Born, as in all other European countries, in the palace and at the desk of the lord—lay or ecclesiastic that he was – in Italy, this culture was condemned to remain there because of, let's say, a shortage of clientele.

Who could read—for example—the "Orlando Furioso" or the "Gerusalemme Liberata" but the lord who maintained the authors, and his flatterers? In Protestant countries, the book spread and, in order to enlarge its market, the authors went nearer to the reader, following his tastes and interests, adopting his language and freeing it from all those classical wastes used in the lord's court. In the Counter-Reformation countries, with Italy in the lead, the culture departed from the public, closing herself in the asphyxial Palace and academic circles, where people wrangled over the values and technique of the hendecasyllable. (My translation)

So dubbing became a medium of political control and censorship, sometimes even without any apparent reason. For example, an American film called *The adventures of Marco Polo* (USA-1938) in Italy was translated as *A Scotsman goes to the Court of the Great Khan*! Not to talk about the use of homely translators (also at those time!) who produced incorrect captions.

Piero Brunetta, a great Italian cinematographic critic and a professor at the University of Padua, often proclaims: "The public is always considered as an informal and passive reality." (My translation)

At this point, it seems clear that an ideal form of collaboration with academia would be to develop a cross-disciplinary professional consciousness in order to set up some kind of standard, not only for the benefit of the users (children in particular, who pass many hours a day in front of a television set), but also for the benefit of the original authors of the works. The latter, seldom present when the work is dubbed, or subtitled, very often find the fruit of their creativity in a jumble, so distorted and disqualified that it cannot be corrected. Above all, the fruition of audio-visual works outside their original borders endows film-multimedia translation with an extremely important role, both from a cultural point of view and on a more specifically linguistic plane.

Some recent work that I have done with my company, the Ministry of Interior Affairs and RAI-Educational (a division of our national television broadcasting company), has shown me how simple it is for a good professional translator to learn how to adapt a script technically for lip synch. It would not have been so easy if I had been dealing with people who were not translators.

We have to admit that the professionals are relatively interested in linguistic statistic and in the story of dubbing; or about that cinematographic critic, often so full of enthusiasm, but overall not really aimed to pragmatic (extra-academic) exigencies. They ask for didactical and cultural means, targeted towards professional training and ongoing professional development.

Theoretical and historical studies on dubbing in Italy more or less stopped in the 1980s, i.e., with the advent of industrial audio-visuals created for broadcasting: telefilms, television movies, soap operas, and telenovelas.

There is, for example, a lack of serious reflection on the factors that have led to the diminution of the importance of the role of the dubbing director. Most of all, there is a lack of reflection on the declining qualities of the client: i.e., the person with the purse strings, who dictates the general criteria under which the professional must work. But it is also important to know the reasons for the numerical prevalence of the most commercial genres on national television. Equally urgent is a reflection on the real reasons why the professional community accepts people with little training and poor cultural understanding.

For us, these are all tasks for academia, not because it is its right, but because it has the moral obligation to indicate which cultural objectives to pursue. I am talking about the purity of the language, of course, but also about comparative study at an international level so that various national experiences will mesh together to establish *a minimal qualitative standard* in the use of the communication systems.

Most of all, academia must be considered as an irreplaceable support for a better reading of the work of art. In our hypothesis, it should be the most influential and prestigious scientific reference point. For those of us working in dubbing, seriously and with acknowledged competence, it could be used to overcome the understandable psychological resistance of those professionals who have operated on the market, validly and for so many years.

If high wages indicate recognition of the value of a particular type of work in economic terms, then it is logical that scientific research tends to free it from the pressures that a certain industry tries to impose on it. Exchanges between working professionals engaged in the active application of the spoken language and those in the academic establishment engaged in related historical and theoretical research could go a long way towards establishing a new way of approaching the problem.

But, of course, it is not a process that concerns only translators and adaptors.

Mario Fabiani writes, in *The Right of the Author in the Digital Era*: "the rights of authors are being confronted with a technological evolution that seems intended to affect ever more urgently the phases of the realisation and utilisation of the products of the intellect." (My translation)

And then: "The romantic image of the author alone with his own torment of creative ecstasy, today is often substituted by the team of authors that, working in entrepreneurial organised structures with more and more elaborate technical contributions, produces works for show business, the audio-visual and the cinematographic sector or even computer software: in short, the realisation of a work into its final shape needs, in addition to a creative effort, the contribution of an industrial activity and of conspicuous investments."

Globalisation, therefore, but not homologation. And a firm refusal to surrender to the verbal medium *par excellence* – the English language that we are using in this prestigious seat of international culture, when it would not be mostly used as a "first knowledge" medium, capable of tempting ulterior close examination and able to create the premises for the saving of the "minor" linguistic heritage.

In the Western world, the United States of America and European countries included, the results of a research study indicated that the younger generations are not very familiar with writing. At a conference in Berlin last year, someone remembered that in the Netherlands they make a peculiar use of subtitling. They subtitle particular national television programmes aimed at youngsters <u>in the same language as that spoken by the actors on the audio-visual show</u>, in order to ameliorate the reading ability of the children.

But it is also important to make a little note of a *must* for our time: in order to live together with people who have arrived from other countries, and who have different habits (sometimes, *really* different and therefore difficult to accept in a short time), we must be able to communicate with them—and they with us—in the broadest possible way, knowing whether they intend 'yes' or 'no' when they give a nod, or paying attention not to reverse the victory sign, etc. In this case, there is no substitute for audio-visual support.

It is certainly the case that a language characterised by such a wide degree of diffusion and being as pervasive as English is, means that it is in the position to develop a very important or maybe even substantial connecting function between the academic laboratory and everyday reality, using the audio-visual language of cinema, television, press, songs, mass-media, etc. This is why it is extremely important that the actual management of multimedia communication systems as a whole will always remain in the hands of professionals who are prepared on *both* cultural fronts.

11

The Translation of Film Dialogues for Dubbing

Zhang Chunbai

—∿—

Introduction

The film dubbing industry is a prosperous one in mainland China, since most Chinese people do not have a good command of foreign languages. Whether it is seen as an art or a craft, film dubbing is subject to a number of special constraints which are worth our attention. In this paper, I will explore those constraints as well as the basic principles and procedures of translating film dialogues for dubbing.

Constraints

The irreversibility of utterances

Unlike the translation of written texts such as novels and short stories, the translation of film dialogues is subject to a number of special constraints. The most striking one is perhaps the irreversibility of the speakers' utterances on the screen. When we are reading written texts, we can return to them from time to time if we find them difficult to understand, but when we are watching a film in the cinema or on television, whatever happens on the screen is irretrievable. Therefore, the language should be easy enough for an average member of the audience to understand.

Matching lip movements

Related to the irreversibility of the speakers' utterances on the screen are the limits of space and time. As dubbed film dialogues must match the speakers' lip movements on the screen, each translated sentence must match the source language sentence naturally. This means that the translator has to calculate how many target language words or characters should be used for each sentence—or even each segment of a sentence, if there are pauses in it. When dubbing an English film into Chinese, for instance, a short English sentence must not be translated into a long Chinese sentence, even though this long sentence may sound very natural. Similarly, a long English sentence cannot be translated into a short Chinese sentence, no matter how perfect it may sound to the Chinese ear. For example:

From *Two Marriages*	
Scott: Dad, I missed you.	斯科特：爸爸，我想你。
Steven: Missed or miss?	史蒂文：現在還想嗎？
Scot: Both.	斯科特：想的。
From *A Man Called Hawk*	
Hawk: Is he your tenant?	霍克：他是你房客麼？
Landlord: Was.	房東：(他) 死了。

In the first example, the sentence "Missed or miss?" would be more naturally translated as 過去想還是現在想？ (Did you miss me in the past or do you miss me now?), but it is translated as 現在還想嗎？ (Do you still miss me?) owing to time and space constraints. Similarly, the one-word answer "Was" in the next example is normally understood as 曾經是的 (once he was) or 現在不是了 (now he isn't), but since only two Chinese characters are allowed here, it is translated as "死了" ([He's] dead) according to what has actually happened in the story.

Matching gestures and movements

Another important constraint on the translating of film dialogues is the need to match movements and gestures, and sometimes even the shapes of the speakers' mouths on the screen. In the words of R. Jumpelt (1961: 24), "... in the setting of film dialogue, the critical factor may well be the necessity of finding expressions that effectively carry the meaning and match most closely the actor's lip movements." If, for instance, the speaker uses an open vowel such as /a:/ when the camera closes in on him, we must also use an open vowel in the target language. If, on the other hand, the speaker uses a sound like /i/ with his mouth only slightly open, then we must not use an open vowel. For example:

Love at First Sight《一見鍾情》

| Stephanie: | Have dinner with me tonight. | 絲黛芬妮：今晚陪我去吃飯。 |
| Michael: | *All right.* And tomorrow night ...
every night ... for the rest of your *life*. | 邁克爾：好啊 (試比較：「行」 或「沒問題」)，只要 你願意，
今生今世，天天一塊 (試比較「起」) 吃。 |

Here, in the original, "All right" (/ɔ:l rait/) and "life" (/laif/) contain three open vowels. The target text uses three similar open vowels in 好啊 (/*hao a:*/) and 塊 (/*kuai*/), which helps to produce natural effects. The result would obviously be very different if these were changed into 行 (/*xing*/) or 沒問題 /*mei wenti*/ and 起 (/*qi*/), in which cases the dominant sound is /i/.

The speaker's gestures accompanying his utterances may also dictate the choice of words in the target text even though this may deviate from the norms of the target language. A typical example is the negative English word "no," which is often translated as *dui* 對 or *shi de* 是的 (both meaning "yes") in Chinese. Let us compare the following examples:

We all shook our heads in agreement.
我們都點頭表示同意。

A: She is not your wife, is she?
B (shakes his head): No, no, no. She isn't.
甲：她不是你太太，是不是 ?
乙：不，不，不。她不是。

The first example is written language. Here "shook our heads" is translated as *dian tou* 點頭 meaning "nodded our heads," because the Chinese normally nod, rather than shake, their heads to express agreement.

In the last example, three "no's" is normally translated as 是的 (yes) in novels or short stories since it is the normal way of responding to such questions in Chinese. In films, however, we may have to change the affirmative 是的 into the negative 不，不，不, despite the obvious deviation from the norms of the Chinese language, if the speaker on the screen is shaking his head all the time. In such cases, the audience will have no difficulty in understanding the sentence since they can see the speaker's head movement on the screen.

Principles

Immediate comprehensibility

It goes without saying that the cinematic art is audience-oriented. Therefore, with a few rare exceptions where, for instance, the speaker is reading a formal legal document or an ancient poem, film dialogues generally use immediately comprehensible spoken language for the sake of the audience. This can be seen clearly if we compare film dialogues with dialogues in novels. The following are two excerpts from the novel *Jane Eyre* with their Chinese translations in the novel and a dubbed film version:

> Rochester: Sometimes I have a queer feeling with regard to you—especially when you are near me, as now: it is as if I had a string somewhere under my left ribs, tightly and inextricably knotted to a similar string situated in the corresponding quarter of your little frame.

> 羅切斯特：我有時候對你有一種奇怪的感覺——特別是，像現在這樣，你靠近我的時候。我左肋骨下的哪個地方，似乎有一根弦，和你那小身體同樣的地方的一根類似的弦打成了結，打得緊緊的，解都解不開。

> From the translation of the novel: *Jane Eyre*

> 羅切斯特：我有時候⋯對你有種奇妙的感覺。當你在我身邊的時候，我就感覺到⋯我的心⋯和你的心⋯完全⋯完全聯繫在一起了，緊緊地連在一起了。

> From the Chinese dubbed version of the film: *Jane Eyre*[1]

Jane: Do you think, because I am poor, obscure, plain, and little, I am soulless and heartless? I have as much soul as you,—and full as much heart!

From *Jane Eyre*

簡：你以為，因為我窮、低微、不美、矮小，我就沒有靈魂沒有心嗎？我的靈魂跟你一樣，我的心也跟你完全一樣！

From the translation of the novel: *Jane Eyre*

簡：你以為我不漂亮、也不富有，就沒有靈魂、沒有愛嗎？我也是有心的人！

From the Chinese dubbed version of the film: *Jane Eyre*

In both examples, the translated novel uses rather literal translations for the sake of fidelity, but we can easily see that they are not very readable. The Chinese, for instance, would rarely use a metaphor like the string metaphor used by Rochester in the first example, and few people would be able to understand it if it were read to them. In the last example, I really cannot imagine anyone using the four Chinese adjectives *qiong* 窮 (poor), *di wei* 低微 (low), *bu mei* 不美 (unattractive), and *aixiao* 矮小 (short) together as in English, and they sound very unnatural to the native ear. In the dubbed film, the translator adopts more colloquial and more natural Chinese sentences for the sake of pragmatic equivalence—though this is done at the expense of the surface meaning. These examples show that film language should be readable and immediately comprehensible. In other words, the translator is more concerned with helping the audience understand the film dialogues with minimal processing effort than with surface fidelity.

Pragmatic equivalence and principle of relevance

According to Katharina Reiss, a screen script is a type of audio-medial text for which an appropriate translation method "must preserve the same *effect on the hearer* that the original has in the source language …" (2000: 46). In other words, the translated dialogues should be able to make the target audience smile, laugh and cry as the original does with the help of non-linguistic media and of "graphic, acoustic, and visual kinds of expression" (43). This goal of pragmatic equivalence, as well as the requirement of immediate comprehensibility discussed above, means that the translator must endeavour to reduce the processing effort of the audience as much as possible. As Gutt (2000: 107) puts it, the translation "should be expressed in such a manner that it yields the intended interpretation without putting the audience to unnecessary processing effort." This principle of relevance, in my view, is especially useful for the translation of film dialogues, considering the nature of film language and the audience. In fact, it should be the guiding principle for film translators.

Specifically, since film dialogues are basically spoken language, the target text must also be spoken language. Generally, any attempt at producing an elegant literary style should be avoided. For example:

From *Jessie*
Jessie: Alex, my mother loves me!
Alex:　Relax, you're in good hands. Besides, you can do nothing about it.
傑　　茜：艾力克斯，開慢點好不好？！
艾力克斯：放心，保你死不了。再說，你害怕也沒用。

From "*No Turning Back*" in *Big Sky*
Davidson: You took off back there. You committed yourself.
Chris:　　Hey, it wasn't the colour of your eyes, fella. It's called self-preservation.
戴維遜：這事你也有份，脫不了關係。
克里斯：嘿，我和你完全是兩碼事。我是自我保護。

Here, the language of the original dialogues is typical spoken English. The Chinese translations succeed in achieving pragmatic equivalence by using natural spoken Chinese.

It should be pointed out that such spoken language should reflect the speaker's personality and level of education, as well as his or her relationship with the hearer. The two examples well illustrate this point.

Occasionally, the source text may contain certain elements for a special purpose: say, to reveal the speaker's personality or to show the seriousness of the matter under discussion. In such cases, the translator may be justified in using more formal language, although he still has to work within the bounds of relevance to the knowledge structure of the target audience. For example:

From the film *Jane Eyre*
Brocklehurst: Who would believe … that the Evil One has already … found in her a servant and agent? Yet such, I grieve to say, is the case.
布洛克爾赫斯特：(但是) 誰又會相信，魔鬼已經附身於她，她成了魔鬼的化身了？而遺憾的是，這的確是個事實。

Brocklehurst: Almighty God, look down upon this miserable sinner, and grant the sense of her weakness. Make your strength to her belief, and seriousness to her repentance. Amen.[1]
布洛克爾赫斯特：啊，萬能的上帝啊，請可憐這個可悲的罪人的脆弱吧，並賜予她信仰和力量，以及悔悟的意念。為她祈禱吧。阿門。

Here, the language used in the first example is slightly more formal than everyday spoken language, and so is the language used in the Chinese translation. The second example is even more formal, but it is still translated rather literally since most Chinese people have sufficient knowledge of Christianity to understand it. In other words, the Chinese audience need not make too much processing effort in order to understand this dialogue.

The translation of metaphors

As regards the translation of metaphors in the source text, the translator has to make judgements about their relevance to the context of the target culture. Here, we have at least five different procedures at our disposal for different contexts.

First, if he can find an equivalent item in the target language, in both form and meaning, the translator can easily come up with a translation that yields "adequate contextual effects" that the audience can understand with "minimal processing effort" (Gutt 2000: 32). For example:

From *Love at First Sight*
Michael: Well, to my mind *coup de foudre* is exactly what I felt when I saw you this morning.
邁克爾：呃，"一見鍾情"正是我早上遇見你時的那種感受。

From *Big Sky*
Harry: Like father, like daughter.
哈里：有其父必有其女。

Here, in the first example, the French idiom *coup de foudre* is
equivalent to the English idiom "love at first sight," which in turn is
equivalent to the Chinese idiom "一見鍾情". The second example is a
slight twist of the idiom "like father, like son," which has an
equivalent Chinese idiom "有其父必有其子". There is a touch of
humour in it. The literal translation here helps produce the same
effect.

Second, sometimes the source text may use the original
metaphors for special purposes. In that case, the translator should
endeavour to keep the original images (Newmark 1988: 112) if it will
not put the audience to "unjustifiable processing effort" (Gutt 2000:
32)—as long as he can manage to match the speakers' lip
movements. For example:

From *Jane Eyre*
Rochester: Since then fortune has knocked me about, and kneaded me
            with her knuckles, and now I flatter myself I am hard and
            tough as an India-rubber ball, with perhaps one small
            sensitive point in the middle of the lump. Does that leave
            hope for me?
Jane: Hope of what, sir?
Rochester: Of my re-transformation from India-rubber back to flesh?
羅切斯特：然而，命運卻在捉弄我，就像…呃，把一個橡皮球給弄硬了一
          樣，但是還保留著球心那柔軟的部分。請問你：你希望得到嗎？
簡：   希望什麼？
羅切斯特："把我從橡皮球變成一個真正的人？"

From *Jessie*
Tim: I made three baskets.
Jessie: Three baskets? You have made three baskets? Who do you think
        you are, Larry Bird?
蒂姆：我投中了三次籃。
傑茜：投中了三次？投中三次籃？你難道是拉利·巴德？

Here, the image of the rubber ball in the first example is the
expressive component of the whole passage, which suggests that the

speaker, i.e., Rochester, is still soft and sensitive at heart despite his "hard and tough" facade. The translator chooses to keep the image since it is not difficult for Chinese audiences to understand it. In the subsequent example, "Larry Bird" is apparently the name of a famous basketball player. It is transferred here since the preceding two questions have prepared the audience for it so that they do not have to make much processing effort in order to see the point. In other words, "Larry Bird" is made sufficiently relevant to the target audience by the preceding questions.

Third, if it is difficult or impossible to keep the original image without overtaxing the processing abilities of the target audience, the translator might have to look for a corresponding or equivalent item in the target language in order to provide adequate contextual effects. For example:

From *Cody*
Cody: Nailing a dealer in a party-town like this is like trying to find a needle on Bondi Beach.
考迪：要想在咱們鎮上找這個毒販簡直就是**大海撈針**。

From *Big Sky*
Robie: You're fishing in the air. It's no use.
羅比：你這是**水中撈月**，沒有用的。

Obviously, the literal translations of the original metaphors "to find a needle on Bondi Beach" (在邦迪海灘上找針) and "fishing in the air" (空中釣魚) would sound too foreign to a Chinese audience and would demand too much processing effort. Therefore, their cultural equivalents, 大海撈針 (to find a needle in the sea) and 水中撈月 (to retrieve the moon in water), are used to minimise the processing effort required of the audience.

Fourth, in the case where it is necessary to keep the foreign flavour in order to provide adequate contextual effects, the translator may have to keep the original cultural image as long as the audience can still work out the speaker's intention. For example:

From *Flamingo Road*
Christie: You ah … make the Weldon house sound like some kind of prison.
Senator: The only difference is that the spoons there are made out of sterling silver.

克里絲蒂：你的話聽起來韋爾登家就像牢籠似的。
參 議 員：唯一的區別是…那兒的調羹是用銀子做的。

The above example comes from the English idiom "to be born with a silver spoon in one's mouth." It is translated literally since the target audience can easily work out what a "silver spoon" signifies even though they do not know the idiom.

Lastly, if none of the above procedures can achieve the goal of yielding adequate contextual effects, the translator may have to reduce the original image to sense in order to avoid putting the audience to unnecessary processing effort. For example:

From *Jessie*
Jessie: Memories are wonderful ... and the good ones ... *stick to you like glue.*
傑茜：回憶是美好的，而好的回憶……將伴你終身。

From *A Man Called Hawk*
Cynthia: We've checked you out, Timmy, juvenile offender record as long as *Constitution Avenue.*
辛茜亞：我們查過了，蒂米，你的犯罪紀錄有厚厚一大疊。

From *Hard Target*
Mary: *The wheels* turn slower here than anywhere else.
瑪麗：我們這兒的節奏比哪兒都慢。

In the example from *Jessie*, the image of "glue" cannot be rendered literally into Chinese (膠水), since to the Chinese audience, it does not have a good connotation. Similarly, a literal translation of "Constitution Avenue" (憲法大街) in the example from *A Man Called Hawk* would be rather unnatural and difficult to understand. The last example describes the sluggishness of the local government. It would obviously be difficult for the Chinese audience to understand it if "the wheels" were literally translated as 輪子.

The translation of puns

Puns are probably the most difficult part of film dialogues, considering all the constraints discussed above. However, this does not mean that it is impossible to produce good translations. In fact, the large common core between Chinese and English often provides us with ample flexibility. For example:

From *Growing Pains*
Jason: I truly believe that you haven't given her a fair shake.
Maggie: I truly hope you haven't.
傑生：我相信你還沒有給她機會試試。
梅琪：但願你還沒試過她。

From *Big Sky*
Chris: Poor old things. They really loved him.
Jimbo: Yeah. Loved him to death even.
克里斯：可憐的人，她們很愛他。
金　波：是啊，都把他愛死了。

Here, the double meanings of the sentences are self-evident. Needless to say, sometimes such literal translation is impossible. In that case we may have to try to preserve the humour at the expense of formal equivalence.

Conclusion

From the above discussion, we can conclude that the overriding concern of the translator of film dialogues should be to produce pragmatic equivalence without putting the target audience to unnecessary processing effort. Accordingly, the translator has to make every effort to come up with immediately comprehensible target language dialogues without deviating too far from the original.

Note

1.   This quotation was transcribed from the VCD edition as it cannot be found in the original novel.

References

Au, Kenneth K. L. 區劍龍. 1993. 〈香港電視字幕翻譯初探〉(A Preliminary study of TV Subtitle Translation in Hong Kong). In Liu Ching-chih 劉靖之 (ed.),《翻譯新論集》(New Theories in Translation). Hong Kong: The Commercial Press, pp. 335–346.

Gutt, Ernst-August. 2000. *Translation and Relevance: Cognition and Context.* Manchester: St. Jerome.

Jumpelt, R. W. 1961. *Die Übersetyung Natuwissenschaftlicher und Technischer Literatur: Sprachliche Masssäbe und Methoden zur Bestimmung ihrer Wesenszüge und Probleme.* Langescheidt Bibliothek für Wissenschaft und Praxis, Vol. 1. Berlin-Schöneberg: Langenscheidt.

Newmark, Peter. 1988. *A Textbook of Translation.* New York: Prentice Hall.

Nida, Eugene A. and Charles Taber. 1969. *The Theory and Practice of Translation.* Brill: Leiden.

Reiss, Katharina. 2000. *Translation Criticism: The Potentials and Limitations,* Manchester: St Jerome.

Zhang, Chunbai 張春柏. 1998. 〈影視翻譯初探〉 (An Initial Survey on Screen Translation). 《中國翻譯》 (Chinese Translators Journal), No. 2, pp. 50–53.

12

Loss of Meaning in Dubbing

Lu Danjun

—ɯ—

Marcel Martin, the French film critic, described dubbed foreign films as "an evil expression of art" in his work *Le Langage Cinématographique*. He went on to list a number of problems caused by dubbing. These include non-synchronised lip movements, mismatched body language, and the loss of the musicality and cadence of the original language. Martin was certainly right in what he said. A film does suffer losses of various kinds when it is dubbed into another language. This is particularly true with regard to the loss of meaning. Although many such problems can often be attributed to poor quality translation, poor handling by dubbing directors and mediocre performances by dubbing artists, there is one aspect of the loss of meaning that just cannot be avoided however hard the translator, the director and the dubbing artists try. This is the loss of meaning caused by the inability to fully convey foreign accents and local dialects which are used deliberately in the original film.

Dialogue plays a very important role in films. It performs the functions of helping with characterisation, strengthening plot development, adding humour or other interesting artistic colour to the story, and even more importantly, conveying the cultural identity of a particular area or a particular social group. What characters say and how they say it not only reflect their social status and educational background, but also indicate other cultural aspects on a higher level. Film-makers are well aware of this special function of dialogue. They often deliberately arrange for one or a number of characters to speak with a regional or even foreign accent on screen so as to achieve a special effect. However, in the dubbing process, more often than not, these special artistic touches and the cultural meanings associated with them are lost to some extent, simply because it is impossible to recreate these subtle features.

In the American Academy award-winning film *The French Connection*, the two American drug squad detectives Jimmy Doyle (played by Gene Hackman) and Buddy Russo (played by Roy Scheider) are monitoring the bugged telephone conversation of the suspected local drug dealer Sal Boca. It is the French accent of the Marseilles-based drug dealer Alain Charnier (played by Fernando Rey) when setting the time of the meeting that makes the two detectives realise that the drugs actually come from France. Here, Charnier's French accent plays a crucial role in the development of the story. Native speakers can easily follow this development. However, when the film was being dubbed into Chinese, we were unable to reproduce this subtle treatment of the dialogue. The best we could do was to ask the dubbing artist to deliberately say the Chinese line in a foreign accent. The result was simply awkward. The Chinese viewers experienced a jump in plot development and wondered how the detectives knew that it was a Frenchman, even though they could follow the story with no difficulty. Here we see a case where the story itself was undermined as a result of an inability to reproduce a foreign accent.

Very often, outstanding actors and actresses deliberately say their lines in a foreign accent to add some special artistic colour to the story. Such delicate treatment of the dialogue is frequently doomed to suffer in the dubbed version. When you listen to the Dutch accent of Meryl Streep in *Out of Africa* or her Polish accent in *Sophie's Choice*, you cannot help but admire her exquisite performing skills and her outstanding language capability. However, when you watch the Chinese version of these two films, you cannot detect any difference in the dialogue. Thus, part of her skill as an outstanding actress goes unnoticed.

Special accents can also play an important role in helping to identify different characters in a film, particularly if there are many similar ones. In *West Side Story*, the two gangs—the Puerto Rican

"Sharks" and the native New York "Jets"—are easily identifiable in the original English version because the Sharks speak English with a Puerto Rican accent. However, in the dubbing process, the dubbing artists, who all speak polished Standard Chinese, do not recognise this accent, and therefore fail to reproduce this difference, although this does not cause the audience any serious problems in following the story. Similar cases can be found in many foreign films that have been dubbed into Chinese. Of course, the fact that translators normally do not take part in the dubbing process is partially responsible for this because in China, most dubbing directors lack sufficient knowledge of any foreign language to recognise such differences. Even if they do recognise some difference, there is not much they can do about it. Some of my colleagues have tried to solve this problem by asking the dubbing artists to say the lines in different Chinese local accents. The result is that the dialogue in the dubbed version sounds awkward and absurd.

Accents are sometimes expertly used in certain films to form not only an interesting contrast between characters but also differences in other respects. One fine example is *Bedtime Story*, in which the characters of the American soldier Fred Benson (played by Marlon Brando) and of the British "prince" (played by David Niven) form an interesting contrast, which is also played out in the development of the story itself—crudity versus refinement. Fred, who speaks colloquial American English, can only win the hearts of innocent, naive girls, while the "prince," who speaks beautiful, polished British English is adept at winning over the upper-class ladies. This contrast not only reflects the different attitudes of these two characters towards life, but also, on a higher level, reflects the cultural differences between the two countries represented by these two characters. In the dubbing process, it is almost impossible to reproduce this unique contrast, and the humour is accordingly lost.

We all tend to have certain fixed stereotyped beliefs or misunderstandings about people from particular places. New Yorkers are flamboyant, Texans are showy and Jews are miserly. In China, too, there are similar stereotypes: Beijingers are self-important while Shanghainese are pragmatic and shrewd. These cultural labels (whether typical or atypical) are usually deeply rooted in the minds of the native people. Film-makers sometimes deliberately employ local accents to impart the cultural identities associated with them. The cultural messages thus conveyed can easily be picked up by native viewers, but usually go unnoticed by foreign cinema-goers. This phenomenon is particularly true in comedies, when the director tends to make fun of a certain type of people.

Cultural identity is another aspect of the dialogue that is often lost in dubbing. This occurs particularly in films that tell of the conflict between two different cultures. In such films, it is common for two social or ethnic groups to come into contact with each other. These different groups use different terms to denote the same object. Each of these terms is associated with the special cultural intentions behind it. In *A Passage to India*, the Indian Doctor Aziz uses *tonga* and Miss Quested uses *carriage* to mean the same thing. This interesting instance not only indicates the difference between the cultural identities of the two characters, but also serves as an allegory of the hidden political tension. However, when translated into Chinese, *tonga* and *carriage* become the same Chinese word, *ma che* 馬車. The original intention of both E. M. Foster and David Lean is clouded and some aspect of the meaning is lost.

It is even more difficult (both in translation and in the dubbing process) to handle the subtlety of social dialects. In the classic film *Cavalcade*, there is a difference between Mrs. Marriott's polished upper-class English and her maid Ellen's lower-class English. Although Ellen later rises in status, her accent still has traces of cockney in it, revealing her social origins and serves as an indicator of the limitations in her understanding of and outlook on the world. It is quite difficult to convey this feature in the Chinese dubbed version. There is really not much that we can do about this, apart from such technical treatment as special diction handling on the part of the translator and change of tonal colour on the part of the dubbing artists.

It is simply unavoidable that a film should suffer certain losses of meaning when it is dubbed into a foreign language. There are many reasons for such losses and the inability fully to express local (and sometimes social) dialects and foreign accents is one of these reasons. It is the responsibility of translators, directors and dubbing artists to recognise this limitation and try to find a way of overcoming it.

References

Balazs, Bela. 1982. *Theory of the Film: Character and Growth of A New Art,* trans. He Li. Beijing: China Film Publishing House.

Bobker, Lee R. 1974. *Elements of Films.* New York: Harcourt Brace Jovanovich.

Marcel, Martin. 1977. *Le Langage Cinematographique.* Paris: Les Editeurs Francais Reunis.

Zhang, Chengshan. 1986. *Film and Film Appreciation.* Shanghai: Tongji University Publishing House.

13

Dubbing and Subtitling—
Art or Craft?

Rupert Chan

—ɯ—

Introduction

Over the past quarter of a century I have done many surtitling/
subtitling and dubbing—essentially script translation—jobs. I have
also translated or adapted some three dozen Western plays for Hong
Kong theatre groups to be staged in the Chinese language. Many of
them were adaptations rather than straight translations, in that I had
transposed the setting to China or Hong Kong: for example,
transporting Shakespeare's *Twelfth Night* and Rostand's *Cyrano de
Bergerac* to the Tang dynasty of ancient China, and Brighouse's
Hobson's Choice to Hong Kong in the 1940s. I was awarded Playwright
of the Year 1990 by the Hong Kong Artists' Guild. Nevertheless, the
same series of questions have been put forward: is translation an art,
or a mere craft? Am I a mere craftsman in all these endeavours, or are
my works of sufficient artistic merit to interest, for instance, this
august gathering of scholars? That, it would seem, is the question. I
propose to share my experience and thoughts with the participants
in this conference, and leave the question for you to answer.

Proscenium Projections

In 1977, the former Director of the Hong Kong Academy of
Performing Arts, Professor Lo King-man, started producing Western
opera in Hong Kong with full orchestral accompaniment under the

auspices of the Urban Council. To help Hong Kong audiences follow the story, he decided to provide Chinese surtitles, and commissioned me to do the translation of opera libretti, from the English rendition of the original Italian or French, into Chinese. I was doubly constrained in this assignment. First of all, I was given instructions to make the surtitles very brief: they had to be just long enough for opera-goers to grasp the storyline at a glance, but not distract them from watching the show. Secondly, the surtitles were to be printed on a roll of transparencies for projection, manually, by a Mr. Xu (who also provided surtitles for Peking opera performances) on the proscenium of the City Hall Concert Hall, the venue for opera productions at that time. The physical restriction was that the projector could only show four lines of eight Chinese characters each at any one time. In such restrictive circumstances, I had to use classical Chinese, which is more concise than modern colloquial Chinese, to make the surtitles brief but still keeping the literary or poetic style akin to the original libretti. For instance, in translating the shepherd's song at the beginning of the last act of Giacomo Puccini's *Tosca*, I used regular four-character lines *à la Book of Songs*. Giuseppe Verdi's *Aida*, set in ancient Egypt, lent itself to rendition in an older style and I did the whole libretto in five-character lines. I believe this worked for Lo King-man's production at the City Hall in the 1980s that catered for a more cultured audience; but when it was reused in a more commercial context by Operama in 1991 at the Stanley Ho Sports Centre of the University of Hong Kong in an open air performance, I suspected that most of the audience found the surtitles hard to follow.

I also experimented with other styles. When Lo King-man produced Gaetano Donizetti's comic opera *Don Pasquale* in English, he asked me to make the surtitles more colloquial to help the audience enjoy this light-hearted production. I used lines such as "Brother, I cannot walk" (行不得也哥哥), a Chinese idiom, and "Loving you turns into harming you" (愛你變成害你), which was the title of a Cantonese popular song at that time. How did the audience react? In addition to being on the receiving end of spontaneous laughter, I was twice scoffed at by some people in local academia. I attended a radio forum on opera and lamented the relative neglect of the literary value of the libretti. A professor of music also present responded, "Perhaps that's because most opera libretti are banal."

And his wife, who had watched the aforesaid *Don Pasquale* production, used the same adjective to comment on my colloquial surtitles! Another ambitious attempt was the production of Benjamin Britten's *Noyes Fludde* (Noah's Flood) by the Hong Kong Academy for Performing Arts (HKAPA) in 1989. The ambition was the Academy's: they wanted to stage the opera, which had a libretto in incomprehensible Old English (as reflected in the title!), in Cantonese. I told them I could render the libretto in Cantonese—a most demanding task because Cantonese pronunciations have definite pitches—but I predicted that when the lines were sung in Western vocal style they would still be difficult to understand aurally.

As mentioned above, my *Aida* translation was reused. Many other surtitle sets of mine were also "recycled" in the 1990s when the HKAPA, and later the Hong Kong Arts Festival, staged the same operas Lo King-man had produced in the 1980s. However, I could not simply "resell" my old translation for use unchanged as in the case of *Aida* (or *Cav & Pag*—which was produced in Taiwan, again by Lo King-man). In the 1990s, there appeared to be a technological improvement in surtitle projections and text as well. I was invariably given a set of English surtitles (approved by the producers and directors) to translate from, which was elaborately numbered line by line: sometimes prefaced by as many as three different serial numbers! I am under the impression that, unlike the aforementioned manual projection of the 1970s and 1980s (which required a projectionist who was familiar with the opera concerned to ensure that the right lines were projected at the right moment), surtitle projection is now technologically synchronised with something (the orchestral score perhaps?) and will always be shown at the right time. However, when I watched these shows I still found moments when surtitles came out too early or too late, so my impression is probably wishful thinking.

When the Hong Kong Cultural Centre opened in 1989, one of the opening programmes was the Cologne Opera production of Rossini's *Barber of Seville*. The "authorities" concerned made a mistake in the Chinese translation of the title: instead of 塞維爾, they rendered "Seville" as 塞爾維亞 (which is the Chinese translation of "Serbia," which is in Eastern Europe). In 1990, I translated the libretto for the Glyndebourne/Stephen Lawless production of Mozart's *The Marriage of Figaro*, a Hong Kong Arts Festival presentation, and I got the Chinese translation of the name "Seville" right, of course. However, the Festival Office for some reason decided to conform to the "error" of the Cultural Centre—possibly under pressure from the same "authorities" who perpetrated it in the first place—and brutally changed the place name to the Chinese translation of "Serbia" again, much to the damage of my reputation as a translator! (A fellow victim was the Hong Kong Repertory Theatre Company, which staged Beaumarchais' play version at the same festival and was subjected to the same perpetuation of this error.) And, believe it or not, there has been unrest in Serbia ever since! By contrast, the other production I am proud to mention is the Festival's presentation of Tan Dun's *Marco Polo* in 1997, which was an original new opera on a Chinese subject. The libretto was by a non-Chinese author who apparently demonstrated his interpretation of what he felt was Chinese philosophy. In the event, I believe this was an opera that baffled all audiences, Western and Chinese alike. As a surtitle translator, I performed what must have been my greatest feat: I managed to translate something that was (and still is) totally incomprehensible to me!

Silver Screen Subtexts

Having established myself as a prolific translator of opera libretti and plays, in the early 1990s, I received new commissions to diversify into translating film subtitles, but the other way round—from Chinese to English. I started with the small screen on television: a Hong Kong television station (TVB) decided to show *The Purple Hairpin* (紫釵記), a Cantonese opera classic starring the celebrated Yam Kim-fai and Pak Suet-sin, on its English channel for the benefit of English-speaking viewers. They commissioned me to do the English subtitles. Screen subtitles were just as constrained, if not more so, as proscenium projections of surtitles: just so many letters per line. This opera classic, written by the late Tong Tik-sang, was rich in classical allusions from the treasure trove of Chinese literature. It was therefore a great challenge to translate it for English viewers unfamiliar with Chinese culture, especially within such restrictive parameters. My tactic was to use classical allusions in Western culture to substitute for the Chinese ones wherever close parallels could be found. For example, the line "誓死憐才，有望夫石不渝之心", in which the heroine compared her fidelity to the legendary rock 望夫石 (literally Yearning-for-husband Rock)—a woman faithfully watching out on a hilltop for her husband to return until she was turned into a rock—was translated succinctly into "I love talent as Eurydice, unchanging till death."

My next assignment was not exactly subtitle translation, but was to act in an advisory capacity for director Tsui Hark's *Once Upon a Time in China* (黃飛鴻), which started his series of kung fu films starring Jet Li as the legendary Chinese kung fu master, Huang Fei-hong. My task was to review all the English and French lines in this film set in late nineteenth-century China (with "foreign devils" cast as villains—except for a good-guy priest played by Colin George from the HKAPA), and to revise any lines where necessary to make them fit into its historical background (the script was done by a young screen playwright): i.e., replacing idioms that were too modern with antiquated expressions of a century ago. The best joke was that Jackie Cheung (the canto-pop singer), who played Huang Fei-hong's stammering pupil, stammered when speaking in Chinese, but miraculously became extremely fluent when speaking long sentences in English!

Among other assignments involving translating subtitles into English, I was flattered to be enlisted to help film directors Clara Lo and Mabel Cheung Yuen-ting, both Hong Kong University alumnae. They were sending their films to international film festivals, and hence required English subtitles of a high quality. In Hong Kong, quality is very often measured by price. There is a regular market rate for translating English subtitles for a Hong Kong film, usually by relatively young translators. A veteran film critic who is Eurasian and bilingual charges twice that market rate when he is called upon to translate subtitles. In my case I charge twice his rate (or four times the market rate). That is why my works are so limited in number. I myself am selective and only accept commissions for good quality films. Very often I confronted similar challenges, as in *The Purple Hairpin*, of cultural differences. One example was a line in *City of Glass*: when a girl disclosed the information that her first boyfriend was named Ah Fung 阿風, she was asked the question "阿風？胡楓、聶風定謝霆鋒？" Literally this means "Which Ah Fung: Woo Fung, Nip Fung or Tse Ting-fung?" Woo Fung is a veteran Hong Kong film and television actor, Nip Fung is a popular comic strip character, and Tse

Ting-fung (Nicholas Tse) is a singer of popular Cantonese songs and
film star. My translation of this exchange involved first rendering Ah
Fung as Michael. The questioning line then became: "Michael who:
Michael Douglas, Michael Jackson or Michael Chang?" Only thus
would it make sense to viewers not familiar with Hong Kong popular
culture.

Rub-a-Dubbing

After a spell of Chinese-to-English subtitle translation, my services
were again enlisted for an English-to-Chinese translation of a film
script: this time for the Cantonese dubbing project of the Disney
production of *Mulan*, which is based on a Chinese folk legend.
Mulan, the daughter, is highly trained in martial arts. She joins the
army disguised as a man to take her aged father's place in a battle
against the Hun invaders. I have a soft spot for Disney's animated
classics and their dubbed versions. I remember taking my children
when they were under ten to see *The Jungle Book* dubbed in
Cantonese, with Sunny Wong, a local folk singer, singing the songs
with Cantonese lyrics. My young kids thoroughly enjoyed the show,
which they could follow, dubbed in their mother tongue. Later, when
they were in their teens, we watched the original English version of
the same film and enjoyed it no less. For this new dubbing project,
Hong Kong pop singer Kelly Chan was commissioned to speak and
sing the part of Mulan, international kung fu star Jackie Chan took
the part of Mulan's captain and lover Li Xiang, and Ge Wenhui, the
DJ-turned-comic actor, was the local substitute for Eddie Murphy as
the voice of Mulan's sidekick, the Dragon.

A dubbing script was something new to me, who was by then an
old hand in the other aforesaid pursuits (and by then I had also
produced two original film scripts). Sound Supply, the dubbing
agency, supplied me with the English script "annotated" by their
experienced colleague, who had counted and marked down the
number of lip movements in each line. The constraint this time was
that I had to observe the number of lip movements and restrict the
number of syllables (i.e., characters, since Cantonese is
monosyllabic) accordingly, in each line. My translation, as with the
scripts I had done for stage plays, had to be colloquial, since it was for
dubbing. I also faced a challenge since, by contrast with translations

for publishing where one can use footnotes to explain puns, double entendres and allusions in detail, a line delivered on stage or in dubbing has to convey the meaning to the audience precisely and instantaneously: there is no time or space for paraphrasing or annotations.

Sound Supply enlisted my services because this was a film based on classical Chinese folklore. My first draft was, while colloquial, also relatively elegant in style, to convey the classical-literary setting. In the event, Jackie Chan came back with a request that his lines be made still more colloquial, since he had difficulty in delivering lines which were too arty-farty ("文縐縐", in his own words). Then, when they were actually doing the recording in the studio, Ge, the stand-up comedian, was up to his old tricks, and altered most of his own lines impromptu!

Spreading the Art of Cantonese Opera

Into the twenty-first century, the HKAPA has launched its own Cantonese opera courses and staged Cantonese opera excerpts regularly as training for its students. My assignment was once again doing Chinese-to-English translation of surtitles, for the benefit of non-Chinese audiences. This proved to be the least restrictive, since I was free to break up each line in Cantonese into more than one line in English. As in Western operas, there are a lot of repetitions in Cantonese opera lines. Also, the singing style is such that very often a single syllable is sustained on a prolonged note or notes. This meant that there was plenty of time for Cantonese opera-goers to read the surtitles.

I should add that, round about the same time I was translating surtitles for these Cantonese opera excerpts for the HKAPA, Lo King-man, now President of the Academy, was producing the first local original operas, viz. *The Divorce* and *The Lamp of Everlasting Light*, based on the Chinese writer Lu Xun's short stories, composed by a couple of young local composers, Lam Shun and Lo Hau-man, with Lo as producer, director and "book" (libretto) writer. I was enlisted as lyricist to write the lyrics based on the dialogues in the original short stories (which were very scanty, so I had to make up extra lines). When the double bill was staged in January 2000, I was also asked to do the Chinese and English surtitles. Instead of line-by-line translation, which might have been too distracting, Lo King-man bade me produce summary surtitles, briefly outlining the story. This has also been the prevailing method adopted for surtitling in musical and commercial stage drama productions in Hong Kong since the 1990s.

In translating surtitles into English for the Cantonese opera excerpts, however, because there was ample time available for reading surtitles, as explained above, I kept to translating the script line by line. The English-reading audiences' feedback supported such an approach, which helped them follow the show closely and enjoy this Chinese art form to the full. The HKAPA is currently planning to take one of the latest excerpt productions, *Monkey King and The Skeleton Demon* from *Journey to the West*, to be staged in Berlin. For this project, my English surtitles will come in handy for a German translator to translate into German. I am therefore most gratified to see that my surtitle translation is contributing to the spread of this ancient Chinese art form to the West.

Finis

I will not end with a conclusion. As I have said, I will leave the question of whether surtitling and dubbing, and indeed the bigger question of whether the translation of opera and drama scripts, is an art or a mere craft, to be answered by other scholars. For my part, it was all in a day's work, and I had my satisfaction in meeting the challenge of making the meaning comprehensible to audiences, and of translating especially difficult lines, in ensuring that I added something original to each translated script, and in collecting the fee I earned. For participants who wish to sample my translation of subtitles for opera and film, I recommend two DVDs on sale: the Universal production of Verdi's *Otello* (2000), for which I did the Chinese subtitles, and the Hong Kong film *City of Glass*, set in 1997 with flashbacks to my own undergraduate days at the University of Hong Kong in the 1970s. For those who are interested in my drama translation/adaptation, I recommend the DVD version of the Springtime Production of George Bernard Shaw's *Pygmalion*, which I transposed to a 1930s Hong Kong setting, with a subtext of 1997: Eliza thanking the Professor for teaching her the "English lady's ways," but being a Hong Kong Chinese she must henceforth walk her own path in life. I believe I (or rather, my Eliza) voiced the sentiments of the majority of the citizens of Hong Kong.

14

Translation Imperative: Synchronise Discipline and Technique

Janet Tauro

—ᴍ—

In the year 1995, *Marimar* entered the Philippine television industry and things were never the same again.

When the Mexican telenovela *Marimar*, which was dubbed into Filipino, zoomed to the top of the ratings chart in June 1996, people saw the country's media giant ABS CBN, with its 3 billion yearly income, down on its knees in defeat. The sizzling *Marimar*, produced by a lowly government-owned station (RPN Channel 9), had unwittingly exposed a crack in the ABS CBN shield. This telenovela hit the big time even though television dubbers and radio talents who had not taken any formal translation course translated it. Even if the multi-billion peso empire of the powerful Lopez family spent millions on research, trying to forecast audience preferences, still its executives would not be able to comprehend the "*Marimar* episode."[1]

Since then, a proliferation of Mexican telenovelas has been translated and dubbed into Filipino. At present, every television station has three to five telenovelas dubbed into Filipino. Outside Hollywood, it is only Latin American telenovelas and Japanese animated series that have become viable television-import projects. The country has consumed these shows with gusto. But media specialists have still failed to divine what this means.

Ironically, research and critical analysis carried out by academicians and research scholars into telenovelas remains nonexistent. Furthermore, academic courses in translation do not figure prominently in the Philippines. In fact, De La Salle University is the only institution in the country which offers a translation programme at graduate and undergraduate levels.

What Venuti (2000) said in *The Translation Studies Reader* about film translation receiving "little scholarly attention despite its potential yield for both linguistics and cultural studies" holds very true in Philippine television.

Why study the translation of the telenovela? Some scholars have asked this question. Because it is there. Such an answer may seem flippant but actually it is precise. The serious academic scholar should study the translation of telenovelas because it is the academic's business to study reality. Scholars should study *Marimar* because it is part of popular culture and popular culture is a reality.

As the Filipino critic Isagani Cruz (1997) said in the *Diliman Review,*

> The scholar who refuses to deal with the popular culture soon finds himself a hyphenated person, an intellectual on campus, an ordinary human being at home. The true scholar must see his experiences as a totality not as fragments.

Thus, there is no need to justify further the significance of this paper on the critical analysis of the text and context of the telenovela *Marimar.*

In the first part of this paper, a critical analysis of the context, the production and the consumption of the text will be presented. The issues that influenced the production and consumption of the text: for instance, the social, economic and political situation of the audience and the television industry, will also be explored and related to the text. In the second part of the paper, a critical reading of the text of *Marimar* as a written text, a visual text and an acoustic text will be presented. In the third part of this paper, the need to synchronise the discipline of academia and the techniques of the television industry will be discussed.

As a result of the textual and contextual critical analysis conducted, an engaging but out of synch *Marimar* was born. But how is it that this out of synch *Marimar* is engaging?

This will be discussed in the first part of this paper, as part of the contextual analysis of *Marimar* that is focused on the issues of production and consumption. There is a need to study the context because it is always part of the production and consumption of the text. The text cannot be understood without the context. As Real (1989) said, in the book *In Super Media: A Cultural Studies Approach*:

> Text always includes contexts. Texts occur only within a culture, a system with subsystems and multiple layers of meaning. Textual interpretation takes text as the center of meaning, but of meaning that is social and historical as well as personal.

Even B.S. Medina (2000), in his book *Sa Ibang Salita, Sampung Sanaysay sa Sining Salin* about translation which is written in Filipino, underscored the need to conduct a critical analysis of the context of a text, since there is a need to know the sense and sensibilities of the country when translating from the language of that country.

The contextual analysis reveals that *Marimar* is engaging because of the production issue: it uses a ubiquitous medium, which is television. According to the *Exposure of Population to Mass Media in the Philippines* website (1996):

> The popularity of television continued to rise in the 90s, as evidenced by the impressive 8.7 percentage point expansion in televiewers (the highest among the 8 mass media forms)- from 48.0 per cent in 1989 to 56.7 per cent in 1996. The increasing trend was reflected in both the urban (1.7 percentage points) and rural areas (5.8 percentage points.)

Aside from being ubiquitous, television is also highly commercialised by nature. In the Philippines, 60 per cent of programmes are soap operas, 20 per cent are news and public affairs programmes, while the remaining 10 per cent are variety shows such as game and sports shows. This prompted the participants in the first Soap Opera Summit in the Philippines, held last February 2001, to call the Philippines the soap opera capital of the world.

The obvious rationale behind the entertainment kind of programming is that it sells. In spite of the millions and even billions earned annually by the top television networks, these networks still want to produce highly commercial programmes that sell. This is the reason why Mexican telenovelas dubbed into Filipino proliferate: because they earn a lot but they do not cost a lot. Translators who are also dubbers are not trained and are therefore paid very little.

Television networks prefer to spend more on the promotion of the telenovelas than on making efforts to make the quality of translation and dubbing of these shows more professional. Rex Lorens, general manager of RPN 9, the government-sequestered television network, admitted that their executives had footed the P1 million-plus-per-day bill of *Marimar* star Thalia's visit to the Philippines in August 1996.

With regard to the consumption issue, *Marimar* is engaging because it satisfies the social and economic needs of the audience. Marimar herself is engaging because this fair-skinned mestiza - with a sculpted nose, luscious lips and expressive brown eyes - captures the imagination of a typical colonial-minded Filipino. Filipino women would like to have the Marimar features. This desire to have the Western look in the Philippines is manifested in the very 'in' and trendy colouring of hair blond or red, and the increasing sales and production of whitening lotion and soap.

Men, on the other hand, are taken with the contours of her breasts thrust against her simple cotton dress and by her legs, creamy and well formed below the short dress. As a result of the Filipino "macho" attitude, women are still viewed as sex objects. Azarcon-de la Cruz (1991) claimed in her book *From Virgin to Vamp: Images of Women in Philippine Media* that television programmes are still about male fantasies and expectations of how women should act, look and position themselves in relation to men.

Marimar is also engaging because of the use of the Filipino language. About 70 per cent of the programmes in the Philippines use the Filipino language. News and current affairs programmes, which used to be in English, now use Filipino. Even in the coverage of the trial of former President Joseph Estrada, most of the television networks used Filipino. Stanford graduate, businessman and former Philippine Stock Exchange President Jose Yulo spoke fluent Filipino when explaining the role of Estrada in the scam. Filipino is considered as an intellectualised language in the Philippines and not just as the language of the *masa* or the poor majority. Medina (2001), in his article in the souvenir programme of the *First Soap Summit for Social Change in the Philippines*, said that "... the telenovela has brought the Filipino language to a commanding level of popular acceptance: imagine the Caucasian white speaking in a native Filipino language."

Other oft-used analysis is that *Marimar* is close to Filipinos' hearts because of the cultural proximity factor, since the Philippines had been a Spanish colony for more than a hundred years. Linguistic affinities and politico-colonial factors may have influenced the phenomenal success of *Marimar*. However, the *Marimar* phenomenon consists of much more than cultural proximity, more than the use of the Filipino language and more than the Filipino colonial mentality.

The *Television Research Council People Meter* survey conducted in July 1996 indicated that the audience of *Marimar* belongs to the middle and lower economic classes of Philippine society. The poor and oppressed Filipinos can relate to the sufferings of Marimar. In the Philippines, being poor is a crime. Sales persons working in shopping malls and utility persons working in offices are asked to take off their clothes before they leave the workplace to make sure that they have not stolen anything from the company. Low-income employees are already accused of committing crimes simply because they are poor. In the telenovela, Marimar is always being blamed for crimes that have been perpetrated by the rich antagonists, just because she is poor. But Marimar fights back, and has been doing so since the beginning of the telenovela, and this is what the Filipinos adore. Battered wives at the Women's Crisis Centre are inspired by the courage of Marimar in fighting back in spite of her status as a woman and as a poor person.

But this is not happening only in the Philippines. Mattelart (1985:4) claimed that telenovelas are also popular with the middle and lower classes of other developing nations:

> This success suggests there are more universal qualities which quite diverse audiences find in telenovelas, perhaps due to their intrinsic temporal rhythms or allegorical character, perhaps due to the result of Globo's experience in the cultivation of audience appeal across and other differences within Brazil, or perhaps some similarity in social desires generated in post-socialist and "Third World" societies alike. A Polish newspaper had a simple explanation: in a situation of social disappointment, the public seeks consolation in fairy tales.

Hence, Marimar is engaging not only because audiences can relate to the oppression that she suffers, but also because they are under the illusion that despite their lowly economic status, they can be like Marimar, they can also fight back.

In conducting a textual analysis of *Marimar*, it is important to note that the telenovela is a translation of a translation of a translation. When RPN Channel 9 bought the rights to *Marimar*, English scripts accompanied it. So from Spanish, it was translated first into English and then into Filipino. However, it was translated twice into Filipino.

The first translation was based on the English script and the second was made during dubbing. Whenever the television dubbers/translators observed that the translated dialogues failed to synchronise with the lip movements, they immediately changed the words in order to match them. There is no printed script for the second translation.

Now for the story of the text: the conflict begins when Sergio, the spoiled son of a plantation owner, conceives a plot to take revenge on his family because they refuse to give him his inheritance. He marries Marimar, a poor innocent girl, in order to humiliate them. As a result, Marimar suffers humiliation at the hands of the rich family who oppose her marriage with Sergio. After being ostracised and thrown out of the house, she has her revenge when her own father, an extremely wealthy man who abandoned her mother, finds her and makes her his heir.

The examples of the translated texts are taken from the ninth episode. This episode was chosen for the following reasons: first, this is one of six episodes which have a complete script in English and Filipino (the translators of the first Filipino version failed to store back-up copies since they used only typewriters, while the translators of the second Filipino version failed to put into print the changes that they had abruptly made, which were therefore inserted by hand); second, because this episode contains one of the major highlights of the telenovela: the break-up between Marimar and Sergio.

In this scene, Marimar is being blamed for the shooting of Chuy. The antagonists, the rich family who actually masterminded the crime, claim that an anonymous admirer of Marimar gunned down Chuy out of jealousy, since the two were always being seen together.

Below is the script of the first three scenes from the ninth episode. Please note that the first line of dialogue in bold letters is from the English script and therefore this is the source text. The second line in bold letters is the literal English translation of the first

Filipino translation. The first Filipino translation being referred to here is based on the English script. The third line in bold letters is the literal English translation of the second Filipino translation. The second Filipino translation was done during dubbing.

SCENE 1
ANGELICA:
God knows if your husband saw you doing something that is not correct and fired at Chuy. (Perfecta exhales) BIZ—STINGER
ANGELICA:
Wala akong ibig sabihin. Nag-aalala lang ako dahil baka nakita kayo ni Sergio na kayong dalawa lang ni Chuy ang magkasama na may ginagawang masama at binaril niya si Chuy.
(I don't mean anything. I am just worried that Sergio might have seen you doing something bad with Chuy and shot Chuy.)
ANGELICA:
Diyos lang ang nakakaalam kung nakita ka ng iyong asawa na may ginagawang hindi tama at binaril si Chuy
(Only God knows if your husband saw you doing something that is not correct and fired at Chuy.)

MARIMAR:
You think that … Sergio? No, don't even say that. (GOES NEAR) **You are evil, evil!** (SLAPS HER) (TENSION MUSIC IN BACKGROUND)
MARIMAR:
Huwag mong pagbintangan si Sergio.Umm. Bawiin mo ang sinabi mo. Hindi lang yan ang matitikman mo kapag hindi mo binawi ang sinabi mo. Masasaktan ka talaga sa akin. Walanghiya ka.Umm
(Don't accuse Sergio … I want you to take back what you have said. That is not the only thing that you'll get from me if you don't take back what you have said.)
MARIMAR:
Sa tingin mo'y si Sergio. Huwag, huwag mong sabihin yan, huwag mong sabihin yan Huwag mong sabihin yan!
(You think? Sergio? Don't, don't say that. Don't say that!)

ANGELICA:
Let go of me, let go of me.

ANGELICA:
Bitiwan mo ako.
(Let go of me.)
ANGELICA:
Bitiwan mo ako
(Let go of me.)

PERFECTA:
Have you gone crazy?
PERFECTA:
Senyoritaaa. Marimar, bitiwan mo siyaa.
(Señoritaa.. Marimar, let go of her.)
PERFECTA:
Anong nangyayari sa 'yo! Tama na! Huminahon ka!
(What is happening to you? That's enough! Be calm!)

MARIMAR:
Let go of me. Let go of me! (PERFECTA SEPARATES THEM AND STRUGGLES WITH MARIMAR) **I am going to pull out your tongue …!**
MARIMAR:
Huwag kang makialam dito. Papatayin ko ang babaeng ito. Pinagbibintangan niya si Sergio. puputulin ko yang dila mo.Bitiwan mo ako, Perfecta bitiwan mo sabi ako. Ummm. Hindi mapapalampas ang ginawa niyang ito.Hindi.Walanghiya ka.Ummm.
(Don't meddle here. I will kill this woman. She accused Sergio. I will cut your tongue. Let go of me. I will not let this pass by, you thick-skinned!)
MARIMAR:
Bitiwan mo ako Perfecta bitiwan mo sabi ako. Puputulin ko ang dila mo. Makikita mo. Walanghiya ka.
(Let me go Perfecta. Let me go, I said. I will cut your tongue. You'll see. You thick-skinned!)

ANGELICA:
Let go of me, let go of me!
ANGELICA:
Ugh.Arayyy.Bitiwan mo ako.
(Ugh. Ouch. Let go of me.)

ANGELICA:
Ugh. araay. Bitiwan mo ako.
(Ugh. Ouch. Let go of me.)

PERFECTA:
You are crazy, crazy!
PERFECTA:
(STRUGGLES/TRYING TO SEPARATE THEM) Tama na! Marimar, tama na!
(That's enough, Marimar. That's enough.)
PERFECTA:
Tama na Marimar, tama na.
(That's enough, Marimar. That's enough.)

SCENE 2 (GARDEN)
RENATO:
(Are you sure, Antonieta?)
RENATO:
Ha? Papaanong. Sigurado ka ba, Antonieta?
(What? How ? Are you sure, Antonieta?)
RENATO:
Sigurado ka ba, Antonieta?
(Are you sure, Antonieta?)

ANTONIETA:
The girl has just said it, she came in screaming and crying that Chuy had been killed.
ANTONIETA:
Oo Renato ... dumating si Marimar galing sa labas at sumisigaw ... binaril daw si Chuy ... at baka patay na siya ngayon
(Yes Renato. Marimar came in from the outside and shouting that Chuy was killed and that he might be dead by now.)
ANTONIETA:
Iyon ang sinabi niya. Pumasok siya. Nagtititili,umiiyak. Napatay daw si Chuy. **(That's what she said. She came in. Shrieking. Crying. Saying that Chuy was killed.)**
RENATO:
Where is he?

RENATO:
Nasaan siya? **(Where is he/she?)**
RENATO:
Nasaan siya? **(Where is he/she?)**

ANTONIETA:
She said by the palm trees.
ANTONIETA:
Naroon sa may niyugan
(There in the palm trees.)
ANTONIETA:
Nandoon sa may niyugan
(There in the palm trees.)

NICANDRO:
Are we going over there boss?
NICANDRO:
Senyor pupuntahan ba natin?
(Señor, are we going there?)
NICANDRO:
Pupunta tayo doon boss?
(Señor, are we going there?)

RENATO:
(TAKES SOME STEPS) **Of course, it's nearby.** (STOPS) **I had
ordered you to go to the alfalfa fields.**
RENATO:
Nicandro. Hindi ba inutusan kitang magpunta sa maisan ngayon?
Bakit naririto ka pa?
**(Nicandro, didn't I order you to go to the cornfields today? Why are
you still here?)**
RENATO:
Siyempre naman malapit lang 'yon. Inutusan ko kayong dalawa na
pumunta sa may taniman sa hacienda?
**(Of course, it's nearby. I ordered you two to go to the field in the
plantation, didn't I?**
NICANDRO:
It was still early boss, I was getting ready to go. (TAKES SOME
STEPS)

NICANDRO:
Maaga pa, Senyor. Naghahanda pa ako ng mga dadalhin ko.
(It's still too early Señor. I am still preparing the things that I'm bringing.)

NICANDRO:
Maaga pa kasi boss, naghahanda pa ako
(It's still too early Boss, I'm still preparing.)

SCENE 3
ANTONIETA: (VOICE OFF) **Is he dead?**
ANTONIETA:
Ayan siya, Renato. Diyos ko. Patay na yata siya.
(There he is, Renato. Oh my God. I think he's dead.)
ANTONIETA:
Patay na ba sya?
(Is she/he dead?)

RENATO:
No, he's just unconscious. (CAMERA RANGE WIDENS TO CUT TO NICANDRO SQUATTING AND ANTONIETA STANDING) Who could have fired at him? (FEDERICO ENTERS ON BOARD A JEEP)
RENATO:
Chuy. Hindi, hindi pa siya patay. Sino kaya ang bumaril sa kanya?
Chuy. No, no he's not dead. Who could have shot him?
RENATO:
Hindi. Nawalan lang ng malay. Sino kaya ang bumaril sa kanya?
No. He just lost his consciousness. Who could have shot him?

ANTONIETA:
That peasant said she didn't see anybody.
ANTONIETA:
Sinabi ni Marimar na wala raw siyang nakita.
Marimar said that she didn't see anybody.
ANTONIETA:
Sabi ng hampos lupang 'yon wala raw siyang nakita.
That lowly creature said she didn't see anybody.

RENATO:
I don't think this boy has any enemies. (FEDERICO GETS OUT OF JEEP AND GOES NEAR)
RENATO:
Sa palagay ko, eh, wala namang kaaway ang batang ito.
I think this boy has no enemy.
RENATO:
Sa tingin ko eh, wala namang kaaway ang batang ito.
I think this boy has no enemy.

NICANDRO:
He must have if he was fired at, perhaps it was out of jealousy.
NICANDRO:
Baka naman binaril siya, dahil pinagseselosan?
Might he have been shot at because of jealousy?
NICANDRO:
Meron siguro kung binaril siya … at maaring sa selos.
He might have, if he was shot, and maybe because of jealousy.
RENATO:
Jealousy?
RENATO:
Teka, ano yong sinabi mong baka pinagselosan …?
Wait. What did you say? Jealousy?
RENATO:
Selos?
Jealousy?

NICANDRO:
Yes, since lately he was always going around with Marimar. (RENATO STANDS)
NICANDRO:
Opo, Senyor Madalas kasi silang nakikitang magkasama ni Marimar nitong mga huling araw.
Yes, Señor. He's always been seen with Marimar these past few days.
NICANDRO:
Opo, dahil nitong mga huling araw, laging silang magkasama ni Marimar.
Yes, because these past few days he's always seen with Marimar.

ANTONIETA:
Why didn't Sergio come with you?
ANTONIETA: Nasaan nga pala si Sergio?
By the way where is Sergio?
ANTONIETA:
Bakit hindi sumama si Sergio sa 'yo?
Why didn't Sergio come with you?

RENATO: (STANDING TO ONE SIDE) We separated a moment ago, he went to town for some seeds. We have to take him right now to a dispensary. Federico, Nicandro, put him in the jeep.
RENATO: Nagpunta siya sa bayan para bumili ng mga binhi. O sige na Nicandro, dalhin na ninyo sa hospital si Chuy. Isakay na ninyo siya sa sasakyan.
He went to town to buy some seeds. Okay Nicandro, bring Chuy to the hospital. Put him in the transportation.
RENATO: Nagkahiwalay kami kanina lang. Nagpunta sya sa bayan para bumili ng mga pananim. Kailangan natin siyang dalhin kaagad sa clinic. Federico, si Chuy.. na ninyo sya sa jeep.
We separated a moment ago. He went to town for some seeds. We have to take him right now to the clinic. Federico, this Chuy, put him in the jeep.

NICANDRO:
Yes boss. (HE STANDS AND GOES NEAR) FEDERICO GOES NEAR AND THE TWO OF THEM TAKE HIM TO THE JEEP (MARIMAR ENTERS AND APPROACHES NICANDRO)
NICANDRO:
Opo Senyor. Federico, halika, tulungan mo ako.
Yes, Señor. Federico, come here, help me.
NICANDRO:
Opo Senyor. **(Yes, Señor.)**

MARIMAR: (EXHALING)
He is dead, right? Is he dead?
MARIMAR:
Patay na ba siya? Diyos ko! Buhay pa ba siya?
Is he dead? Oh my God! Is he alive?

MARIMAR:
Patay na ba sya? Anong sa tingin nyo?
Is he dead? What do you think?

RENATO:
(PICKS UP JESUS' HAT) No girl, he is just wounded.
RENATO:
Buhay pa siya …
He's still alive …
RENATO:
Hindi hija, may sugat lang sya.
No hija, he only has wound.

MARIMAR:
Are you taking him to the doctor?
MARIMAR: (WORRIED / CRYING) Dadalhin ba siya sa doctor?
Are you taking him to the doctor?
MARIMAR: Dadalhin nyo sa doktor?
Are you taking him to the doctor?

RENATO:
Yes.
RENATO:
Oo.
Yes.
RENATO:
Oo.
Yes.

MARIMAR:
But why is that, who could have done it, why did they fire at him?
MARIMAR:
Sino kaya ang bumaril sa kanya? Bakit siya binaril?
Who could have shot him? Why was he shot?
MARIMAR:
Pero sino ang gumawa sa kanya noon? Bakit siya binaril?
But who did this to him? Why was he shot?

ANTONIETA:
No one should know better than you.

ANTONIETA:
Ikaw lang ang nakakaalam niyan
Only you know that.
ANTONIETA:
Walang ibang nakakaalam niyan kundi ikaw.
Nobody knows better than you.

MARIMAR:
No, well, I did not see who it was.
MARIMAR:
Hindi ko nakita kung sino ang bumaril.
I did not see who shot him.
MARIMAR:
Ano? Pero wala akong nakitang iba.
What? But I didn't seen anybody.

ANTONIETA:
You caused this situation, don't deny it, it was your fault. (SOFT BACKGROUND MUSIC)
ANTONIETA:
Ikaw ang may kagagawan ng lahat ng ito. Kasalanan mo ito.
You caused this situation. This is all your fault.
ANTONIETA:
Ikaw ang dahilan bakit nangyari ito huwag ka ng magkaila. Kasalanan mo ito.
You are the reason why this thing happened, don't deny it, it was your fault.

MARIMAR:
Me ... my fault? (EXIT RUNNING) (RENATO AND ANTONIETA TAKE STEPS TOWARD THE JEEP WHERE JESUS IS ALREADY ON BOARD)
MARIMAR:
Kasalanan ko? Hindi ... (FADES OUT) Hindiiii
My fault? No. No.
MARIMAR:
Kasalanan ko?
My fault?

NICANDRO:
We will take him to the dispensary boss, you don't worry about it.
NICANDRO:
Opo, Senyor Sige po, aalis na kami.
Yes Señor. Okay we will go now.
NICANDRO:
Dadalhin na namin kaagad sa clinic si Chuy. Boss huwag kayong mangamba.
We will bring Chuy right away to the clinic. Boss don't worry.

RENATO:
All right Nicandro, keep me abreast of what is happening. (THROWS HIM HIS HAT)
RENATO:
Sige na Nicandro. Dalhin na ninyo siya sa hospital. Balitaan mo lang ako kung ano ang nangyari.
Okay Nicandro. Bring him now to the hospital. Just keep me informed of what is happening.
RENATO:
O sige, Nicandro. Balitaan mo ako kung ano ang nangyayari.
Okay Nicandro. Just keep me informed of what is happening.

RENATO:
Who could have done this?
RENATO:
Sino kaya ang may kagagawan nito?
Who could have done this?
RENATO:
Sino kaya ang gumawa nito?
Who could have done this?

ANTONIETA:
I think the same as Nicandro, it must have been your son, Sergio. (RENATO LOOKS AT HER DISCONCERTED)
ANTONIETA:
Baka nga totoo ang sinabi ni Nicandro, na may nagselos kaya binaril si Chuy. Baka ang anak mo, si Sergio.
What Nicandro said might be true, that somebody got jealous and shot Chuy. It might have been your son Sergio.

ANTONIETA:
Tulad ng iniisip ni Nicandro, maari ang anak mo, si Sergio.
Like what Nicandro is thinking. It might have been your son, Sergio.

In critically analysing the text of the three scenes, I focus first on the paralinguistic components, such as the tone and clearness of the dialogues being delivered (acoustic). Clearness means that the delivery of the dialogues should be slow enough to be heard and understood. My second focus is on the correctness, coherence, emphasis and clarity of the written text (print), hence, the translated words should be short and conversational. My third focus is on communicativeness and on the appropriateness of the translated text to the visual medium (visual). Dialogues should be visually clear and should take into consideration that the medium is television, hence, image is already pervasive and translated text should not be redundant. The three samples that have been chosen for each of the above topics were considered to exemplify best the problems in the translation of the text.

First, for the acoustic text:

1. The entire first scene is a fighting scene; however, this is no excuse for the poor clarity of the dialogues being delivered by Marimar, Angelica and Perfecta.

2. In the first scene, take note of the first translation of Marimar's dialogue:
   "Don't accuse Sergio. I want you to take back what you have said. That is not the only thing that you'll get from me if you don't take back what you have said."
   This is very long, especially in Filipino, and therefore not acoustically clear. Now for the second translation of Marimar's dialogue:
   "You think? Sergio? Don't, don't say that. Don't say that!"
   This is shorter, more natural and conversational.

3. In the first scene, take note of Perfecta's dialogue:
   "Señoritaa. Marimar, let go of her."
   This line is more acoustically appropriate and clear considering that Marimar is already hitting Angelica. However, the second translation was used:
   "What is happening to you? That's enough! Be calm!"

The first translation is better than the second translation because this line has in it the five-syllable Filipino phrase *huminahon ka* (be calm), which is very long, not conversational and not acoustically clear.

Second, with regard to the printed text:

1. In the second scene, Renato says:
   "*Where is he?*"
   The Filipino translation is "*Nasaan siya*," which is quite confusing: using the word *siya* does not make it clear who has come in, since the Filipino word *siya* can refer to a male or a female, so it could refer to Marimar or to Chuy.

2. In the second scene, Nicandro says:
   "*Señor, are we going there?*"
   From the perspective of the audience, for Nicandro to ask whether they should go to the scene of the crime is ridiculous. Although this is the meaning of the message in the source language, the audience will surely shout and say, "Of course you should go there! The crime happened in your plantation and Chuy is one of your workers."

   From the perspective of the writer, the translator has the right to create another message with a similar, though not identical, meaning. It should have been "Are we going there now?" or "Do you want us to go there now?"

3. In the third scene, Marimar's speech in the first translation is:
   "*Is he dead? Oh my God! Is he alive?*"
   From the perspective of a writer, this speech is histrionic and may sound funny, hence the second translation of Marimar's dialogue is more appropriate and conversational:
   "*Is he dead? What do you think?*"

Third, concerning the visual text:

1. In the first scene, Angelica says:
   "*I don't mean anything. I am just worried...*"
   This line is not synchronised with the character's facial expression. She appears to be furious, but what she says is very subtle and calm. The translation fails to take into account the visual component of the text.

2. In the second scene, the first translation of Antonieta's speech is:

   "*There he is, Renato. Oh my God. I think he's dead.*"

   This line is completely unnecessary. Television is a visual medium; hence there is no need to say, "*There he is.*" This is only done on the radio, since the audience cannot see the characters and their entry into the scene has to be announced.

3. Also, in the same first translation of Antonieta's speech:

   "*There he is, Renato. Oh my God. I think he's dead.*"

   In this example, the character's speech in the first translation is not synchronised with her facial expression. It is the right decision to change the first translation, since Antonieta's face appears stoical while her use of the phrase "*Oh my God*" suggests that she is horrified ...

On the basis of the critical analysis of the sample dialogues presented above, I suggest that the translators have failed to translate *Marimar* as a printed text, as a visual text or as an acoustic text.

First, as a written text, it is important to note that, unlike the reading of a book, in which the reader can go back if there is something that he or she does not understand, once something has been viewed on television, the audience cannot rewind it and see it again. In critically analysing the text as a printed text it was pointed out that in some instances in the three scenes examined, the first translation appears more correct. Why is this? Because it has coherence, clarity and emphasis. Since the second translation was done haphazardly during dubbing, so from the point of view of a writer, it would be difficult to study and scrutinise the text for coherence, emphasis and clarity.

Second, in an acoustic text the television industry is supposed to be aware that paralinguistic components such as tone and clarity are important. In fact, the syllables are counted to make sure that the words are understandable, familiar, conversational and that the actors will not become tongue-tied when pronouncing the words. There are some cases in which the second translation is more acoustically appropriate because the dialogues are shorter. The clearness in the delivery of the dialogues suffers when the translated words are very long. Even if the dubber were a professional it would still be difficult, since he or she would be uttering the words very quickly in an effort to synchronise them with the lip movements.

Aside from the very long dialogues, there were also some cases in which the tone of the dubber was not clear and not synchronised with the actor's facial expression. According to Vangie Labalan, dubbing director of *Marimar*, the same dubber dubs the voices of two or three characters in the telenovela. Since this is the case it will indeed be difficult for the dubber to synchronise with and modulate his or her tone according to the facial expressions of three actors, even if he or she is a professional dubber.

Third, when we examined it as a visual text, it was observed that there are some words in the first translation which are redundant. Taking into consideration the fact that television is a visual medium, there is no need to make the dialogues very detailed because the audience can already see what is going on. Visual images are very pervasive, especially for Mexican actors, since they are very passionate when they are executing a scene. Vangie Labalan has admitted that, since their translators are actually radio experts, the words chosen in the first translation are those that are often used on the radio which become redundant if used on television.

Aside from the redundant text and its not being applicable to the visual medium, it has also been observed that there is much focus on synchronisation. With any visual text it is important to make sure that the translated text is synchronised with the actor's lip movements. It distracts the audience and makes them laugh if the actor's mouth is still opening and shutting when they can no longer hear anything, or vice versa.

However, from the samples examined above, it appears that as a result of such a strong focus on exact synchronisation, the clarity of the message has suffered. Synchronisation is important from the point of view of helping the audience understand the message, not in order to convince them that the actors know how to speak Filipino. The audience is aware that the actors are not really Filipino; hence, they do not know how to speak Filipino. So why the need to ensure that there is exact synchronisation?

Luyken et al. (1991), in their book *Overcoming Language Barriers in Television*, recommend that dubbing as a form of translation on television be used with either very young or very old audiences, since it is difficult for them to read written translated texts on the screen.

In order for the dubbed text to be understandable by the very young and very old, there is a need to consider the text of *Marimar* as a printed text, an acoustic text and a visual text. However, the critical analysis presented above reveals that there are problems in the translation of the text as a visual text, an acoustic text and as a printed text.

The issues and problems have been discussed and presented against the background of the critical textual and contextual analysis of *Marimar* conducted above. It is now time to underscore the need for the academic community and the television industry to synchronise the action they take to address these issues and problems in an effort to develop the future dubbing industry.

It has been emphasised that there is a need to synchronise theory and practice. In her book *Translation Studies*, Bassnett-McGuire (1980) states:

> The need for systematic study of translation arises directly from the problems encountered during the actual translation process and it is as essential for those working in the field to bring their practical experience to theoretical discussion, as it is for increased theoretical perceptiveness to be put to use in the translation of texts. To divorce the theory from practice ... would be tragic indeed.

If there is a need to synchronise theory with practice, there is also a need to synchronise the activities of the academic community and the television industry.

That it is disastrous to separate theory from practice means that it is also disastrous to separate translation as a discipline from translation as a technique. Hence, discipline, which comes from academia, and technique, which comes from the television industry, should be synchronised, since translation is both a discipline and a technique.

From the critical analysis conducted, *Marimar* appears engaging but out of synch because the translation of telenovelas is regarded as a technique and not as a discipline by both academia and the television industry.

Since it is both a discipline and a technique, the academic community and the television industry should put equal emphasis on the acquisition of the theoretical background of the discipline and practical skills. Both practitioners and academicians should think about the underlying, deeper issues of linguistic transfer. Since it is both a discipline and a technique, academia and the television industry should be able to explain and justify their decisions regarding translation and to take part in the ongoing, multi-faceted and often contradictory debate as to the true nature of translation. Translation as a technique and a discipline is a source of new theories, ideas, concepts, trends and issues that the academic community and the television industry should be aware of. Indeed, there is a need for the television industry and the academic community to put their acts together to serve the needs of the coming industry of television translation.

Note

1. The very rich Lopez family who also owns businesses in other industries in the country owns ABS CBN. While ABS CBN earned P3 billion in 1995, its closest competitor GMA Channel 7 only earned P800 million. The government under the administration of former president Corazon Aquino on the other hand sequestered RPN Channel 9. The network was identified as one of the ill-gotten wealth of the family of the former President Ferdinand Marcos.

References

Azarcon-de la Cruz, Pennie. 1988. *Images of Women in Philippine Media.* Manila: Asian Social Institute.

Bassnett-McGuire, Susan. 1987. *Translation Studies.* New York: Methuen.

Cruz, Isagani. 1985. "Splitscreen." *Diliman Review.* Manila: University of the Philippines Press.

Hatim, Basil and Ian Mason. 1997. "Politeness in screen translating." In *The Translator as Communicator,* pp. 78–96. London: Routledge.

Luyken, Georg-Michael, et al. 1991. *Overcoming Language Barriers in Television: Dubbing and Subtitling for the European Audience.* Manchester: European Institute for the Media.

Mattelart, Armand. 1985. *Transnationals and the Third World: The Struggle for Culture.* Greenwood Publishing Group.

Medina, B. S. 2001. *Sa Ibang Salita, Sampung Sanaysay sa Sining Salin.* Manila: De La Salle University Press.

———. 2001. *The Philippine Soap, A Story. First Soap Opera Summit for Social Change.* 2001. Manila: De La Salle University Press.

Real, Michael. 1989. "Structuralist analysis 1": Bill Cosby and recoding ethinicity. In *Super Media: A Cultural Studies Approach.* Newbury Park, CA: Sage Publications.

Venuti, Lawrence. 2000. *The Translation Studies Reader.* New York: Routledge. http://www.exposure.pop.mass.media

15

Translating Understanding and Non-understanding through Subtitling: A Case Study of a Finnish Subtitled Translation of *Comme des Rois*

Kari Jokelainen

—ɷ—

The aim of this case study is to illustrate some practical solutions to the problem of transmitting several languages and cultures in one particular film and the extralinguistic messages they present. The presentation is based on a subtitled translation of a film called *Comme des Rois*.

General Guidelines for Finnish Subtitles

The basic rules for a subtitle are that the text should be clear, that it should be a comprehensible, logical unit, and that the time coding should be accurate. The duration of each subtitle must be sufficient for an average reading speed. YLE Public Television sets a minimum duration of 16 characters per second. Inevitably this means compression of the original text. Here, the translator should aim for coherence while choosing the essential information relayed by the speech and preserving the original style.

The translation should therefore present in the target language an equivalence of the style, content and effect of the original text. In the case of a film, for instance, a written translation of oral and often casual speech inevitably means balancing between these two registers. The work requires a good sense of style. Producing colloquial language as such in a written form is quite impossible for a television subtitle. Slang and dialect are specifically oral and the transliteration of these is hard to perceive in the space of a few seconds. The translator therefore has to recognise the registers and the style of the original language and create an illusion of different forms of speech in the target language. The use of slang and dialect as well as vulgarisms in the translation should be considered carefully, because in writing they tend to make a stronger impact than in oral speech.

A Finnish subtitle should be in good Finnish. This means that it should sound natural and contain an appropriate choice of words, and use Finnish idioms and syntax. In short, it must give the impression that it was written in Finnish in the first place. The structures of the foreign language must not be copied in the translation. A central characteristic of a good subtitle is that the viewer does not even notice that he is reading it.

Case Study of *Comme des Rois*

Comme des Rois (A Day as a King) is a French-Polish comedy directed by François Velle in 1997. In Finland it was broadcast in April 2001 by YLE Public Television. The subtitled translation for the Finnish audience was made using a videotape and a dialogue list in French.

The film concerns two Polish brothers, Roman and Edek, who are looking for a better life in France after the collapse of the Berlin Wall. They try hard in Paris, but without any real success. At the point of despair, when they have actually decided to go back home, they suddenly end up at a film festival, where they pretend to be an Icelandic director, who at that moment has not yet arrived, and his interpreter.

One of the main comedic elements of the film is the confusion created by the use of several languages. In different situations the characters speak Polish, French, Hungarian, Icelandic and English. Amusing situations arise when several languages are used in the same scene and the characters in it partly or completely misunderstand what has been said.

The film is full of action and the viewer is kept constantly in suspense. The big question is whether the festival administrators will ever find out that the two brothers are impostors and, if they do, when and how this will happen. The viewer of the original version sees the story through the eyes of the brothers and knows exactly as much as they do, which is more than the other characters at the festival do.

All these factors present a special challenge to the translator. In the same way as the original, his script must keep the foreign viewer in the position of the brothers and, at the same time, as the master of the situation. The viewer has to know what is going on even when the characters do not and he must be able to distinguish between what the characters understand and what they do not. To make this possible, the translator has to be one step, if not two, ahead of the situation and he must analyse carefully the different functions of the languages used in the specific scenes.

As for the layout of the text, the subtitler has very few means for expressing different types of speech. Basically, the subtitle consists of two lines of normal white text, and for special occasions all we can add are italics. For example, colours or different text fonts are not in use for normal subtitling in Finnish television broadcasting. The solution must be found in the combination of normal text and italics. It is anyway quite possible that variation in text types would be too confusing for the spectator.

The use of italics and normal text should be consistent and there should be—if possible—one basic idea to guide the choice. In this particular case our idea is: when the dialogue is comprehensible to all the characters involved in the scene, the text should be normal. When only some of the persons understand, the subtitles are in italics. Thus, the italics tell the viewer immediately that there is something special going on and with a consistent application of our basic rule he will quickly get the meaning of it.

The main language of the film is French. French is therefore subtitled into Finnish in normal text. However, this does not necessarily mean that all the other languages should automatically be set in italics. At the beginning of the film, for example, there is a short sequence where the brothers make plans to leave Poland and this sequence is played in Warsaw. In this environment, Polish is the language naturally understood by everybody, and therefore there is no need to change the normal method of subtitling.

Example 1: (Brothers watching French television and finding out about the collapse of the Berlin Wall.)

ROMAN (Polish): Edek, w lewo, bardziej w lewo! Nie, nie, wróc, wróc! Edek, wracaj w lewo! Wracaj bardziej! Nie no, jeszcze raz, w lewo, w lewo, Edek, w lewo! Nie, nie, nie, wróc! Edek, wracaj powrotem, w lewo! Stop, nie ruszaj sie! No tak, wspaniale, wspaniale! Telewizja francuska! Jezu! Mur! Rozwalaja mur berlinski!

(Subtitles in Finnish)	(English)
Enemmän vasemmalle, Edek!	More to the left, Edek!
Liikaa! Takaisin, Edek!	Too much! Turn back, Edek!
Vielä vasemmalle!	Still to the left!
Takaisin! Vasemmalle!	Back! To the left!
Stop! Pysy siinä.	Stop! Stay there.
Upeaa!	Great!
Tämä on Ranskan televisio.	This is French TV.
Nehän kaataa	But they are
siellä Berliinin muuria!	demolishing the Berlin Wall!

When the brothers come to France, they immediately switch to French, even between themselves. This might sound a bit strange, but the viewer is given an explanation: the elder brother has forbidden the younger the use of Polish in order to improve his French. This, of course, is a clever trick by the director to make it easier to present the film to the French audience and it makes things easier for the subtitler as well.

At the end of the film, the brothers move to California and start speaking English in its natural environment. This again is normal, and basic subtitling will do. Even in a sequence where they meet a French actress whom they know and the dialogue suddenly changes into French, there is no need to emphasise this by changing the text. It all happens naturally and it does not cause problems to the characters of the film. As for the viewers, those who can distinguish between these two languages will understand the change, while others will not. However, there is not much harm done. In this case the choice of language does not have a special message. The main thing is to make the viewer understand the dialogue.

Example 2: (Scene at Los Angeles Airport)

ELIZABETH (French): Alors, vous êtes là pour faire des repérages pour un nouveau film?

EDEK (French): Oui, je prépare un road movie. Sur comment c'est' difficile pour un travailleur immigré dans l'Amérique.
ROMAN (French): Qu'est-ce qu'il raconte?
ELIZABETH (English): He's preparing a road movie. You know this is Mr. Nielsen I've mentioned to you so much before.
PRODUCER (English): No joke, it's great to meet you.
EDEK (English): Great to meet me.
PRODUCER (English): Elizabeth is your biggest fan. You know, we've got to get to that meeting with Spielberg at Dreamworks.
ELIZABETH (French): Cette fois-ci je ne vais pas vous laisser partir. Vous allez venir avec nous et on ne va plus se quitter.

(Subtitles in Finnish)	(English)
Valmisteletteko uutta elokuvaa?—Joo...	Are you preparing a new film?—Yes.
Siitä tulee *road movie* siirtolaisten vaikeuksista.	It will be a *road movie* on the problems of immigrants.
Mitä se höpisee?	What is he talking about?
Valmisteilla on *road movie.*	He's preparing a road movie.
Tässä on herra Nielsen, josta olen puhunut paljon.	This is Mr. Nielsen I've talked so much about.
Mukava nähdä teidät.	Nice to meet you.
—Mukava nähdä minut.	—Nice to meet me.
Elizabeth on suuri ihailijanne.	Elizabeth is your great fan.
Pitää lähteä Dreamworksiin tapaamaan Spielbergiä.	We've got to leave for Dreamworks to meet Spielberg.
Tällä kertaa en päästä teitä käsistäni. Enää emme erkane.	This time I won't let you go. We won't part anymore.

The situation is different when two languages are used in the same sequence to create an amusing situation. Soon after their arrival at the film festival, Roman and Edek end up on the stage at a press conference. Edek is forced to pretend to be the Icelandic director, Olaf Nielsen, and Roman acts as his interpreter, Jürgen Jürgenson. Both brothers, of course, understand the questions asked by the journalists in French, but in order to play his role well, the "interpreter" has to say something to the "director" in "Icelandic"— which is actually Polish. In the dialogue between themselves, they try to work out in Polish how they should answer. The journalists do not understand their words and cannot distinguish between Icelandic and Polish. In this case, the content of the discussion between the brothers is comprehensible to the viewer, but not to the journalists. Changing the text into italics can convey this message: it hints to the viewer that there is something special going on and that those two characters have changed the language in order to plot something together.

In the original version, a French viewer would readily notice the change into Polish. As the information given by the Polish dialogue is important, this sequence most probably would be subtitled in French. On the other hand, a Finn watching the film would not necessarily make a distinction between French and Polish on the basis of a few sentences. Thus it is essential to help him to understand the change by using a different layout.

Example 3: (The press conference at the festival)

M. Fouilles, L'Ecran Intérieur
JOURNALIST (French): Ma question à M. Nielsen part d'un sentiment ambivalent que j'ai eu en voyant son très beau film. C'est cette quête de liberté vécue par contraint et pas par l'absence de contraint. Ce sont bien-sûr les grands espaces, la banquise, qui sont une prison extérieure face à une liberté qui, elle, est intérieure. Le héros est libre dans sa prison et il est emprisonné dans sa liberté, si vous permettez ce paradoxe barthésien. Ma question est, le couple prison-liberté, est-il la motivation souterraine de votre film?
EDEK (Polish): Mysle, ze trzeba ci bylo jedenastego roku na uniwersytecie, co?
ROMAN (Polish): Poczekaj, ja ci przetlumacze, kurka wodna.
EDEK (Polish) Co ty przetlumaczysz?
ROMAN(Polish): Poczekaj, zaraz zobaczysz.
(French) Ça, c'est une question qu'on nous pose souvent et je peux répondre sans demander à M Nielsen. La réponse à la question est: "Non."

(Subtitles in Finnish)	(English)
Kysymykseni kumpuaa	My question arises from
siitä ristiriitaisesta tunteesta—	the ambivalent feeling—
jonka koin	I experienced

nähdessäni elokuvanne.
Kyseessä on vapauden etsintä—
jota ohjaa pakonomaisuus
eikä suinkaan sen puute.

Tietenkin
jääkentän avara vapaus—
on eräänlainen ulkoinen vankila
päähenkilön sisäiselle vapaudelle.
Hän on vapaa vankilassaan
ja samalla vapautensa vanki—
käyttääkseni
barthesilaista paradoksia.
Onko tämä vankilan ja vapauden
teema elokuvanne perusajatus?

Vielä yksi vuosi yliopistossa
ei olisi ollut nyt haitaksi.

Saamari, odota että käännän.
Mitähän sinä mahdat sanoa?
Odota,
kohta näet.
Tätä kysytään usein ja voin
vastata kysymättä ohjaajalta.

Vastaus on: "Ei".

watching your film.
It is about a quest for freedom—
lived through constraint
and not through the absence of
it.
Of course
the vast liberty of the ice floe—
is a kind of outer prison
to the inner freedom of the hero.
He is free in his prison
and imprisoned by his freedom
—to use
the Barthesian paradox.
Is the theme of prison and liberty
the hidden motivation of your
film?
One more year at the university
wouldn't be a bad idea now.

Damn it, let me translate.
I wonder what you're gonna say?
Wait
and see.
We're asked this often and I can
answer without asking the
director.
The answer is: "No."

In the above example, there is another kind of non-understanding. The journalist, an intellectual, asks a long question, reasoning in a very abstract way and using erudite words which are completely incomprehensible to the brothers. So the incomprehensibility in this case is not the result of a foreign language being used, as the monologue is in French. So there is no reason to use italics. Instead, the translator must create the difficulty of understanding by means of a highly complicated text, which will leave the viewer perplexed.

There is a similar situation when a group of Polish film purchasers suddenly arrives. At this point Roman pretends to be an

Icelandic film agent and negotiates with the Polish buyers. The discussions are conducted through an interpreter, because obviously Roman cannot admit that he, too, is actually Polish. However, the Polish interpreter is highly incompetent and does not understand French properly. What Roman says in French is subtitled in the Finnish translation in normal text. The interpreter's translation is written in italics. This contrast tells the viewer that Roman's message does not reach his partner. Knowing perfectly well how poorly his message has been interpreted, Roman finally gets tired of it and—to everyone's amazement—starts to speak fluent Polish. Now his speech has to be in italics as well in order to make the viewer understand that he has changed his language.

Now the whole dialogue is conducted in Polish and everyone understands what is being said. Still the subtitles are in italics. Outwardly, this might seem to contradict our basic rule. But having started the scene with French as normal and Polish as italics, the subtitler has no choice but to carry on consistently that way. A change in this system would confuse the viewer.

Example 4: (Negotiating with the Polish)

ROMAN (French):
Je répète que je peux faire moins cher si vous me payez 10% en cash demain.
INTERPRETER (Polish):
Powtarzam: Od jutra bedzie 10 procent drozej.
ROMAN (French):
Mais non! Je dis que je peux faire 50% moins cher, si vous me payez en cash demain et pas après un mois!
INTERPRETER (Polish):
Pan Jurgensson mówi, ze to bedzie o 50 procent drozej, jezeli to 10 procent zaplacimy za miesiac.
PURCHASER (Polish):
Jest Pan tego pewien?
INTERPRETER (Polish):
Tak, tak powiedzial. Zaraz ... spytam sie.
ROMAN (Polish)
Alez nie, ja tak nie powiedzialem. Powiedzialem, ze jezeli zaplacicie mi 10 procent gotówka, to bedziecie mieli 50 procent taniej film, i to

powiedizalem! Tak, ja mowie troszeczke po polsku, bo moja babcia byla troszeczke polka. Ale Panowie, obudzcie sie! Chcecie robic biznes, to trzeba reagowac szybko! Komunizm sie skonczyl! Czas to pieniadz, a ja, prosze pania, nie mam czasu.

(Subtitles in Finnish)	(English)
Annan alennusta, jos maksatte 10% huomenna käteisenä.	I'll give you a discount, if you pay me tomorrow 10% in cash.
Huomenna	Tomorrow
hinta nousee 10%.	the price will go up 10%.
Eipäs!	No!
Lasken hintaa 50%, jos maksatte käteisellä huomenna.	I'll reduce the price by 50%, if you pay me in cash tomorrow.
Ei ylihuomenna eikä ensi kuussa!	Not the day after or next month!
Jürgensson sanoo,	Jürgensson says,
että hinta nousee 50%—	that the price will go up 50%—
jos maksamme	if we pay
10% ensi kuussa.	10% next month.
Oletteko varma?	Are you sure?
—Niin hän sanoi.	—That's what he said.
Kysäisen vielä kerran.	I'll ask once again.
Ei se niin mene!	It wasn't that way!
Sanoin että jos maksatte huomenna 10% käteisenä—	I told you, if you pay tomorrow 10% in cash—
saatte elokuvan	you'll get the film
50% halvemmalla!	50 % cheaper.
Puhun pikkuisen puolaa, kun isoäiti oli pikkuisen puolalainen.	I speak a bit of Polish as my granny was a bit Polish.
Herätys, herrat!	Wake up, gentlemen!
Nyt tehdään bisnestä!	We're doing business now!
Kommunismi kaatui jo.	Communism has collapsed!
Aika on rahaa	Time is money
eikä minulla ei ole sitä.	and I don't have it.

Apart from italics and normal text, the subtitler has another Shakespearean choice to make: "to translate or not to translate?" And if he does not translate, should he insert a subtitle in the original language or leave the spoken lines without a subtitle?

Here is an example. Trying to make a living in Paris, Roman decides to give private lessons. There is a French lady who would like to learn Hungarian. Roman does not know a word of Hungarian but decides to take the job and the risk because he thinks that—Polish or Hungarian—the lady in question will not be able to tell the difference anyway. The lady wants to know how to say in Hungarian, "Give me a kiss." Roman teaches her to say it in Polish—"Daj mi buzi"—pretending that it is Hungarian. During the lesson, they repeat the Polish phrase several times, which helps the viewer to memorise it. When the Polish phrase is used again in the next scene, the viewer recognises it easily. The subtitler should have it written down in Polish: translation is not needed because we already know what it means.

Shortly afterwards, a real Hungarian, the lady's boyfriend, comes in. The lady now repeats the phrase both she and the viewer have learned but which is incomprehensible to the Hungarian. Instead, he understands that the teacher is a fake and decides to test his skills. He says a short line in Hungarian, which Roman of course does not understand. All this makes for an embarrassing and amusing situation. To emphasise the embarrassment and non-understanding of Roman, the translator can insert a subtitle in the original Hungarian. Then the viewer is in the same situation that Roman is experiencing and understands better how he feels. In this particular case, the "Hungarian" line the film-maker has chosen is just Hungarian-sounding nonsense. However, there is no point in presenting a false language in written form. I feel strongly that all it would show is a lack of respect. So the subtitle is modified to the nearest possible real Hungarian phrase. A normal Finnish viewer will not notice the difference.

Example 5: (Teaching Hungarian and the arrival of the real Hungarian)

LADY (French): Vous savez, c'est très important pour moi. Il faut que je puisse parler hongrois le plus vite possible.
ROMAN (French): Croyez à László Eszterházy! Dans trois jours vous parlerez hongrois comme moi.
LADY (French): Voilà, je me suis permise de noter les principales expressions que je tiens absolument à connaître. Bien-sûr, "Je

t'aime." "Embrasse-moi tendrement." "Prends-moi dans tes bras."
"Comme tu es fort."
LADY (French): Vous pensez qu'il y a un problème?
ROMAN (French): Aucun problème! Et comme on dit a Budapest:
"Zaden problem!"
LADY: Zaden problem.

—

ROMAN and the LADY: Dai mi buzi.
LADY (French): Heureusement que vous avez pu rester toute la
journée. Je ne savais pas qu'il y avait tant de nuances de
prononciation en hongrois.
ROMAN (French): Vous savez, madame, Hongrie, c'est un pays de
nuances et de romantisme. Et de l'amour.
LADY (French): L'amour ... Je ne devrais pas vous le dire, mais si
j'ai apporté du Tokay, c'est que j'ai une surprise pour vous ce
soir.
ROMAN (French): Le Tokay ... Nous les Hongrois, on adore le
Tokay. Et les surprises aussi.
LADY (French): Ah, d'ailleurs, le voila. Un compatriote à vous
László. Péter, mon fiancé qui arrive aujourd'hui de Budapest.
ROMAN (French): Oh, merde!
LADY (French): Péter est venu à Paris pour le championnat du
hockey sur glace.
PETER (Hungarian): Jó napot, László.
ROMAN (French): Peter, on est a Paris, on doit parler français,
eh!
LADY (French): Oui, et c'est moi qui vais parler hongrois. Daj mi
buzi. Peut-être que je n'ai pas assez arrondi les lèvres comme vous
m'aviez dit?
ROMAN (French): Certainement, certainement ... Oh, mon dieu,
j'ai oublié! J'ai un rendez-vous très important. Au revoir.
PETER (Hungarian): He, László, nem kersz egy kis tokaji bórt?

(Subtitles in Finnish)	(English)
Tämä on hyvin tärkeää.	It's very important.
Minun	I have to learn
on opittava nopeasti unkaria.	Hungarian quickly.
László Esterházy! Kolmessa	László Esterházy! In three
päivässä puhutte jo kuin minä!	days you'll speak like me.

Kirjasin tähän ilmauksia, jotka	I wrote down expressions
haluan ehdottomasti oppia.	I want to learn absolutely.
"Rakastan sinua",	"I love you",
"suutele minua hellästi"—	"kiss me tenderly"—
"sulje minut syliisi",	"take me in your arms",
"sinä olet ihanan vahva" …	"you are so strong …"
Onko asiassa ongelma? -Ei!	Is there a problem? - No!
Kuten meillä Budapestissä	Like we say in Budapest:
sanotaan: *Zaden problem!*	*Zaden problem!*
Daj mi buzi.	Daj mi buzi.
Onneksi teillä	I'm happy
oli koko päivä aikaa.	you had the whole day.
Unkarin ääntämys	The pronunciation of
	Hungarian
on täynnä vivahteita.	is full of nuances.
Unkari on vivahteiden,	Hungary is a country of
romantiikan ja rakkauden maa.	nuances, romance and love.
Toin teille tokaijia,	I brought you some Tokai
koska minulla on teille yllätys.	because I have a surprise for you.
Me unkarilaiset	We Hungarians
rakastamme tokaijia ja yllätyksiä.	love Tokai and surprises.
Sieltä se yllätys tuleekin.	There he is.
Maanmiehenne. Peter	Your compatriot. Peter has
tuli tänään Budapestistä.	come today from Budapest.
Peter tuli Pariisiin	Peter has come to Paris
jääkiekon EM-kisoihin.	for the hockey championship.
Jó napot, László!	Jó napot, László!
Puhutaan ranskaa,	Why not speak French
kun Pariisissa ollaan!	since we're in Paris!
Aivan! Ja minä puhun unkaria.	Yes! And I'll speak Hungarian.
Daj mi buzi.	Daj mi buzi.
Ehkä	Perhaps I didn't
en pyöristänyt tarpeeksi huulia.	round my lips enough.
Aivan niin!	That's it!
Muistuikin mieleen,	Now I remember
että minulla oli menoa.	I have another meeting.
Näkemiin.	Goodbye.
He, László, nem kersz	He, László, nem kersz
egy kis tokaji bórt?	egy kis tokaji bórt?

This is another example of a situation where the translation of a line is unnecessary. At the end of the film, the real Icelandic director arrives completely unaware of the hassle and the total chaos. He is amazed and all he can do is repeat his name in Icelandic: "Ég heiti Ólafur Nielsson" (My name is Ólafur Nielsson). Subtitling his line in Icelandic emphasises the absurdity of the situation and the amazement of the real Icelandic director. As a rule Finns do not understand Icelandic, but the message of this line is clear. It is short and it contains a familiar name in its Icelandic form (Ólafur) and therefore most Finnish viewers will easily be able to guess what he says and in which language. Another helping factor is that the corresponding expression in Swedish, the second official language of Finland, looks a bit similar.

Example 6: (The real Olaf Nielsen arrives)
ROMAN (French): Olaf Nielsen, champagne!
DIRECTOR (Icelandic): Já?
EDEK: Olaf?
DIRECTOR (Icelandic): Ég heiti Ólafur Nielsson.
EDEK (French): Oui! Enfin!

(Subtitles in Finnish)	(English)
Olaf Nielsen! Samppanjaa!	Olaf Nielsen! Champagne!
Já?	Já?
Olaf?	Olaf?
Ég heiti Ólafur Níelsson.	Ég heiti Ólafur Nielsson.

In this translation we have Finnish subtitles in normal text and in italics. Additionally, we have subtitles in Polish, Hungarian and Icelandic. The translator should ask himself if this might not be too confusing for the viewer. Will the viewer really be able to recognise the three foreign languages and understand the message they carry? Fortunately, the subtitler is not alone. He has the setting, the sound, the gestures and the mimicry of the actors for support. On the other hand, translating these subtitles would actually destroy the comedy of the situation, as the spectator will regard them as normal speech.

As I have already mentioned, the subtitler has limited possibilities available to enable him or her to express different kinds of speech by means of a subtitle layout. Thus the choice of italics needs to be considered carefully in order not to give it too many meanings in the same film. It is essential that the translator analyses the different functions of different kinds of speech as well as their different situations, creates a basic rule for the use of italics and sticks to it consistently.

References

Comme des Rois. 1997. A 95-min French-Polish comedy directed by François Velle, written by François Velle and Mariusz Pujszo and produced by Nicolas Velle and Ludi Boeken, Koba Films, Raphael Films, TF1 Films Productions and W Produtions. Cast: Stephane Freiss, Maruschka Detmers, Mariusz Pujszo, Thierry Lhermitte, Louis Velle, Jacques Sereys, Christian Bujeau, Pauline Macia.

Comme des Rois, French dialogue list.

Jokelainen, Kari. 2000. *Herrojen Elämää.* A Finnish subtitled translation of *Comme des Rois,* for YLE Import, Finland.

Ohjeita Tv-kääntäjille (Guidelines for Finnish Subtitling). 2000. YLE Import Department, May 30, 2000.

16

Translating Subtitles for the Hong Kong Audience: Limitations and Difficulties

Shu Kei

—ɯ—

Before embarking on a discussion of my proposed topic, I think that I should clarify my position. I must confess that I am neither a professional translator nor a professional subtitler, despite the fact that I have, indeed, translated subtitles for over thirty feature films, either from English to Chinese or vice versa. The first film I translated was a little known 1973 Western called *The Deadly Trackers* (the Chinese title was 亡命大追殺), directed by Barry Shear and written by Samuel Fuller, which was offered to me as a part-time job by a publicity person at Warner Brothers—one of my contacts from whom I obtained the professional materials I needed to write a regular column on upcoming foreign films in a monthly film magazine. I was still in high school at the time, doing all kinds of work to earn my tuition fees, and the job proved most welcome. His comment on my work afterwards was that my translation was "too literary" and contained too many Chinese particles, such as *de* 的 and *le* 了; I was never offered a subtitling job by him again.

I began to venture regularly into subtitle translation only after I had become a distributor of specialised or art-house films in the mid-1980s, mainly for the films made by my own company. The reason was obvious: it would save me a lot of time *and* money to do the job myself. I have to admit that I was becoming more and more dissatisfied with the subtitles of most of the foreign films at the time—there were very few non-English speaking films, and most of them were dubbed, often badly. Also, I was unable to find any "professional" subtitler for the job: almost all practising subtitlers were staff members of the distribution companies who were more than happy to earn some extra income. Some of them took up the job after their retirement, *and* became "professional." Thus, this paper only presents a short summary of some of my personal experiences as an amateur subtitler.

Subtitling is a particular mode of translation. A close look at the process of subtitling may help to reveal the limitations and difficulties faced by the subtitler which, according to Nornes conspire to form "an array of challenges that seem to lead down the path of corruption." (Nornes 1999: 20) What I would like to do is to examine these limitations in the context of the local film industry and reveal the helplessness, as well as the haplessness, of being a subtitler.

The process goes like this. First and foremost, to enable and facilitate translation, as well as the pressing of the text onto the film, the dialogues to be subtitled are segmented into individual lines; the breaks are marked according to the speed (i.e., the temporal length) of their delivery by the actor. Nornes notes that it is "the translator (who) determines the length of each unit of translation down to the frame." (ibid.: 20) I am not quite sure how subtitles are done in Japan, or to what extent the subtitler can exercise his power in the process (Nornes himself has been engaged in subtitling in Japan since 1991 and according to his description, subtitlers—at least the most famous ones—do acquire a certain kind of prestige status.) However, as far as my experience goes and according to my knowledge of local subtitling conditions, the subtitler has very limited power. Instead, he will be provided with a dialogue script or subtitle list, in which the dialogue has already been broken up into individual lines and marked with serial numbers in most cases. (In Hollywood, there are companies that specialise in doing this.) This serves as the source text for the translation.

In a typical *combined* script which includes continuity, dialogue and spotting list, there is a full transcription of the released version of the film on the far left, including a detailed description of its titles, scenes, shots, spoken dialogues, as well as the marks of the footages of each scene (the unit of measurement here is a foot but the practice nowadays is to use electronic time code). Next is the "title no.": i.e., the serial number of each line to be translated, inclusive not only of the dialogues, but also of other titles/intertitles or important texts which appear in the film and which are crucial to the plot, such as a written note, the headline of a newspaper and so on. Each subtitle line is marked with the start and the end of the footage, which we call "spotting." From the length of the footage provided, an experienced subtitler can determine the length of his translation: i.e., the number of words or characters to be allowed on each line. (Nonetheless, a restriction on the length of the translation has often been imposed by the subtitling method itself. We will discuss this point later.) The last column of the combined script shows the actual lines to be subtitled. Dialogues will be slightly trimmed for their occasional redundancy, and so will some meaningless utterances. Some items of information are provided to help the subtitler better understand the lines, such as who the speaker and addressee of the dialogue are, the mode of delivery, as well as detailed explanations of slang, idioms, the underlying meanings of words and the syntax.

But there are cases in which the script is just a plain subtitle list and nothing more. In this case, the subtitler is undoubtedly handicapped in many ways unimaginable to the audience.

In the old days, veteran subtitlers would start translating immediately upon receipt of the combined script, or just the subtitle list. No demand would be made to preview the film. In this case, the translation of subtitles would pretty much be reduced to a basic word-for-word pattern; the mode of subtitling, in areas such as the relationship between the image, the sound and the text ("the audiovisual punctuation"), the timing of each line, the mood of the utterances, the social background of the characters that dictates the subtitler's choice and usage of words, the implications and references of the text, would be given minimal or no consideration by the subtitler. Nowadays, more responsible subtitlers always request a preview of the film before they start the translation. However, my own experience is that a single viewing is far from adequate to grasp every turn of phrase and comprehend a film fully. An obligatory tool of translation, in my opinion, is a sample videotape of the film, to which the subtitler can always refer in case of doubt and uncertainty. Unfortunately, no Hollywood studio, as far as I know, is willing to hand over a videotape, not so much for fear of piracy as from pure arrogance. Local distribution companies more or less follow a similar policy. As we shall see, such bureaucracy can only lead to all kinds of unnecessary and embarrassing mistakes that make translators cringe and the audience furious.

As pointed out by Nornes, there are three methods of putting subtitles on a film (ibid.: 20). The oldest method is to make a leaden block from each typeset line, which is then burnt into the tissue of the celluloid. The temporal length of each line, i.e., the number of frames each line will take up, is guided by the spotting list. The technician will make a mark on the celluloid with chalk, which will be wiped off later. Subtitles done using this method have a shiny, silvery look on the screen. The disadvantage is that the words will become illegible if they are projected against a whitish background in the image. Also, the font size is fixed and unusually large. In the case of dual-language subtitles, the lines will occupy almost one-fifth of the frame and create a lot of visual nuisance. (It is customary in Hong Kong for non-English speaking films to carry subtitles in *both* Chinese *and* English.)

With the advent of modern technology, over the last two decades computer-controlled laser has been introduced, to incise subtitles onto the celluloid. (Hong Kong, however, did not have laser subtitling until about 1995.) In terms of their appearance and the accuracy of their timing, laser-made subtitles are definitely a huge improvement over the burning method. The problem of illegibility of subtitles projected against a whitish background is also solved by the ability to cast dark shading around the fonts by laser. However, both methods limit the space to only 14 Chinese characters, inclusive of punctuation marks. Double lines in Chinese are not feasible in the burning method and are severely discouraged in laser subtitling, although for reasons I have hitherto found inexplicable, since double lines for English subtitles are acceptable and manageable with both methods. There is also a substantial difference in price: both methods are charged at HK$7.50 (slightly less than US$1.00) per line for single-language subtitles, but the burning method is charged at only half-price for successive prints (mainly because the blocks can be reused), whereas there is no reduction in price for successive prints with laser subtitling. For dual-language subtitles, the burning method is charged at HK$8.50 (US$1.10) per line, whereas laser subtitling costs HK$13.50 (US$1.70) per line, a full 59 per cent more than the former.

The third method of subtitling is to photograph the subtitles optically, develop them as negatives, splice them together in order, then have them sandwiched and printed with the image and sound as a third film strip. This is the most expensive method because it involves at least a shooting session, a laboratory and an editor. Locally it costs around HK$30,000 (US$3,850) to make a set of subtitles this way. This method is employed only when there is a demand for a massive number of subtitled prints: for instance, when the film is to be opened at many cinemas at the same time. Then the average cost of subtitling for each print becomes much lower than when using the former two methods. With Hong Kong films it is most usual to find the optical method used to print dual-language-subtitled copies to be distributed both locally and in the Greater China region. Recently, some Hollywood studios have started to employ this method to produce subtitled prints for the same regions, using a "standardised" set of translations (Mandarin). Undoubtedly, the motive behind this policy is economic; however, most probably unbeknown to the studios, it has also created a subtle cultural problem, which we will discuss later.

One big advantage of the optical method is the high degree of clarity it gives to the subtitles. There is also plenty of space available for the text. Translators no longer have to condense their translations drastically. For example, up until recently, translators have had to use such northern Chinese dialect words as *sha* 啥 (what), to replace the more colloquial *shenme* 什麼, and *beng* 甭 (need not), as a condensation of *buyong* 不用. Indeed, the restriction of 14 characters within a single line has more often than not forced the translator to perform, in Nornes' words, acts of "corruption" on the subtitles, such as the reduction of meaning and the exclusion of texture and materiality.

Compared with their Japanese counterparts, the Chinese subtitlers are in a much more unfavourable situation. Nornes points out several advantages for subtitling inherent in the Japanese language: "... for one thing, Japanese does not waste precious space on gaps between words, and can even break a line in mid-word." (ibid.: 20) *Kanji* (Chinese characters) carries multiple meanings in a syllable; "neologisms and abbreviations are easily accomplished through the creative combination of *kanji*. Even better, Japanese often leaves out the subject, direct object or other parts of speech, saving much needed space.... Finally, in addition to italics, Japanese has the enviable ability to be inscribed both horizontally and vertically...." (ibid.: 21). It is this last characteristic that I would like to discuss here as a possible model for future Chinese subtitling. Chinese texts used to be written vertically and read from right to left. It was not until the turn of the last century that written Chinese took on a horizontal format after the manner of Western languages. In fact, many Chinese books nowadays are still printed in the vertical manner.

Personally, I always find it visually more pleasing to the eye to have Chinese texts placed vertically on the sides of a frame, rather than compressed horizontally at the bottom, especially if the film is photographed in the widescreen or vista-size format, because horizontal subtitles tend to make the composition of the image look crowded, busy and give a heavy and weighty feeling, owing to the fact that Chinese characters are made up of strokes rather than curves. By contrast, vertical subtitles would always find space at the side, and have the further advantage of flexibility: being able to jump between the two sides to match the position of the speaker and to balance themselves with the composition of the image. Imagine a big close-up of an actor: horizontal subtitles would almost inevitably disrupt the composition of the shot with the text superimposed on the mouth, if not the nostrils, whereas vertical subtitles would at most just cover the ear.

However, the biggest challenge a subtitler has to face still involves the craft and skill of translation. Citing Goethe, Nornes emphasises the fact that an ideal subtitler "identifies strongly with the source text and the culture in which it was produced, so much so that he cedes the particular powers of his own culture to accomplish a translation that invites the reader/spectator to a novel and rich experience of the foreign." (ibid.: 29) Nornes' suggestion is, for me, the best solution to a controversy among many subtitlers in Hong Kong: i.e., whether it is right or "legitimate" to employ colloquial Cantonese, the local dialect, in film subtitling, and if so, to what extent it should be used. As we all know, Hong Kong is a city dominated by a Cantonese-speaking population. Despite the efforts of the SAR government to promote putonghua as an official language, colloquial Cantonese continues to dominate not only in our everyday life, but has also permeated practically every aspect of our culture, whether high or low, including literature, music, journalism and all kinds of writings. It is perhaps important to point out that the Cantonese used by the people of Hong Kong in general is actually far removed from the standard Cantonese, or *Guangfuhua* (廣府話), spoken in Guangdong, a province in South China.

Over the years, Hong Kong Cantonese has developed into a self-contained language mixed with many foreign languages and other Chinese dialects, including English, Japanese, Thai, Vietnamese, Chaozhou, Hakka, putonghua, etc. Slang and idioms are being created almost every day. One example is the term "pork chop" (豬扒 or 豬排), an offensive or derogatory word recently coined to describe young females who are either overweight or downright unattractive. Hong Kong Cantonese is ruthless in seizing whatever resources it can lay its hands on to enrich itself and to express the temperament of the times. This has made it one of the most animated and lively languages in the world. As a result, it is very natural to employ it in screen translation, the bulk of which contains everyday conversation and colloquial expressions that cry out for an equivalent in the target language cultures to match them. Only by exploiting the full power of the language can we "intensify the interaction between the reader and the foreign," which, for Nornes, is one of the most important functions of subtitle translation, and hence, one of the greatest pleasures of cinema-going (ibid.: 29).

As you can see, there are still limitations to this relatively free style of translation. Audiences from other regions of China, especially those in Taiwan and mainland China, most of whom speak only putonghua (or Mandarin), will probably find the subtitles largely incomprehensible owing to the amount of colloquial Cantonese used. But this might be a dilemma we will have to live with. I mentioned earlier that some Hollywood studios are using a standardised set of subtitles in putonghua to make optical prints for circulation in the Greater China Region (Taiwan, mainland China, Hong Kong, Singapore, and Malaysia). Reading the subtitles of these prints, I cannot help but feel strangely detached and uninvolved. They may not be inappropriately translated, but they certainly are irrelevant to this viewer, failing miserably in "achieving perfect identity with the original" (ibid.: 29). Like Nornes, what I am advocating is that the subtitler should take into consideration the interaction between cultures.

Another limitation is actually concerned with Cantonese itself, and that is, a lot of Cantonese sounds still have yet to find their written equivalents. This is unfortunate, but most probably the problem will not be solved as long as Cantonese remains a dialect and its syntax is left unexplored and unstudied.

The third and last limitation has to do with censorship. Local film censors have adopted a three-tier system since the mid-eighties, in which films are divided into three categories[1]. Individuals below 18 years of age are not permitted to watch Category III films. However, there are no clearly written rules according to which the censors determine a film's category. From the beginning, the censors adopted a double standard in categorising local and foreign (Western/non-Asian) films. The most blatant examples concern the use of obscenities, foul language and the four-letter word in films. Local films containing any of these, whether in the dialogue or in the subtitles, will certainly be given a Category III classification, whereas foreign films in similar situations will almost always be classified as Category II. For this reason, obscenities are always watered down; the subtitler is forced to adopt a much tamer mode of expression in the form of euphemism or homophone. This is a pity, because Cantonese is perhaps the language that contains the largest number of obscenities, which are used with a high degree of imagination and flexibility.

Note

1. The Hong Kong Television and Entertainment Licensing Authority (TELA) issued a three-level rating system in 1986, which was revised to include three levels of main ratings, and two subratings for one level: Category I are films which are "Suitable For All Ages"; Category IIA are those classified as "Not Suitable For Children" and parental guidance is required. Category IIB are those films "Not Suitable for Young Persons and Children." Category III films are for "Persons Aged 18 and Above Only."

Reference

Nornes, Abé Mark. "For an Abusive Subtitling." *Film Quarterly*. 52.3 (1999): 17–34.

17

Surtitling for *Xiqu* (Chinese Opera) in the Theatre

Jessica W. Y. Yeung

—ɯ—

Introduction

This paper examines the functions of surtitles for *xiqu* performance. For a theatrical form as culturally specific as *xiqu*, the provision of surtitles in foreign languages for the international theatre circus carries much significance. It not only enhances the aesthetic and theatrical experience for the audience, it also affects the representation of Chinese culture by this theatrical form. Good surtitles in foreign languages[1] are an effective means to promote a cross-cultural understanding of the aesthetics of *xiqu*, and also of the values embodied and the stories enacted in this form. In order to present an overview of *xiqu* surtitling, this paper is structured in three parts: first, reporting on the situation of surtitling for *xiqu* performance; second, articulating the considerations in the process of surtitling for *xiqu;* and third, examining the role of *xiqu* surtitles in the overall theatrical experience.

The Apparatuses

The first surtitles for *xiqu* were done for a national rather than an international audience. The variety of regional *xiqu* is huge. Scholars have diverse views as to the exact number of regional forms, but it is generally accepted to be within the range of 200 to 450. These regional variations share the same basic theatrical and dramatic principles. One reason for this is that they have originated from religious and folk practices that were geographically and anthropologically very close to each other. Moreover, centuries of mutual influence and exchange have brought these variations formally very close to one another, to the extent that an audience of one regional form can easily identify aesthetically with another regional form. The only barrier to their viewing lies in the local dialect each regional variation is performed in. It is therefore very common for theatre venues and presenters to provide Chinese surtitles when they accommodate touring companies performing in regional forms other than the local ones.

Before the era of computerised surtitling systems, the OHT type of projection system was often used for *xiqu* performance. The libretto was handwritten, vertically, according to the traditional system of Chinese writing and printing, on transparencies to be projected on one side (or both sides, if two projectors were available) of the proscenium arch on the front of the stage. Therefore (as opposed to surtitles), "side-titles" would be a better description. In order to boost the aesthetic quality of the side-titles, the text was usually written in a beautiful hand, sometimes in stroke style and with felt pens, imitating the effect of traditional calligraphy in ink. Since the text was written vertically, a special kind of transparency was used. Such transparencies were merely a few inches wide but they extended to dozens of metres in length. They were rolled up compactly like film reels. A spinning mechanism was built into the projector so that the text on the transparency would unwind in exactly the same way a film reel unwinds in the film compartment of a camera. Such an apparatus catered specifically to the needs of *xiqu* and was therefore not usually included in the standard technical provision of performing venues. Most touring companies possessed their own projection equipment and took it along with them on tour. Indeed, it was one of the standard items in their touring paraphernalia.

It is also increasingly common to provide surtitles or side-titles for *xiqu* performances even for the local audiences of regional forms. As the range of entertainment and cultural activities expands, the number of *xiqu* connoisseurs is diminishing. Most audiences attending performances are not familiar with the librettos and often find the texts of traditional pieces written in classical Chinese difficult to follow. Many newly written pieces also adopt a classical style of language in accordance with an overall archaic convention of the form. It is therefore very common for performing companies and presenters who want to attract new audiences to provide surtitles in Chinese to help audiences acculturate into the form. As the technology for digital display has made significant advances since the final decades of the 20th century, surtitling has become easy and affordable.

In the 1990s, a company in the Chinese city of Taiyuan in Shanxi Province produced a computerised display apparatus that dramatically improved surtitling for *xiqu*. The system consists of a digital display box connected to a computer. The display box is about 8 x 3 feet square, and can be placed vertically to display two rows of eight Chinese characters at any one time, or horizontally to display two rows of twelve English letters of the alphabet. Although many performance venues have digital display boards, most of them are placed above the proscenium arch at the front of the stage. Texts are displayed horizontally. Although a horizontal arrangement of Chinese characters is not uncommon in modern printing, this arrangement is considered undesirable for *xiqu* performances by many people since it does not accord with the overall archaic style of the form. With the new apparatus, a display box can be placed vertically on one or both sides of the stage. Such a display conforms much more closely to the reading habits of readers of Chinese. Its position at the side of the stage also affords better sightlines for the audience than display boards on top of the stage do.

This new apparatus also made full bilingual surtitles in Chinese and English for *xiqu* much easier. The problem before was not so much to do with the availability of translation but with finding suitable operators for the English surtitles. *Xiqu* training has been highly exclusive and limited to those performers committed to the profession at an early age. It is very difficult to find people who are sufficiently familiar with the theatrical form and who also have the required command of and sensitivity to English. Like subtitling for films and surtitling for other theatrical forms, the effectiveness of *xiqu* surtitles depends heavily on the timing of the display. Knowledge of the theatrical form, of that particular piece of *xiqu*, and of the English language are all necessary for the operator, so that s/he can anticipate the timing of the lines to come. Such knowledge is particularly important for *xiqu* because it is a rather common practice for *xiqu* artists to exercise some degree of flexibility in their performance, which could result in considerable deviation in the lines being sung from the script already input as surtitles. Operators who are not very knowledgeable about *xiqu* would find it very difficult to cope. But with the new apparatus produced in Shanxi Province, this problem was easily solved. One needed only to connect a second display box to the system, placing it horizontally, to display English. The computer program is set to facilitate the simultaneous display of the corresponding Chinese and English lines. All that it is necessary to do is to type two lines of Chinese into the computer, followed by their equivalents in English, also in two lines. The two versions will each be displayed on one display box, one placed vertically for the Chinese and one horizontally for the English. Since the lines in both languages are synchronised, the operator does not need to worry about the English. It is customary for a crew member from the performing troupe to operate the surtitles. Timing is judged on the basis of the Chinese texts.

Advancements in computer technology have offered an increased variety of possibilities for display in the theatre. Powerpoint software affords one of the most powerful devices in this respect. In the theatre of the 21st century, one can display any combination of languages, any number of words in any position on the stage. I have seen performances in which the surtitles have become an essential part of the set, accentuating the asynchronism of the archaic form in respect of modern reality. [2] It is highly possible that more and more theatre makers will include the surtitles in their overall aesthetic construction rather than seeing them merely as a functional device.

The Considerations

Reading the surtitles in the theatre places much more strain on the spectator than reading the subtitles of a film. Without close-ups and zoom, figures and objects onstage appear relatively smaller than those shown on the cinematic screen. The *xiqu* audience has to keep their focus fixed on relatively smaller things and for a longer period of time, since a full-scale *xiqu* is seldom shorter than three hours, while most films are under two. The three-dimensionality of the stage also adds to the complexity of the vision. The position of the surtitles display imposes another demand on the audience. On the cinematic screen, the subtitles span the entire width of the bottom of the screen. The image and the text embrace each other and form an integrated whole in the audience's field of vision. But surtitles in the theatre are put on either the sides or the top of the stage. The audience have to look away from the image onstage to see them. The surtitles are at the same time a help and a distraction. Over-frequent changeover of the surtitles and the flashing of new lines on the display board only complicate the requirement on the audience's vision, so that the whole experience can become an irritation rather than a definite enhancement of the theatrical experience.

This limitation does not really affect the Chinese surtitles, since there is not much flexibility available if the decision has already been made to show the full libretto. Moreover, the language used in *xiqu* librettos is often very condensed, conforming to the style of classical Chinese. But the English surtitles are often longer, because English words take up much more space than Chinese characters, and also because many stock images and cultural items easily understood by the Chinese audience need to be explained and elaborated for the non-Chinese audience, who rely on the English surtitles. Therefore, in order to limit the length of the English surtitles and the frequency of their changeover, functional and grammatical words are sometimes omitted, especially when the lines are spoken or sung very quickly in very fast-paced episodes. Helping the audience to follow the narrative should take absolute priority.

Once the narrative has been addressed, the surtitlist often finds herself/himself facing similar difficult translation decisions to those confronted by many other literary translators. *Xiqu* librettos have inherited the convention of Song Dynasty lyrics, loaded with a plethora of allusions to early poetry. Many of them refer to historical figures and events, others to images of nature. If the surtitlist is to preserve them all and to explain them adequately in English, s/he will produce an extended text, probably of a length impossible to be used as surtitles. Good surtitlists, like good literary translators, succeed in discriminating intuitively between images in terms of their importance in relation to the narrative and the emotional states of the characters. I would also suggest that a hierarchy should be established in terms of what I would describe as "the intensity of corporeality" among the images. This means retaining those images that can evoke the most intense physical sensation: for example, images of sharp colours or scents, and also concrete images of flowers and birds. The phenomenological power of the libretto can thus be best preserved.

The Presence

Having described how surtitling is done for *xiqu*, I would now like to ask the question: In what ways have surtitles contributed to the overall theatrical experience of a *xiqu* performance? Their most obvious function is surely to help the audience follow the story. This explains the narratorial function of surtitles, and of the theatre. Indeed, the narratorial approach to the theatre has dominated theatre studies for a long time. The various units in a theatre production, including the text and the surtitles, are understood mainly through their narratorial function. However, in the last decades of the 20th century, the proliferation of postmodern performances called for new approaches to theatre studies in order to articulate the meanings in those works that traditional narratology had failed to elucidate. In particular, the studies by Bert O. States and Stanton B. Garner focus on the overall experience of viewing a theatrical performance (States 1985; Garner 1994). They both emphasise the idea of theatrical experience as a process of intending, in the phenomenological sense[3], the stage content, both human and inanimate, and both mobile and static. The set of a performance, its properties, the human bodies, the colours, the lighting effects and all spatial and temporal happenings occurring onstage are viewed as components of an experience that has an overall structure. This structure is experienced simultaneously in its totality and through its many fragments. Both States and Garner believe that by taking into account the process of intentionality in theatrical experience, we can get one step closer to the heart of the theatre aesthetic. We can explore the ground that narratology and semiology have left untrodden.

A related and very useful concept that will help us investigate the phenomenological function of surtitles is that of consciousness, which characterises human experience as a complicated structure receiving multiple sensory stimuli. The concept takes into account the issues of concentration and distraction, and of attention and distraction. John Searle defined consciousness as "those subjective states of sentience or awareness" occurring when one is awake. It is similar to what Husserl called "psychic life" in *Phenomenology* (Kearney and Rainwater 1988: 17). Searle went on to make the distinction between consciousness and intellectual mental activities, since "many states of consciousness have little or nothing to do with knowledge," and "it is not generally the case that all conscious states are also self-conscious" (Searle). According to him, consciousness, knowledge, self-awareness and intellectual mental activities all operate simultaneously like a cluster of experiential processes. The arena of these activities is the individual subjectivity. Searle assumes this subjectivity to exist as a unity and a totality, otherwise these activities would not remain in their own place and schizophrenia would be the norm of human behaviour and much more common than it is now. He calls this subjectivity a "unified conscious experience"; one can also understand it in terms of what Kant calls "the transcendental unity of apperception." According to Searle, "unified conscious experience" has two important features. First, all mental processes operate side by side with one another and contribute towards a unified subjectivity, although they might not be working towards a singular comprehensive consciousness at any one time. This plurality of sentience results in something like a conglomeration described by Searle as "a field of consciousness." This "field" has a "centre and periphery." The centre is the location of maximum attention. The periphery is the "background" against which the centre becomes the focus of attention. Consciousness is therefore a hierarchical structure. It is not like a seamless single-celled egg with a smooth surface. On the contrary, it is more akin to a conglomeration of items of irregular shape and with undulating surfaces. Second, Searle characterised the totality of experience as a structure with a temporal dimension. In other words, we can talk about instances of "unified conscious experience," and understand consciousness as being made up of instances of heterogeneous intensity of attention focused on different intentional objects, to borrow the phenomenological term.

If we examine theatrical experience in the light of consciousness, all the entities onstage, including surtitles, will reveal themselves to us in a completely different way. One question to ask is: Where are the words in a *xiqu* performance located in our consciousness: at the centre or at the periphery? For a native audience, the script is of paramount importance. It is the starting point of everything and provides an anchor to all stage business. However spectacular the players' movements and however expressive their voices are, without the words they are empty shapes and sounds. It is the text that renders specificity to what the physical elements signify. To fully understand a piece of *xiqu*, the intellectual faculty related to linguistic comprehension has to operate vigorously and this intellectual mental activity has to occupy the central position in the audience's consciousness, together with their visual and audio perceptions. For the non-Chinese audience, if there are no surtitles, the composition of their consciousness will be completely different. The meaning of the players' actions, movement and sounds, which constitute the dramatic structure of the piece, will be lost without the linguistic codes being processed by the intellectual faculty of the mind. As a result, the sensual elements will fill in and occupy the centre of consciousness. However, without the meanings provided by the words, what they see will be no more than floating contours, flashy colours and flamboyant sounds. The environment provided for *xiqu* viewing sets the parameters for how the piece can be understood. In time it can even condition the mode of reception of the art form. The less frequently the audience are given the content, the less important they will find it. Reception of *xiqu* as mere spectacle does not promote cross-cultural understanding, but simply reinforces the stereotype of the Chinese as being those people with nimble feet and slitty eyes.

On the one hand, surtitles bring the performance and the audience closer to each other, but on the other, they accentuate the distance between them. States observes that in the theatre, every piece of property has two identities: what it signifies onstage, and what it really is (States, op. cit.: 20). To have the surtitles in English flashing in front of the audience in a *xiqu* performance creates a strange alienating effect, reminding the audience that there is a here and now in the theatre, and that their comprehension of the piece is mediated by an entity (a foreign language in its physical presence as the surtitles display) completely external to the piece, but internal to the audience experience of it. This results in a tug of war. The audience is simultaneously pulled towards the performance and pushed away from it. What is established is a healthy space of cultural contact, in which both cultural distance and the effort to bridge it are made visible rather than being masked or dismissed.

Notes

1. Most surtitles for *xiqu* for non-Chinese audiences are done in English,
    for the simple reason that English surtitles travel well in the
    international theatre market.
2. In a controversial production of the traditional *xiqu* piece *The Outcast
    General* [*Tiao Huache*] by the Hong Kong experimental theatre company
    Zuni Icosohedron, the traditional embroidered backdrop was replaced
    by a screen with the Chinese and English texts projected onto it. A
    striking aesthetic effect was created when the traditional acting by the
    players was set against the background of modern technology.
3. In the simplest terms, to intend an object in the phenomenological
    sense means to approach it with our senses. Edmund Husserl defined it
    in a very specific manner:

    > The terminological expression, deriving from Scholasticism, for
    > designating the basic character of being as consciousness, as
    > consciousness of something, is *intentionality*. In unreflective holding
    > of some object or other in consciousness, we are turned or directed
    > towards it: our "*intentio*" goes out towards it. The phenomenological
    > reversal of our gaze shows that this "being directed" is really an
    > immanent essential feature of the respective experiences involved;
    > they are "intentional" experiences. (Husserl 1988: 16)

    A comprehensive explanation of this concept is given by Hammond,
    Howarth and Kent:

    > Experience, as it were, always refers to something beyond itself, and
    > therefore cannot be characterized independently of this.
    > (Conversely, it is claimed, no straightforward sense can be given to
    > an outer, external world of objects which are not the objects *of* such
    > experiences.) One cannot, for example, characterize perceptual
    > experience without describing what it is that is seen, touched,
    > heard, and so on. This feature of conscious experience is called by
    > phenomenologists its "intentionality"; and what it is that is
    > experienced—such as the cocktail that Sartre perceived—is often
    > termed the "intentional object." (Hammond, Howarth, and Kent
    > 1991: 2–3)

References

Dolby, William. 1976. *A History of Chinese Drama.* London: Elek Books
　　Ltd.

Garner, Jr. Stanton B. 1994. *Bodied Spaces: Phenomenology and Performance in
　　Contemporary Drama.* New York: Cornell University Press.

Hammond, Michael, Jane Howarth, and Russell Kent. 1991. *Understanding Phenomenology*. Oxford: Basel and Blackwell Ltd.

Husserl, Edmund. 1988. "Phenomenology." In Kearney and Mara (eds.), *The Continental Philosophy Reader*. London: Routledge, pp. 3–22.

Kearney, Richard and Mara Rainwater, eds. 1988. *The Continental Philosophy Reader*. London: Routledge.

States, Bert O. 1985. *Great Reckonings and Little Rooms: On the Phenomenology of Theater*. Berkeley: University of California Press.

18

The Pedagogy of Subtitling

Corinne Imhauser

—ɯ—

In Europe, hundreds of programmes are now available 24 hours a day, through cable or satellite and DVDs, making it possible to watch a film in any number of languages. In Europe, the U.S. and in developing countries, subtitling is increasingly used to improve language proficiency or to encourage young children to read (Koolstra 1993). Subtitling also allows the hard of hearing to have access to information and culture, and helps ethnic minorities foster their own cultures and languages.

Consequently, subtitling can no longer be regarded as a minor form of translation, and today a large number of higher education institutions or universities are setting up courses in subtitling.

On the basis of twenty years' experience both as a practitioner and as an academic, in this paper I discuss pedagogical and technical challenges with regard to subtitling. It is a reflection on some of the basic skills involved in subtitling, on the tools that can be used or developed for teaching and, broadly speaking, on pedagogy.

Curriculum Development

Some professional translators or academics believe that any translator can become a subtitler. Nothing could be further from the truth—just as a good interpreter is not necessarily a good translator, all translators/interpreters do not make good subtitlers.

However, before dealing with the specific translation skills involved in subtitling—which are closely linked to the different framework in which the translator will work—it should be noted that it is essential that students already have a good command of traditional translation techniques (Card 1998) before specialising in subtitling. Our ten-year experience at Institut Superieur de Traducteurs et Interpretes (ISTI) has indeed shown that few undergraduate students achieve satisfactory results in subtitling because of a number of additional parameters which make translation even more challenging.

New parameters

1. Semiotics

While translation courses are for the most part based on written text, in subtitling other parameters come into play that should be granted equal status: i.e., the semantic weight of image, sound and prosody (Barthes 1977; de Linde 1997; Schröder 2004).

Just as the interpreter must take account of the speaker's body language as well as intonation and pauses when translating, subtitlers should therefore always bear in mind what appears on the screen and what is heard by the viewer. This should reduce the number of frequent mistakes made by translators who use the dialogue list as if it were a normal text[1] and who do not always realise that visual or auditory clues may alter the meaning of the written dialogues.

Such clues are also useful for dealing with polysemy or direct references to what can be seen on screen but is vague in the written transcription. In addition, relying on visual or auditory content will make condensation easier since part of the information normally available in a written translation can be either seen or heard by the viewer. Finally, the rhythm of the film/programme or of certain scenes is also meaningful and should be matched by the rhythm of subtitles.

2. Technical constraints

Students must learn to respect *technical constraints* so that viewers can read subtitles easily. These parameters are, for example[2]:

- space (32 characters/line, for example)
- duration (6 seconds maximum / 1.5 seconds minimum)
- reading speed (6 seconds = 70 characters)
- one or two lines
- cuts
- rhythm

Specific Skills

On the basis of the above-mentioned parameters, it is possible to identify a number of basic skills to be acquired or developed.

Linguistic skills

- breaking the sentence into appropriate semantic/grammatical units
- condensation/adaptation: developing the ability to produce shorter sentences without losing information[3] through the use of synonyms or by relying on redundant information on screen
- aural comprehension—sometimes poor among translators

Technical skills

- image and sound awareness
- time and space management
- spotting
- (+ the manual projection of subtitles often used at film festivals).

Tools

After a two-year trial and error period, we found that if students were taught how to use the subtitling software at the very beginning of the course, it made it more difficult for them to acquire some of the new skills identified above: namely, chunking (Katan 1999), sound/image awareness, and time/space management. Students indeed tended to focus on becoming expert users rather than on producing good translations.

Another reason why we find it important to avoid being too closely tied to technology is that public higher education budgets in

Europe have been slashed in the last few years. Consequently, if too much emphasis is placed on the acquisition of sophisticated, up-to-date tools, higher education institutions/universities face several dangers:

- being compelled to increase registration fees in order to cover the costs of equipment, thereby limiting access to higher education;
- being too theoretical because of a lack of equipment, thereby challenging the quality of academic training; and
- limiting access to information owing to corporate sponsorship imposing control over course content.

Simple tools

Image and sound awareness

Experience has shown that students first need to become "active viewers," in that they should learn to analyse image and sound at various levels. It is indeed striking that as "passive" viewers, students are not always aware, for example, of cuts or of the difference between cuts and scene changes. They also fail to pay attention to body language, gestures, colour codes, music, icons, posture, facial expression or eye gaze; object communication such as clothing hairstyles or even architecture; symbols and infographics prosodic features of speech such as intonation and stress and other paralinguistic features of speech such as voice quality emotion and speaking style (Poyatos 1997: 361).

This is why we decided to begin with tailor-made drills using ordinary equipment such as PCs, sound cards, video/DVD players and TV/video programmes/films or excerpts. The first objective was to develop the awareness that the above-mentioned parameters might have a bearing on the future content of subtitles, while using tools that students were familiar with, so that they would not be distracted by the intricacies of technology.

As mentioned above, given the semantic weight of sound and images, it was considered essential that—when students work on the translation of dialogues at a later stage—they are given permanent access to the corresponding videotapes or files. To this end, the course is given in the computer lab, or students receive copies if they wish to work at home.

Space management, subtitle breaks and reduction

Space limitation is a permanent constraint in subtitling. It means that if the maximum number of characters per line is 35, for example, the translator will have to tap all the resources of his/her mother tongue to convey the message in no more than 35 characters without betraying the original or leaving out information—a common criticism among viewers. As mentioned above, many undergraduate students who tried their hand at subtitling realised that this one constraint explained why subtitlers must have a perfect command of their mother tongue and of translation techniques.

Another consequence of space limitation is that it is often necessary to break a sentence into several subtitles. Surprisingly, not all students/translators are aware that breaks must be made in accordance with basic rules—like respecting sense blocks, logic or the grammatical rules of the language they are translating into.

| Example: | Suddenly, he discovered the house was on fire. | Tomorrow, she will go to the dentist in downtown Brussels. |

At the beginning of the subtitling course, we therefore devote several hours to "chunking": i.e., how to break a sentence into correct grammatical units or sense blocks. To allow students to become familiar with space limitations, we have again used ordinary PCs, reducing the window of the Word document in such a way that only a certain number of characters can appear.

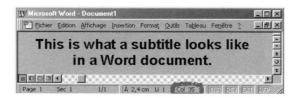

Time awareness spotting

Another dramatic difference between subtitling and other types of translation is the importance of time in subtitling: i.e., the duration of an utterance, the duration of a scene, and the amount of time needed by the viewer to read the subtitle—or "reading speed." For the first time, translators must thus take time into account before translating in order to calculate the number of characters they will be allowed to use in each subtitle and to synchronise the subtitles with the original dialogue. They should therefore be shown how to measure time and constantly link it to images and the soundtrack.

At this stage, any media player in a PC can be used with beginners:

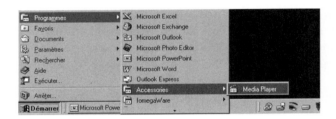

- it allows them to measure time, since minutes and seconds are displayed
- the slide bar makes it possible to
  - identify cuts
  - measure the duration of an utterance and therefore calculate the corresponding number of characters.

When students have understood the importance of time and are able to decide when a subtitle will appear or disappear, they are ready to understand the 'spotting' process that will be explained when they use real subtitling software.

The manual projection of subtitles

Apart from the fact that learning to project subtitles manually is an excellent pedagogical tool, it is also becoming a plus for translators in terms of working opportunities, since an increasing number of film festivals, theatres or opera houses now display manually projected intra-lingual or interlingual subtitles and surtitles (Dewolf 2001).

In order to be able to 'launch' subtitles from an ordinary PC, one simply needs to save each subtitle on a separate page in a Word document.

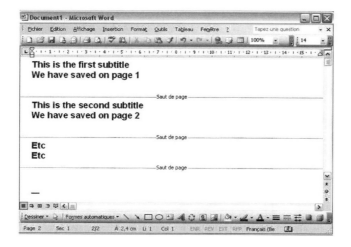

Then, it is possible to display them one after another on the computer screen by clicking the "page down" button.

This exercise is useful for several reasons:

- Students get used to establishing a constant relationship between subtitles and images
- They become aware of rhythm
- They can check whether their subtitles are readable
- They can practise on any computer, including their own computers at home, if they want to
- They can rehearse before projecting their subtitles during their internship.

In-house digital subtitling software

Ten years ago at ISTI, since it was financially impossible to buy subtitling software for all our students, we decided to develop our own digital tool. It is the result of a two-year interdisciplinary project based on our own professional experience in subtitling and on the expertise of our programmer. Although it is far from being perfect, it has not only proved to be a valuable tool for teaching subtitling, but it was also successfully used by Canal+ Belgium, a major European cable TV channel, thereby showing that it was a reliable tool.

Today, a number of websites offer free or demo versions of more sophisticated software which make it possible for students to become familiar with the latest developments.

As to our subtitling software, it is a simplified version of other professional programmes available on the market. It allows students:

- to view the digitised video files to be subtitled on any ordinary PC
- to cue in time codes
- to type in the subtitles
- to 'simulate' and edit, and
- to print subtitles or send them by email.

So far, this in-house tool has enabled our students to understand the rationale behind most professional software. When faced with other software during their internships or after they have graduated, they are then able to adapt swiftly.

Conclusion

In this paper, we have tried to show that it is possible to use the equipment already available at many institutions or universities to develop basic subtitling drills. We have also indicated that it is possible to develop one's own tools—a digital subtitling programme, for instance. This requires sound professional experience and an in-depth analysis of course content together with an interdisciplinary approach.

It is obvious that this does not mean that students should not have access to professional subtitling equipment before they graduate, but it does mean that, even if some institutions cannot afford it, alternative solutions can be found. It is possible, for example, to invite software developers to show their products, to obtain a trial version of new software, or to receive older equipment from subtitling companies or TV stations upgrading their working tools. At our institute, we negotiated with the festival organisers who work with our students during their traineeship so that our students would have the opportunity to subtitle some of the films in a professional studio. These are but a few examples of solutions that do not jeopardise the financial balance of public education while creating links between academia and practitioners.

If higher education is to survive, we must adapt, but not at any cost. Should we yield to pressure from industry, training will slowly take over from education. Training is useful but it should not supersede education. Traditionally, the role of universities has been to graduate students who are flexible, creative and proactive, so that they might adapt swiftly to changing working environments. That is why we have found it necessary at ISTI to develop a one-year course where language, culture, pragmatics and translation are associated with workshops and lectures by practitioners on new market trends and working conditions.

Notes

1. Unfortunately, subtitling agencies increasingly consider it too expensive or time-consuming to send a copy of the video file and simply email an Excel sheet with a transcription of the original dialogue in one column and other empty columns for each language in which the translation is to be made.

2. Such parameters may vary according to the TV channel, the country, the public, or the company style guide for example; they should be specified before translating.

3. Reduction is not necessarily synonymous with omission; poor subtitlers often leave out information because they do not master their mother tongue or relevant translation techniques.

References

Barthes, Roland. 1982. *Image- Music–Text*, trans. Stephen Heath. London: Fontana Paperbacks, first published 1977, third impression.

Card, Lorin. 1998. *Je Vois ce que Vous Voulez Dire : Un Essai sur la Notion de Ll'équivalence dans les Sous-titres de « 37°2 le Matin » et « Au Revoir les Enfants »*. Université Mount Allison, Sackville, Canada, Meta, XLIII, 2

de Linde, Zoe. 1997. *Linguistic and Visual Complexity of Television Subtitles*. PhD thesis, University of Bristol.

Delabatista, Dirk. 1989. "Translation and mass communication: Film and TV translation as evidence of cultural dynamics." *Babel*, 35: 4, pp. 193–218.

Dewolf, Linda. 2001. "Surtitling operas. With examples of translations from German into French and Dutch." In Y. Gambier and H. Gottlieb (eds.),

(*Multi*) *Media Translation: Concepts, Practices and Research.* Amsterdam: John Benjamins, pp. 179–188.

Gambier, Y. 2000. " Le profil du traducteur pour écrans," Daniel Gouadec (éd.) Formation des traducteurs, Actes du colloque international de Rennes, 24-25.9.1999. Paris : Maison du Dictionnaire, pp. 89–94.

Imhauser C. 2001. *Les Outils D'aide à L'enseignement du Sous-titrage,* ed. Daniel Gouadec. Formation des traducteurs (2), Actes du colloque international de Rennes, 2000. Paris : Maison du Dictionnaire, pp. 47–56

Katan, D. 1999. *Translating Cultures—An Introduction for Translators, Interpreters and Mediators.* Manchester: St. Jerome.

Koolstra, Cees M. 1993. *Television and Children's Reading: A Three-Year Panel Study.* PhD thesis, Centre for Child and Media Studies, Leiden University (Short version in *Reading Research Quarterly,* 32/2, April-June 1997, pp. 128–152).

Metz, Christian. 1974. "The modern cinema and narrativity." In Michael Taylor (trans.), *Film Language: A Semiotics of Cinema.* Chicago: University of Chicago Press, pp 185–227.

Poyatos, Fernando, ed. 1997. *Nonverbal Communication and Translation. New Perspectives and Challenges in Literature, Interpretation and the Media.* Amsterdam: John Benjamins.

Schröder, M. 2004. "Speech and emotion research: An overview of research frameworks and a dimensional approach to emotional speech synthesis." PhD thesis. Vol. 7 of *Phonus,* Research Report of the Institute of Phonetics, Saarland University.

Stam, Robert, Robert Burgoyne, and Sandy Flitterman-Lewis. 1992. *New Vocabularies in Film Semiotics: Structuralism, Post-Structuralism and Beyond.* New York: Routledge.

Whorf, B. L. 1956. *Language, Thought and Reality.* Cambridge, MA: MIT Press.

Roundtable Discussion

—˷˷—

Participants were asked to comment on the state of their profession in their respective countries.

Asian-Pacific Area

Angeline Oyang
AOY International (Australia)

As a latecomer to the profession, I escaped all the angst of development that everybody else seems to have gone through. Over the last few days, I have heard much about various aspects of subtitling, and this hinges on how you work, what your working environment and your status are, and how you regard yourself. I'll start off with the place where I work, its social and political environment, and the amenities that are available to me in that environment.

I work with the Special Broadcasting Service (SBS), the multicultural and multilingual public broadcaster of Australia. This service is the result of twenty years of development and we have just celebrated our twentieth anniversary. As a former social worker, I was a part of the movement that pushed the government to accept the concept of multiculturalism. I am very happy to be enjoying the fruits of my past life. SBS was first established to cater for the needs of a linguistically diverse population to have programmes in their own languages, starting off with radio and then television.

SBS was incorporated in 1991, which meant that they could show commercials and accept sponsorship. It is a leaner brother of the government station, Australia Broadcasting Commission (ABC), the wealthier and better-looked-after public broadcaster. The following Act of Parliament lays down the function of SBS:

> The principal function of SBS is to provide multilingual and multicultural radio and television services that inform, educate and entertain all Australians and, in doing so, reflect Australia's multicultural society.

So everybody is entitled to a diversity of linguistically and culturally appropriate programmes. This frees us from various commercial pressures, and we just aim for the highest standards possible. We do not have any time limits, although we have general guidelines on how long it should take to subtitle a programme, feature or documentary. But the subtitlers are well recognised, and have complete control of the programme. We view the feature at least three times: first to preview it, then time-code it with software, and finally subtitle it. We also summarise the content of the film to determine the censorship rating and the quality of the film subtitles, and whether it needs to be redone or not. We have an in-house production team to redo it, or to do anything technical to it.

After the subtitling, we discuss our work with the editors, who are really our advisors. I am a China-born Hong Kong local, and probably would best appreciate the meaning and the cultural context of a film from Hong Kong. Therefore I am the meaning conveyor, the cross-cultural communicator. The editor is a good, local native speaker, who knows if my expressions will be acceptable to the audience or not. After each piece of work, we have a meeting. We can argue about it. I don't have to accept the editor's opinion, and he has to take into account what I think, and what the producers or what the characters are really saying. We exchange views and review the whole thing again. After it is offline, we see it again. So we are very thorough and the set-up is very good. We have our own studios, and are given a timeslot. We can work in them 24 hours a day if we like, except on Sundays. So we have a very flexible working arrangement and we work on a faith and trust basis.

As far as the amount of work goes, SBS buys 57 per cent of its television programmes, so it has local English-speaking programmes 43 per cent of the time, and that comes to about 6,500 hours of airtime per year. According to the annual report of SBS, Chinese

(Cantonese and Mandarin) programming takes up about 400 hours a year, depending on the prevailing audience preferences. At present, there are more Mandarin programmes than Cantonese programmes. It also depends on how the buyers can negotiate for our programmes. Now they are dealing with the Chinese government, and bureaucracy plays a part in how much work we can get.

Compared to Vietnamese, we are not doing too badly, but compared to French and German, we are not as good. European programmes seem to be preferred by whoever is organising the programming. Recently, SBS established a language service, and they are marketing themselves as well. We employ about ten full-time editors, 12–13 part-time editors and 20–40 subtitlers, for the most part on a contractual basis because of the ebb and flow of the preferences and the migrants, etc. After the Tiananmen Incident in 1989, Australia acquired 20,000 new Chinese immigrants, mainly former students, who brought in their parents, fiancés, uncles and aunts. Over the past ten years, we have observed a marked increase in mainland Chinese immigrants.

The last part is about our working conditions. SBS treats all contractors as employees who come to be superannuated. The salary of a subtitler is equivalent to that of a teacher, a junior university lecturer, or a senior nurse. Not too bad, but not excellent either. It is balanced by good working conditions. There is flexibility in the job, as you can come and go when you like, and can do part of your work at home, such as previewing. I think that it compares favourably to what Shu Kei has said about the scene in Hong Kong, where subtitlers are paid around A$6,000 for a 100-minute feature. As Australia is a multicultural nation, we cater for 58 languages.

Qian Shaochang
Shanghai International Studies University (China)

For about twenty years, I was a surgeon in Shanghai's biggest hospital. During the Cultural Revolution, my parents and relatives were badly persecuted, and I also spent a few years in jail. As an ex-convict I was not able to return to medicine and had to switch to teaching English. In any event, I am the only Chinese professor of

English who was once a doctor. Gradually, in my spare time, I started translating films and television programmes.

In China, dubbing rather than subtitling is our preferred mode of screen translation. Every year we have a few films and television programmes that are subtitled, but ninety per cent of them are dubbed because the audience prefers dubbing to subtitling. There are a number of reasons for this. Most Chinese do not know a foreign language. Before 1949, English was taught in all schools. After the Korean War, which started in 1950, English was replaced by Russian. In the 1950s, no foreign language was taught, so after China was opened to the outside world in 1978, its people were eager to learn English. However, the majority of Chinese people are still unable to understand foreign films in English. This is the first reason. The second reason is that, with subtitles, you have to read them and watch the picture at virtually the same time, which divides your attention. Sometimes the subtitles are quite long, so actually you are not watching the picture but reading the subtitles. The third reason is that sometimes the synchronisation is poor, so you have to guess which person is saying which sentence.

In China, many people are illiterate or semi-literate, and cannot read subtitles at all. Besides, the ethnic minorities in Tibet, Inner Mongolia and other places cannot read Chinese, even though they might speak it. For them, subtitling poses problems. It is also difficult for children, who cannot read very well. That is why, in China, we generally dub rather than subtitle.

Before 1978 there was very little screen translation as imported films from the West were not allowed. All our films came from the Soviet Union and some Eastern European countries. During the Cultural Revolution, we only had three to four films shown per day: two Russian, one Vietnamese and one Albanian film—four films for a country as large as China. Now the situation is quite different. The most important films are American, from Hollywood, so the government has made some arrangements to limit the number of Hollywood films so that they do not account for more than fifty per cent of all imported films and television programmes.

Most American films have very high box office ratings because of the high cost or advanced techniques involved in shooting these films. But the ratings of foreign television programmes are falling fast. Now ratings hover around five to ten per cent for foreign films.

This is because the quality of imported programmes and films is getting poorer. There are also other reasons for this development, such as an increase in alternative forms of entertainment.

The pay for translators of television programmes used to be very low. Now it is higher: the pay for each episode ranges between 300 and 3,000 yuan, depending on the experience and quality of the translators.

Shu Kei
Film-maker and Distributor (Hong Kong)

As I discussed subtitling foreign films in my paper for this conference, today I would like to talk about subtitling for local films. Those who are familiar with Hong Kong films would know that almost all of them carry bilingual subtitles, in English and Chinese. This is a kind of tradition that began in the 1960s and continues today. I think basically the reason for this is market demand. From the early days of the local film industry, Hong Kong films were exported to Southeast Asia and to Chinatowns in Europe and the U.S. The political climate of Southeast Asia in the 1960s dictated that Hong Kong films be subtitled in both English and Chinese. Since the language of Hong Kong is Cantonese, the main language of Hong Kong film production until the late 1960s was Cantonese.

Some Asian countries, such as Singapore, Taiwan and Malaysia, at this time gradually started to forbid the import of films produced in Cantonese. There were two ways to get around that: the first was by subtitling the films in written Chinese and the second was to dub them into Mandarin. Starting in the late 1960s almost up until the present, not only are the majority of Hong Kong films subtitled in English and Chinese, but they also have two versions—the original Cantonese version and a dubbed Mandarin version.

The subtitling department is perhaps the most poorly equipped department in a Hong Kong film production. One reason for this is the time allowed for doing the subtitles. Most Hong Kong films are produced in a rushed and hasty manner. It is almost a tradition, starting with little or no pre-production, no script, and everything is done almost simultaneously. The shooting, pre-production, the writing of the script and everything else are still going on during the post-production stage. Everything is done in such haste, so you can imagine that there is no way that subtitling can be done in the manner we would like.

In post-production, as soon as the editing process begins, the dialogue will be transcribed either by the assistant director or the continuity person. Since everything is going on at the same time, the film will be dubbed and edited reel by reel. Then the transcript will be sent to the subtitler reel by reel. In the 1970s and 1980s, the people who did the subtitling called themselves a company, but actually it was just a family business. The father shot the negative, while the son was responsible for the translation, and he might only have received a secondary school education. Those who translated the subtitles into English never had the opportunity to see the film. They translated the film reel by reel, and the transcriptions were sent with an audio tape, and sometimes the job even included translating the Cantonese into Mandarin. In the late 1970s and 1980s, it became a tradition for the Chinese subtitles to be in spoken Cantonese. The subtitlers would also have to transcribe another set of Mandarin subtitles for films exported to Taiwan, Singapore or Malaysia.

Naturally, this method would lead to all kinds of mistakes, as it was not easy to understand the film with just an audio tape. For example, it was easy to get the gender of the speaker wrong. In the 1980s, most people would ignore the English subtitles so that mistakes would never be noticed, or if they were, no attention was paid to them. So when these films were shown at international film festivals there would be all kinds of embarrassment. My good friend John Sham produced a film called *People's Hero* (人民英雄), and when he viewed it during the Toronto Film Festival, he discovered all the mistakes. There is a line where someone actually says, "Can someone provide him with some aid." However, the subtitle reads: "Can anyone provide him with AIDS," the last word being in capital letters.

For a discussion of some interesting mistakes, I recommend that you read David Bordwell's book on Hong Kong cinema entitled *Planet Hong Kong: Popular Cinema and the Art of Entertainment.* There is a chapter on that which is very funny. Anyway, after the translation had been done, they would typeset, get negatives of it, and send them to the laboratory for processing. The editor would then check on how the subtitling had been done. More formal companies were set up in the late 1970s and early 1980s, but these were still often two-man outfits, with mainly in-house translators who were not very experienced, so similar kinds of mistakes continued to be made. For better productions, and as more Hong Kong films were invited to international film festivals, better translators were invited to subtitle films. These were experienced film critics, sometimes coordinators of the Hong Kong Film Festival, and sometimes scholars, like Professor Rupert Chan, who talked about his experience of translating the film *City of Glass* during the conference.

Even though that was the case, there was no idea of spotting and no idea about how long the sentence would appear on the screen. The spotting was given to the translator by editors, who did it by listening to the dialogue alone, so the subtitles might be all wrong. The translator would have little sense of spotting because he was not in the profession. Spotting in Chinese films is particularly important since Cantonese is spoken very fast, much faster than Mandarin, and much faster than most other languages in the world. Maybe Italian is the closest to Cantonese in rhythm and also speed. So there is another difficulty of subtitling.

This is generally how things have been done since the late 1960s. The whole process, from transcription to translation to spotting to the shooting of the subtitles, can take as little as three days, or even less, as everything is going on simultaneously. One reel of the film is dubbed, taken to the lab and then released.

The total cost of the subtitling that the subtitling company charges is around HK$35,000, which includes the cost of the translator. Rupert Chan charges four times as much as a regular translator. If an outside freelance or experienced translator is used, the range will be between HK$10,000 and 20,000. Only very occasionally, a specialist is asked to do the translation of some important or good quality film. Chuang Ying-ting, who also presented a paper in this conference, cited *Farewell My Concubine* (1993), which I also distributed. In that case we asked Linda Jaivin, who lives in Australia, to subtitle the film. With her Chinese language ability and extensive knowledge of China, she was able to do a concise translation of the dialogue and put in additional information so that Western audiences would understand the film better, because the film is about contemporary Chinese history. This is the general situation of Hong Kong films in our industry.

Yumiko Kato
SDI Media Hong Kong Limited (Hong Kong)

As opposed to many other countries in Europe and America, nearly a hundred per cent of the motion pictures released in cinemas in Japan are subtitled. Most Japanese prefer subtitled films to dubbed ones, mainly because they wish to listen to the original voices of the actors so that they can fully appreciate the vibes and the subtleties of the films, even though they do not understand the language.

There are also other reasons, such as the relatively low cost of subtitling compared to dubbing. As the majority of films are in English, subtitling allows the audience to become accustomed to everyday conversational English. With the current wave of globalisation, the ability to comprehend and communicate in English is becoming crucial in most international undertakings. Accordingly, the number of students and adults who study conversational English has increased rapidly and private schools for English have proliferated. Some schools even use Hollywood films as teaching materials. In addition, Japan's high literacy rate makes subtitling accessible to most of the population.

Therefore subtitling is in great demand in Japan. However, it is extremely difficult to be a subtitler as there are a plethora of strict technical rules, and there exists a kind of "guildship" in the industry. It is said that there are three ways to become a subtitler: to attend a private institution specialising in teaching subtitling translation; to be apprenticed to an experienced subtitler; and to work for a film distribution company, learning on the job while developing connections in the industry.

As I have just mentioned, Japanese subtitling has many strict technical rules and regulations. Generally, one subtitle must not exceed thirteen characters in a maximum of two lines when it is shown horizontally, and ten characters in a maximum of two lines when shown vertically. The most basic and implicit rule for a subtitler is "four characters for every second." The audience feels comfortable reading four characters a second, any more and they cannot read the whole title before it disappears. This is the formula based on consideration for the audience: that they should enjoy the film without being disturbed by the subtitles. It is impossible to translate dialogue word for word, for inevitably this would result in a violation of this rule. Therefore, the subtitler must encapsulate the meaning of the dialogue and express it in a felicitous, natural way and yet convey the original context.

I totally agree with Professor Karima Fumitoshi, who stated in his speech on Thursday that, "subtitling is not translating." Japanese film subtitling is not translating dialogues spoken in foreign languages, but is rather like recreating film scripts in a summarised manner. The subtitles are therefore normally written not in the literary style but in the colloquial style, so there is a big difference between them and those that you see here in Hong Kong. The colloquial style provides the quality required by the subtitlers to express the feelings of the characters in the film and the context to the maximum degree possible, given the limited number of characters.

Accordingly, one must have the ability to understand the film in depth and consider the background of the characters: for example, the character's age, gender, occupation, educational background, personality, the current situation etc., in order to produce good quality subtitles. Also, the visual effect of subtitles must be carefully considered. The Japanese language consists of three kinds of characters: the ideographic Chinese characters known as *kanji* and phonetic characters known as *hiragana* and *katakana*. *Katakana* is mainly used for foreign words, while Chinese characters and *hiragana* are used for composing sentences. For an ideal subtitle, a well-balanced use of those three kinds of characters is desirable, as well as the most appropriate use of wording.

Word order must also be taken into account, for generally, in the English language, the word order is of a subject followed by a verb, whereas in Japanese a verb comes at the end of a sentence. Therefore, one must strive to structure the subtitles so that they are synchronised with the original dialogue and the picture. In the case of a comedy film, for example, the timing is crucial to enable the audience to understand the jokes in context.

There are other technicalities in Japanese subtitling, such as the use of italic font to display the lyrics of a song, or telephone dialogue as spoken by someone on the other end of the phone, dialogue on television and radio, etc. Double quotation marks are used to display such things as the names of books, road signs, and quotations of phrases uttered by other characters.

Japanese subtitling is also known for its strict time coding.

Japanese production houses and distributors require extremely precise time coding and they will not tolerate even one frame of deviation between the dialogue and the subtitles. Accordingly, it is said that Japanese audiences in general are so used to precise time cueing that they automatically feel uncomfortable if there is a deviation of ten frames, which is only a little over 0.3 seconds in duration.

The technicalities I have just mentioned are just the tip of the iceberg. As you can see, Japanese subtitling is a very complicated and sophisticated process. Some experienced subtitlers say that it takes ten years for one to become a really established subtitler. Despite all the painstaking attention to detail that the subtitler has to pay, the ideal subtitles are supposed to be like the air that we breathe, so that at the end of the day the audiences do not even recall having read any subtitles and have simply enjoyed the film.

Shim Hoo Sang
SDI Media Hong Kong Limited (Hong Kong)

I am responsible for the Korean language section of SDI Media Hong Kong Limited. I will discuss some issues and challenges and also provide a brief introduction to the dubbing and translation industry in Korea.

Currently, there are seven cable and satellite broadcasting companies in Korea. However, programmes are usually locally produced for the domestic market. To my knowledge, a channel dedicated solely to foreign content does not exist in Korea at this time. Obviously some channels may choose to broadcast more foreign productions than others, but owing to the language barrier, Korean audiences have a strong preference for local language programmes. Until recently, the Korean audience preferred dubbing over subtitling. But these days we are seeing a strong trend towards subtitling. The main reason for this trend is the public interest in learning English, in addition to the lower cost of subtitling in comparison to dubbing. Inevitably, we have to dub children's cartoons and other programmes. With globalisation, English is definitely the language needed to get ahead, but it is also needed just to keep pace with the rest of the world, hence the surge in public interest in learning English. To become a translator in Korea, one must have mastery of English, Japanese, Chinese or other foreign languages. However, owing to the lack of truly fluent, multilingual human resources in the country, just a little knowledge of a foreign language can help one get a high salary at a prestigious corporation.

It is thus difficult and highly competitive to find capable and experienced translators in Korea. With this shortage of talent, numerous language schools for budding translators have popped up, with graduates receiving professional certificates at the end of their training. But there seem to be issues of reliability and curiosity in general. Slang is unique to each particular country and is frequently used in films. It is the most difficult part of a language to translate, especially for translators who do not have experience of living in that particular culture.

As far as I know, there are few academic programmes in translation at universities in Korea. At present, the translation and interpretation programmes at Hangul University of Foreign Studies produce highly regarded professional translators with expertise and knowledge. The translators at SDI Media are not only proficient in foreign languages but the majority of them also have overseas experience, either as students or as long-term residents, so they have mastered the slang and have the ability to translate the language as it is actually spoken.

As you are aware, the Korean and Japanese languages are similar in syntax and expressions, showing the similarities between the two cultures. However, Korean language and culture are quite different from the English or Chinese languages and cultures. Therefore, incorrect Korean translation of English texts will result in very odd expressions in inappropriate places. For instance, in Korea, it is not customary to use the word "killing." So rather than using this word, we use the expression "to get rid of." Many Hollywood films contain explicit language and swear words that we cannot translate and broadcast in their entirety. We must change creatively, in order to get the essence of the scene, or the entire film is compromised.

Date conventions are also different. In the U.S., it is month, then day, then year; in Hong Kong, it is day, month, and then year. In Korea it is year, month, and day. For example, my family almost became illegal immigrants last year because we thought that the date on the Hong Kong visa on our passports (11/5/00) meant 5 November 2000, instead of 11 May 2000.

Next, I'll give you a brief introduction to the dubbing scene in Korea.

There are approximately twenty production houses in Korea, a considerable number of which have state-of-the-art facilities. However, they operate on a certain business model. Apart from the network stations with their internal subtitling and dubbing departments, integrated subtitling and dubbing service providers like SDI Media do not exist in Korea at present. The dubbing profession in Hong Kong is not the highest paid profession, but in Korea dubbing artists are very popular, if not more popular than actual film stars. To become a dubbing artist, you must go through a voice test which you cannot prepare for. Then you have to undergo ten more radio tests to see if you are a born talent. It is also very competitive to enter the profession. Another reason for the popularity of dubbing as a profession in Korea is the low level of stress and the high salary relative to other professions. The opportunity to become famous is another attraction.

Most of the dubbing artists in Korea have their own fan clubs, believe it or not. For well known and popular dubbing artists, there are great opportunities to start a professional dubbing school, another potential source of income. In addition, dubbing artists have formed a trade union that dictates pay levels and fee structure. The budding dubbing artists, in their desire to become famous and successful by working for the major networks, become union members. Compared to Southeast Asia in general, even to Japan, production costs for dubbing are much higher in Korea since the artists' fees are so much more. Usually the costs are calculated per minute, but in Korea, they are calculated in ten-minute units. For a one-minute programme they would charge for ten minutes.

Korean films are gaining more of a name for themselves and are becoming more widely distributed, so issues related to subtitling and dubbing will become more prominent.

Janet Tauro
De La Salle University (The Philippines)

I used to be a journalist, but am now a professor at De La Salle

University, which, according to a survey by *Asiaweek*, is the number one private university in the Philippines. I am also the Vice Chairperson of the Department of Literature and Philippine languages, which offers translation programmes at undergraduate and graduate levels. We have only fourteen undergraduates studying translation and three students at graduate level, so translation is quite new in the Philippines.

Hatim and Mason claimed, "The world of the translator is inhabited by an extraordinary number of dichotomies ..." (1997: 1). Ironically, however, this diversity of the translation world is not seen in the fields of dubbing and subtitling in the Philippines. Translation is considered only as a technique, or a skill. This is how the academic community and the film and television industry view translation.

My thesis is based on the textual and contextual critical analysis of the telenovela *Marimar*, which, although entertaining, is out of synch because its translation is treated more as a product of technique only, and not of technique and discipline. I will now delve more deeply into a contextual analysis, that is, an examination of the consumption and production of both dubbing and sub-titling in the television and film industry and in the academic community.

Let me first talk about dubbing. Dubbing as a form of translation is very popular in our country for television rather than in films. For a contextual analysis of dubbed programs in the Philippines, I will take a quick look at the economics and programming of the two top-rating television networks.

The ABS CBN network continues to dominate ratings reviews, taking up almost half of the viewers, while its closest competitor, JMA Channel 7 (JMA 7), has only a third of its share. In 1995, ABS CBN earned 3.8 billion pesos from advertising compared with only 205 million pesos raised by JMA 7. ABS CBN registered double-digit revenue growth in the first half of 2001 despite the sluggish business environment.

Now let us take a look at those programmes which are dubbed into Filipino. ABS CBN has three Mexican telenovelas and five cartoons; JMA 7 has three telenovelas, five cartoons and the American series, *Sesame Street*. Fifty per cent of dubbed programmes are Hollywood television series. But these are not translated, since the majority of the Filipino people know how to speak English. These dubbed programmes comprise only 10 to 15 per cent of the networks' programming and the majority are scheduled during prime time.

I would, however, like to stress that these networks earn huge sums and have the means to produce their own telenovelas or improve the translation in the television industry. But they still prefer to import telenovelas and employ radio talents and dubbers as translators. These television empires are spending millions of pesos on research. Their focus, however, is not on improving the quality of their translation but on audience preferences and ratings.

Mexican telenovelas and Japanese animations dubbed into Filipino proliferate because they reap high profits, while not costing much to buy. Translators who are also dubbers are not trained and their pay is low. Seven years after the screening of *Marimar*, no training workshop or seminar has been organised to improve television dubbing by any of these top networks.

Television networks prefer to spend more money on promoting telenovelas than on making efforts to improve the quality of the translation and dubbing of these shows. Rex Lorens, general manager of RPN 9, admitted that their executives were footing the P1 million-plus-per-day bill of *Marimar* star Thalia's visit to the Philippines in August 1996. This year, the star of JMA 7's *Monica Brava* was invited to the Philippines, with all expenses paid for by the network, in an effort to promote the telenovela. "Monica Brava" appeared in almost all JMA 7 broadcasts, even in its news and public affairs programmes.

Now let us move on to subtitling. Subtitling in the Philippines started in 1981 during the Manila Film Festival. Since then, it has been used in Filipino films that are nominated or invited to take part in international film festivals.

In my interview with Clodualdo del Mundo, a highly acclaimed scriptwriter in the Philippines, he admitted that, like dubbing, subtitling is viewed more as a technique than a discipline. He said that a translator is hired to do the subtitling of a film. When asked to give the profile of such a translator, he claimed that he or she would have a background in translation through subtitling and in the technical aspects of film such as editing and dubbing. Again, they learn as they go along. But there are some instances, according to Del

Mundo, when either the scriptwriters themselves or the directors do the subtitling and the quality is far better than that of the subtitling done by the translators.

Translation through subtitling has two steps. The first translation is based on the script and is done by the scriptwriter, or by both the scriptwriter and the director, or by the translator. The second translation is based on the video and is done by the director, who views the film with the technical advisor. However, there are some instances, according to Del Mundo, when the director leaves the translation in the hands of the translator alone, which is not a very good idea.

Del Mundo observed that translation through subtitling is viewed simply as abbreviated translation. Translators, according to him, are not aware of the academic discipline of translation studies and just learn on the job. Del Mundo, who is also an academician, having been a professor for ten years, claimed that he had not heard of any study made on subtitling in the Philippines. He emphasised the need for such studies if media translation is to become professionalised in the Philippines.

Research into dubbing and subtitling remains non-existent. Furthermore, academic courses in translation do not figure prominently in the Philippines. In fact, De La Salle University is the only institution in the country that offers translation courses at graduate and undergraduate levels, although its graduate programmes will close shortly.

With this state of dubbing and subtitling existing in the Philippines, there is a pressing need to establish some sort of synchronisation between the academic community and the television industry. Synchronisation is crucial for film and television translation. It should not, however, be confined to actual translation practice, but should be extended to those working in the academic community so that each will benefit from the expertise of the other. This is important in order to improve translation in television.

Reference

Hatim, B. and Mason, I. 1997. *The Translator as Communicator.* London: Routledge.

Paul Yu
E-Zen Hall Communication Company (Taiwan)

My company, E-Zen Hall, deals with film subtitling and dubbing. About 80 per cent of the dubbing work is done in Taipei, where there are about 250 recording studios, excluding musical studios. Those studios serve four television stations in Taiwan. They also serve cable television stations, including channels in Singapore, Hong Kong and China. Subtitlers have their own unions. These unions help us to deal with basic salary issues, provide health insurance, and help the government regulate the dubbing profession. These unions also produce professional magazines to popularise and raise the status of the profession in the eyes of the public.

There are three different kinds of studio in Taiwan. The biggest has an integrated operations system. Having received the tape, we will first do the translation, then the dubbing and proofreading, and finally we will mix the dialogue with the sound effects. The smaller studios deal with the sound. They dub award ceremonies and entertainment shows. There are also dubbing companies that only dub advertisements.

Now I will focus on the translation part. Larger companies have their own translators. These in-house translators are usually more flexible and more willing to arrange their schedule according to the needs of the company. Smaller recording studios do not deal with translations. Sometimes their clients will provide translations themselves, or they will look for a translation agency. Because of the economic downturn in Taiwan, many channels have abandoned dubbing, so they will use the original sound. These channels include JET, the Japanese movie channels and AXN.

But there are some foreign channels, such as the HBO, "Cinemax," and Hollywood channels which still have their own Chinese subtitlers. Some smaller channels that do not have their own translators will outsource the translation to outside companies. These translation agencies do not have high standards and are less flexible. So, generally speaking, those channels with their own translators will be more able to fulfil the customers' needs.

There are two kinds of translation: dubbing translation and subtitle translation. In subtitle translation, the meaning is pinpointed in as short a sentence as possible. For dubbing, we require dubbers to reflect the story and action of the film, in the oral performance of the actors and actresses. With regard to subtitling, most of the channels will deal with it themselves; otherwise they will outsource it to private companies. Companies that have an integrated system can easily fulfil the client's needs by changing the font, colour and length of the subtitles.

Regarding dubbing, audiences usually have a very good interactive relationship. In Taiwan we have websites for Chinese dubbers. These websites have been established with the support of our audiences. We all draw information from these sites. China has similar websites, where they invite experts to critique and compare dubbings from various films. So we obtain constant feedback on our work. In addition to having highly trained personnel, our equipment is all digitised. Most of the large-scale studios have digital systems. My company has a system equipped with O2R and BAT systems. These systems can process animations such as cartoons and some simple dramas. We also have D8B for production purposes. These systems can process large-scale animated films and foreign movies and dramas. In fact, there are many excellent dubbing professionals in Taiwan. They are also very hardworking people with websites and programmes especially designed for dubbers. We also have on–the–job training for dubbers. Senior dubbers will give instructions and advice to their younger brethren. Unfortunately, as a result of the economic downturn and an extremely competitive environment, the salary of dubbers in Taiwan is not high. In a better economic environment, I believe that dubbers in Taiwan will have a bright future, and dubbing and translation will both be enhanced. I sincerely hope that the dubbing and subtitling industry will attract more attention so that subtitlers and dubbers can both contribute in their own fashion to serve customers, and give Taiwanese audiences more language options.

Europe

Corinne Imhauser
Institut Supérieur de Traducteurs et Interprètes (Belgium)

I graduated as an interpreter and translator. At the moment I teach interpreting at undergraduate level at the *Institut Supérieur de Traducteurs et Interprètes* (ISTI) in Brussels, which is the French-speaking translators and interpreters' school. I set up a subtitling course six years ago at ISTI and now it is part of a master's degree in multimedia translation that includes not only normal subtitling, but also surtitling for the opera, and subtitling for the deaf, which is unique. I believe that in Europe there is no training in subtitling for the hard of hearing. In the master's programme, we also have localisation and website translation which is the new market in translation, at least in Belgium.

Belgium lies between France and Germany, which explains why there are two language communities in Belgium—one speaks Flemish, which is close to German and Dutch, while the other speaks French. There is a legendary rivalry between the two, and this also explains why the situation is a bit different. Belgium is one of the smallest countries in Europe, yet we do a lot of subtitling and dubbing. Now the situation is quite different if you are dealing with the Flemish community (or the Flemings, as we call them). Historically, Flemish was a minority language, so the Flemish community has always been used to subtitling. Also, for economic reasons they could not subtitle that many films. In the south, with the French-speaking community, we are a bit more like the French in that the public usually prefer dubbing. But this is changing, and in Brussels, which is the capital, the situation is a compromise between the two. If you go to the cinemas in Brussels, the films are always in the original language, with subtitling in French and Flemish. This is probably one of the reasons why in general people prefer using Belgian subtitlers, since we are used to using one line and are more experienced in reducing and adapting translations. On the other hand, the French subtitles in France normally have two lines, which means that the translators place too much information in the subtitles so that you can either read the subtitles or watch the film, but it is very difficult to do both. So this is the situation as far as dubbing and subtitling in Belgium are concerned.

I say that things are changing in the French community as more and more people are watching subtitled films for the same reasons that were given this morning: i.e., more young people study English, travel, and prefer to see original films. Now I would also like to make a distinction between television and cinema in terms of subtitling.

Actually, I do not work in dubbing: I always worked in subtitling before teaching. I used to work for the main public service television broadcaster, a little bit like SBS or Finnish Television. Being a public service channel, its policy has always been quality-based, similar to the Australian situation. This means that in the French community we have two different situations. On the one hand, there is a language policy that the public service channel should air films twice a week: either the original versions with subtitles or the dubbed versions. We broadcast the two versions on two different channels simultaneously, so you can choose either one or the other. I tried it with my sons, who were used to watching dubbed films, and I said, "why don't we try the subtitled version, to give it a try," and they said "we don't want to." But when they heard the real sound with the real actors, they were astounded. "This is incredible," they said, "this is completely different!" So progressively we would watch the subtitled version, and come back to the dubbed version, and now they watch only the subtitled versions and are very proud of it. They tell their friends that they should watch the subtitled versions because they are better. So this is a very positive development in public service television.

The opposite situation applies to commercial television. The quality of subtitling is very bad indeed because just anybody does it and it doesn't comply with any rules. We also have cable television in Belgium, which means that we can watch at least fifty different channels coming from all over the world. This is quite important, because this means that the number of programmes available has really exploded, which is quite a favourable development for subtitling because television stations can no longer dub everything. The result is that now we see more and more subtitling on television. Another important development in television is that we are now beginning to subtitle more and more through teletext for the hard of hearing. This is the result of consistent lobbying by the hard of hearing lobby group. In the near future, at least on public television channels, it will be compulsory to broadcast at least 50 per cent of the programmes with closed captions. This is an important development for us because it means that we have to be practical, and it is a new market, and that is why we included it in our master's degree.

Belgian cinema is completely different. In Brussels, for example, there are only five people who subtitle everything that is shown in the cinema. It is a very small world, so the market is not big. We used to have good quality subtitles in the cinema, but now it is done quite quickly, whereas the opposite is true for television.

Now, talking about the market, I tell my students that cinema is rather limited, but television, DVD and video are really booming, so this is where they will be able to work in the future. Another possibility is film festivals. We have a lot of film festivals in Belgium and Europe. This doesn't mean that you will make money there, as film festivals have a very limited budget. But it is a good opportunity to meet people and to help new directors and new producers to get their films known, and sometimes to get rewards. This is an important thing that I am trying to work towards at the moment, because there are festivals where they allow anyone to do the subtitling because they don't have any money. So we are trying to inform festival organisers and to make them aware that if they do not pay enough attention to the quality of subtitles, they could jeopardise the success of a film, and, as has just been said, there are not enough distributors who pay enough attention to this issue.

As far as working conditions are concerned, they vary considerably according to your actual working environment. There are some television channels that have in-house subtitlers, which is the case with French-speaking public service television. There used to be five and now there are only two, but there are also freelance translators. Now with Flemish public service television the situation is completely different. They have 45 full-time translators plus 12 working solely for the hard of hearing. So their subtitling department is really big. Apart from television channels, we also have subtitling companies, and the situation can vary markedly from company to company.

In some cases, the good subtitling companies have translators who work in-house, a bit like SDI, so even if you are a freelance translator, you may go to the company and use their equipment. In Belgium it is usual for the subtitler to control the whole process: that is to say, we do the spotting, we do everything simultaneously, nothing is separated, you use your computer, you watch the film on your computer, you do the subtitling and of course you have someone review your work, but on the whole you control the whole process. The opposite situation also exists, with some new subtitling studios working on hijacking the market in their attempts to break into it. They charge their clients a lot, but offer the subtitler extremely low prices: three Hong Kong dollars per subtitle and a maximum two-day time limit to do the work. So you see that the quality is going down; but we are trying to oppose this and hopefully we will improve working conditions in the future.

The worst situation is probably with DVD. Some DVD companies, or subtitlers working for DVD companies, use the same cueing for fifteen different languages. Obviously this does not work because each language has its own syntax and its own semantic units, but they still have to respect the cueing. Usually they use German as the guide, as it has the longest words. Another argument given is that it is impossible for technical reasons.

Lastly, the way in which we are now attempting to enhance quality in Europe is by improving education in subtitling. When I started teaching subtitling six years ago, it was the first subtitling course in Belgium. Now, there are three universities offering subtitling courses in the French-speaking part and the same number on the Flemish side. France has at least four universities offering subtitling courses, so it is really a growing profession, and is continually improving.

Annika Jarvinen
Finnish Public Broadcasting Company (Finland)
Kari Jokelainen
Professional Translator (Finland)

The Finnish screen translator has the great responsibility for the whole process of making the Finnish version of the programme. The materials that he normally has for the translation and editing of the programme are a videotape, a script, or a dialogue list when one is available. If the film distributor cannot deliver a dialogue list, the translator has to work on the audio-visual material alone. One of the main tasks of the Finnish screen translator is to make subtitles according to the criteria set down in the country. The translator also time-codes the subtitles for an automated broadcast, using subtitling software. With documentaries, the first task is to translate and edit the text of the narration for the Finnish audience from the point of view of the local cultural background and the Finnish tradition of narration. As the information provided by the author of the documentary is sometimes inadequate, the translator has to check all the essential facts. Normally, the same translator also works as a director in the sound recording studio with a narrator and a sound engineer. If the documentary includes sequences with interviews, they are subtitled in Finnish. In this case, we hardly ever use a voice-over.

As the Finnish screen translator is the author in every phase of the project, the full responsibility for quality lies with him or her. This is true also for animated cartoons. The work starts with the translation and adaptation of the text to coincide with the movements of the characters. The next step is recording with dubbing actors and an assisting sound engineer. It should be mentioned that the cast of actors is selected in cooperation with the translator and the production coordinator. After the actual recording phase, the translator and the engineer create the final mix of the Finnish version with dialogue, music and sound effects.

The adapting of the Finnish translation is particularly demanding because the structure of the Finnish language is completely different from those Indo-European languages that we usually translate, such as English, German, and Scandinavian and Romance languages.

To emphasise the comprehensive responsibility of the translator, the last subtitle or the credits always include the name of the translator. In Finland, television translators always hold the copyright to their translation, with the television company having the right to one showing after paying the appropriate fee.

Sergio Patou-Patucchi
Italian Association for Translators and Interpreters (Italy)

In Italy we dub around 90 per cent of everything. Most dubbing is done in Rome, with the remainder being carried out in either Milan or Turin. I will talk principally about television programmes, because in Italy, only 100 hours per year of cinematic films are dubbed. It is better to leave these to a particular kind of translator and adaptor.

There are many terrestrial and satellite television stations dealing with all kinds of broadcasting: sport, entertainment, educational, and so on. Then we have a 24-hour paid-for channel for information concerning work. The Vatican also has its own broadcasting network. We have subtitles for festivals; we do subtitling using teletext and normal broadcasting for the hard of hearing and soundtracks for the blind. This work is accomplished by dubbing companies and freelancers. We also have a national agreement with actors, directors, dubbers and dialogists, who are organised into unions. So everybody gets the standard minimum wage.

As the main activity in this sector, dubbing is used by the distributors to change the story. For example, if the distributors get a picture that they don't like but one that has a good cast of actors, or something very marketable with an unconventional story, they will ask the dubbing actors to modify the story so that it becomes a whole new picture.

We have been said to do the best dubbing in the world, at least up until 1986. However, when television programmes became more important than films, we became average at everything, although my technicians did do some excellent work on one project: the Ministry of the Interior asked us to prepare educational material for new immigrants to Italy. We had to prepare a thirty-minute video, a thirty-minute audio-cassette, a brochure and a vocabulary list. They did the whole thing in Italian, then gave it to me and said that they wanted it translated into seven languages: Albanian, Arabic, Chinese, English, French, Filipino and Spanish. The first thing I had to do was put them in alphabetical order. It is impossible to dub into Chinese in Italy, so I had to find possible translators, train them to dub, and explain to them what a dubbing director does in the dubbing studio. Then we had to find actors to act out the dialogue. We had difficulty in finding actual dubbing actors, so we had theatre actors taking the roles of principal characters, and for the secondary roles we had some people who could play new immigrants to Italy. They had to have good pronunciation, of course.

Nobody has spoken about voice-over technique. We have done experiments with the use of the original voice under the voice-over. You may hear the original voice, you may be able to distinguish the tones of the original voice, but you have a kind of translation put over the top. It is an act of dubbing of course, and the intention and inflection are there, but it is something between speaking and acting, so it is difficult to achieve compatibility between the two voices.

I want to say one more thing: what we have today is globalisation, not homogenisation. I firmly refuse to surrender to the notion that the only verbal medium par excellence is the English language.

Jan Ivarsson
TransEdit (Sweden)

The first thing to say about subtitling and dubbing in Sweden is that we dub only for small children who can't read. We dubbed some films in the 1940s and 1950s which were complete commercial flops—people wanted to hear the actual voices of the actors, to see them acting in a normal way, and not experience the synthetic feeling that you always get with dubbing. So when television arrived in the mid-1950s, there was no question that foreign programmes would be subtitled.

So how much do we subtitle in Sweden? That is extremely difficult to calculate. We have two state channels, where almost 50 per cent of the content on first transmission is of foreign origin. Then we have eight or nine other free-to-air channels that are subtitled, some of them are on 24-hour-a-day with lots of reruns. We have subtitled news and current affairs programmes and so on. We subtitle 50 per cent of Swedish programmes to assist the hard of hearing, and organisations are pressing for 100 per cent (but that will probably never be quite possible). We subtitle news for the hard of hearing; one of our channels even has one news transmission that is subtitled in direct, which means that the subtitlers write online with the aid of a syllable keyboard. Quality will always be questionable, of course, but text comes immediately.

We also have films, of course. There are some 300 films a year, imported mainly from America. We have the whole video and DVD market, and the actual figures are very hard to calculate. I would say that at least 500 hours of first-run subtitled films and television programmes are broadcast per week in Sweden. That means something like 30,000 hours a year, which is quite a lot. If we try to compare this with written translations and say that one hour of television translation corresponds to thirty printed pages (which is a very low estimate, it is probably more like 50-60 pages), that number of hours would correspond to four or five thousand books of 250 pages each per year. So we translate considerably more for the screen than for printed books. However, subtitlers do not exist for the average person. If you say at a dinner that you are a subtitler, people will say "how interesting" and "you know the other day I saw on television somebody who had translated this and this very badly..."

The Swedish Academy gives out several prizes to translators every year, but no subtitle translator has ever got one, apart from one internal television language prize—but that is the only recognition of this kind, in spite of the fact that television subtitlers translate Shakespeare, Molière and the Bible and other highly literary figures. It is extremely difficult to render blank verse into subtitles. The translator who translated the *Muppet Show* and subtitled it is a genius, but she has never won a prize.

So, for whom do we subtitle? We do not only subtitle for the normal Swede. We have immigrants who are not very fluent in Swedish. We have people who are hard of hearing, many more than most people would imagine. Up to 25 per cent of the television audience has difficulty in hearing dialogue, as there are lots of old people who watch television. People who work watch much less television. In addition, we subtitle for children, who are not fast readers. So you have to be very considerate about whom you are translating for and you should think also of those categories of the audience.

How many translators are there? I have tried for a couple of years to note down every name and I came up with something like 500. I would say that half of them work part-time, very part-time. There are about 11 full-time translators on Swedish television who do a lot of other things besides translating. (Our situation is very much like that of Finland in many ways.) We also have 70 freelance translators. On the commercial side, there is SDI which employs about 100 translators, most of whom are freelancers. That is bigger than Swedish Television. There are of course lots of smaller producers, and I have no idea how many might work on the translation of pornographic films.

How are these people trained? Those working for television would have something like a B.A. or M.A. in languages, but it is not a formal requirement. They are trained in subtitle translation in-house, and sometimes there are actual courses. I have taught a couple of these, talking to groups of 10 or 12 or even 15. I have also taught similar groups for a couple of other companies. Then at university there are translation programmes that give short courses on the basics of screen translation, but as they don't have proper subtitling equipment, they cannot give full training for the job.

How do Swedish translators work? They usually have access to good electronic equipment, and practically always do the whole job in all companies, including the cueing (or timing).

There are rules of language to follow. That is very important, because our young people to a large extent learn how to write Swedish by watching television, and if something is accepted there, that is seen as correct. That is where private companies sin very badly, because they have no concept of quality control, and almost anything goes. I am not talking about translation errors, but language errors, which are very much more important than translation errors.

How are Swedish translators paid? In television and film companies they are well paid, usually according to text equivalent. They earn roughly something equivalent to HK$10 per text. But in private companies this is not the case: they pay a lot less and I must say (and I regret that SDI is a bad sinner in this context): they are pushing down salaries and text pricing in Sweden.

Swedish translators own the copyright and can have their names attached to their work. So if you are a serious translator, you don't mind if your name is up there in the credits.

DVD is dangerous because we have seen a tendency to translate into 15 different languages. Made by translation bureaux in Hollywood or Los Angeles, the subtitles are simply done by someone who "knows Swedish," and who just follows the pre-cued format, and the results are disastrous but cheap.

Contributors

—⚊—

Kenneth K. L. AU is currently Assistant Professor at the Department of Chinese, Translation and Linguistics of City University of Hong Kong. He teaches theory of translation, audio-visual translation, and commercial and financial translation. His research interests include audiovisual translation, financial translation and translation studies. He translated *Corporate Finance: Flotations, Equity Issues and Acquisitions* and authored a number of papers on refereed journals. He is a PhD candidate working on audiovisual translation at Department of Translation, the Chinese University of Hong Kong.
(Email: kenneth.au@cityu.edu.hk, Address: Department of Chinese, Translation and Linguistics, City University of Hong Kong, 83 Tat Chee Avenue, Kowloon Tong, Hong Kong.)

Rupert CHAN is a university administrator and freelance translator, playwright, writer and lyricist. He hosts the Sunday Opera on Radio Hong Kong, and is an adviser of the Leisure & Cultural Services Department of Hong Kong on opera and drama. Of his forty plus drama translations, three are musicals (*Cabaret*, *Pygmalion* and *Little Shop of Horrors*) for which he also wrote the lyrics in Chinese. Chan has translated over 30 opera libretti for Chinese surtitle projections, and in 1989 has translated Britten's Old English libretto of the opera *Noyes Fludde* for the HKAPA production in Cantonese. In 2000 he wrote the lyrics of the original Chamber Operas based on Lu Xun's short stories, *The Divorce* and *The Lamp of Everlasting Light* with the libretto by Lo King-man and Rupert Chan. An award-winning project is the lyrics in Mandarin of *Nine Regions Singing As One* composed by Professor Chan Wing-wah for the 1997 Hong Kong Reunification (sung by Warren Mok and Choir), which won the Most Performed

Original Local Serious Work Award from the Composers and Authors Society of Hong Kong. Chan received the Hong Kong Artists Guild "Playwright of the Year Award" in 1990. He now sits on the Board of Directors of the Chung Ying Theatre Company. His scripts already published include *Twelfth Night, Hobson's Choice, L'Hotel du Libre Echange* and *Cyrano de Bergerac*.
(Email: rkychan@hkusua.hku.hk)

Chapman CHEN (Ph.D. in Literature, M.A. in Translation, B.A. in English) has taught for ten years translation, interpretation (English, Cantonese, Mandarin), and comparative literature in various universities in Hong Kong and Taiwan. Before that, he had worked for almost nine years as a court interpreter for the Hong Kong Judiciary. He has published twenty-four academic articles in international refereed journals, four books, and four translations (two by John Benjamins). His research interests include drama translation, Finnish culture, subtitling, Cantonese language, and comparative literature. He is now a translator, interpreter and researcher.
(Email: kivilonnrot@yahoo.com)

CHUANG Ying-ting is currently Assistant Professor in the Department of English & Graduate Institute of Interpreting and Translation, at the National Kaohsiung First University of Science and Technology in Taiwan. Her research interest is mainly concerned with multi-modal translation and approaching translation from a social semiotic perspective. At present, she is working on a theoretical framework to address the impact of technology and globalization, to explore new forms and new environment of translation, i.e., to deal with the new interrelationships between sign activities and the social and cultural environment and the new interpersonal factors in the translating process.
(Email: ytchuang@ccms.nkfust.edu.tw; Address: Department of English & Graduate Institute of Interpreting and Translation, NKFUST, 2, Cho-yueh Road, Kaohsiung 811, Taiwan.)

Gilbert C. F. FONG graduated from The Chinese University of Hong Kong and received his M.A. and Ph.D. from the University of

Toronto. Afterwards, he taught Chinese Language and Literature at the University of Toronto and York University in Canada, and he was Professor with the Department of Translation, The Chinese University of Hong Kong. Presently he is Professor and Head of Translation at the Hang Seng School of Commerce. He has written many articles on modern and contemporary Chinese literature and literary translation. An acclaimed translator, he translated many plays by Gao Xingjian, winner of the 2000 Nobel Prize for Literature, into English; they are published in *The Other Shore, Snow in August, Cold Literature: Selected Works by Gao Xingjian* (with Mabel Lee), *Escape and The Man Who Questions Death*, and *Of Mountains and Seas.* He also translated into Chinese Samuel Beckett's *Waiting for Godot,* Jean Genet's *Haute Surveillance,* Dale Wasserman's *Man of La Mancha, Burning Patience* by Antonio Skármeta and Arthur Miller's *Death of a Salesman.* He was editor of several books, including *Studies on Hong Kong Drama, Plays from Hong Kong,* and he is currently editor of two academic journals, *Hong Kong Drama Review* and *Journal of Translation Studies.*
(Email: gilbert.fong@gmail.com; Address: Hang Seng School of Commerce, Hong Kong.)

FUMITOSHI Karima is an experienced subtitler of Japanese films and teaches the history of Chinese cinema and contemporary Chinese culture in Tokyo.

HE Yuanjian is Professor at the Department of Translation, The Chinese University of Hong Kong. He teaches translation, translation studies (including translation criticism) and comparative language studies. Author of *An Introduction to Government-Binding Theory in Chinese Syntax* (1996), *Generative Linguistics and Chinese Grammar* (with Shen Yang and Gu Yang, 2001), *The Verb-Complement Constructions in Chinese* (with Lingling Wang, 2002), *Generative Linguistics for Chinese Grammar and Translation* (2007) and of over 40 research papers in journals and book chapters covering Chinese linguistics, language typology and translation studies. His new works include *Translating China* (co-edited with Luo Xuanmin). He is also a research fellow at the Centre for Chinese Linguistics, Peking University and an adjunct professor at the Department of Chinese Language and Literature, Sichuan University, China.

(Email: yuanjianhe@cuhk.edu.hk; Address: Department of Translation, The Chinese University of Hong Kong, Shatin, N.T., Hong Kong.)

Corinne IMHAUSER graduated in interpretation at EII (University of Mons-Belgium). She has always been working both as a professional interpreter/translator and in academia. For ten years, she was a translator/subtitler with the main French-speaking public TV channel and is now working with independent producers both in subtitling and voice-over. She worked at EURO AIM, a MEDIA project of DGX (EU Commission) for the support of independent cinema and TV producers. She is now a consultant with the EU and the European Parliament. She taught interpretation at the Universidad Central de Venezuela in the 1980s. She set up a subtitling course at ISTI in 1994 and developed the first subtitling course for the hard of hearing in Europe. She was Head of the postgraduate studies in multimedia translation at ISTI in Brussels until 2006 and is now Head of the Interpretation Department. She is also involved in voice coaching at the EU and other international institutions and has given lectures and workshops all over the world to raise awareness on the need to develop a specific pedagogy and to bridge the gap between the academe and practitioners. She was Chair of the IFT (International Federation of Translators) Media Committee from 2003 to 2005. She has been a member of the Steering committee of the "Languages and the Media" conference for the past ten years. She has published numerous articles in academic journals on subtitling research and teaching.
(Email: cimhauserbxl@hotmail.com)

Jan IVARSSON studied at Uppsala University. He has been Lecturer of Swedish at the Christian-Albrecht University in Kiel (1960–1963), at the Sorbonne and the École Supérieure d'Interprètes et de Traducteurs in Paris (1963–1970). During 1970–1978 he was Secretary-General of the Swedish Cultural Centre in Paris. After 1978, he worked in Stockholm as a TV and film subtitler, mostly for Sveriges Television. He also contributed largely to the creation of a new, computerized, time code-based subtitling system at the SVT, in collaboration with ScanTitling/Cavena. In 1995 he retired. He has

translated poetry, plays and books from French, German and English into Swedish as well as many TV programmes. In 1992 he published *Subtitling for the Media—A Handbook of an Art* and, together with Mary Carroll, *Subtitling* in 1998. In the period 1992–1996, he was a member of the Working Group on Language Transfer of the European Institute for the Media and in 1995 was one of the founding members of the ESIST (European Association for Studies in Screen Translation. He has lectured on different aspects of media translation at numerous conferences and has taught subtitlers in Stockholm (SVT and Språkcentrum), Berlin (SFB), Riga (UNDP project) and in Xalapa.
(Email: jan.ivarsson@transedit.se. Website: http://www.trans edit.se)

Kari JOKELAINEN is a professional screen translator working on a free-lance basis mostly for the Finnish Television (YLE) in Helsinki since 1986 after graduating at Jyväskylä University as Master of Arts in Philology. His target language is Finnish and main source languages Italian, French, Russian, Catalan, Estonian and English. His assignments include all main programme fields, like subtitling films, serials, documentaries; translation for voice-over speakers; translation, adaptation and direction of cartoon-dubbing. In addition, he makes occasionally surtitles for Russian theatre troupes performing in Finland. At present he participates also in filmmaking in an Estonian crew charged with travel and shooting arrangements and interpretation.
(Email: kari.jokelainen@saunalahti.fi)

LEE Young Koo received his BA degree in Chinese from Hankuk University of Foreign Studies, and Master degrees in Chinese from Seoul National University and from National Taiwan University, and Ph.D. in Chinese from Yonsei University. He has been teaching at Hankuk University of Foreign Studies (HUFS) since 1982, and served as Director of Academic Office of Graduate School of HUFS, and President of Korea Esperanto Association. He has been researching in Chinese literature and cultural studies for about 27 years. Presently, his research focused on Korean war-time literature, contemporary and modern Chinese Literature, and overseas Chinese writers. His major works include four books: *World Novelist- Nobel Prize*

Winner Gao Xingjian and his World in Novels, Gao Xingjian's The Case
for Literature, *The Origin of World Literature, La Literatura Mondo de
Elpin* and a number of Chinese articles on Gao Xingjian and other
contemporary and modern Chinese writers. Prof Lee is also active in
cultural exchange between Korea and China. He is currently
Director of Institute of Foreign Literature of HUFS, President of
Academic Association of Global Cultural Contents and President of
The Society of Chinese Studies.
(Email: ykli@hufs.ac.kr)

LU Danjun studied English language and literature at Changsha
Railway University, China and drama and anthropology at the
University of California, Berkeley. He is currently Associate Professor
of English at Central South University, China. He has also translated
more than 100 English works into Chinese and won several national
awards, specializing in translating musical literature. In addition, he
has translated more than 300 foreign films into Chinese and taken
part in dubbing more than 50 of them.

Sergio PATOU-PATUCCHI works as a Docent of "Theory and
technique of the cinematographic language," Interpreting and
Translation faculty of the Libera Università degli Studi "S. Pio V" in
Rome. He is the Coordinator and a Docent of the Masters post-
lauream: "Translation and Adaptation of Audiovisuals and
Multimedia for Dubbing and Subtitling" and "Production & Set
Translator and Interpreter for Cinema and TV." He works with RAI
(the Italian National Broadcasting Co.) as a dubbing director and
translator-adaptator of dialogues from English, French and Spanish
and is a director and author of many radio programmes. He is also a
freelance translator, a screenwriter, director and writer for the
theatre, writer of librettos of ballets and operas. For the C.N.R.
(Italian National Council of Researches), he was Manager-in-Charge
of the scientific research "The true influence of TV and motion-
picture language on every-day Italian speaking." At the moment, he
is the Vice-President and National Coordinator for Literary and
Audiovisual Translation of the AITI (Italian Association of
Translators and Interpreters—member of FIT, Fédération
Internationale des Traducteurs).
(Email: patucchi@tin.it)

QIAN Shaochang was born in Hangzhou, China and graduated from St. Xavier's College in Shanghai in 1947, and from Shanghai Second Medical University (formerly medical school of St. John's University) in 1954 with MD degree. He worked as a surgeon at Shanghai People's Hospital for 20 years. He was persecuted during the Cultural Revolution (1966–76) and lost the job. Later he switched to teaching English at the Shanghai International Studies University, of which he is presently a professor. He has written two books, published more than 50 papers and translated more than 10 million words, among which are some 700 hours of moives and teleplays.

SHU Kei started as a film critic and began writing scripts for television when he was studying in university. He made his directorial debut in 1981 and so far has made six films, including *Sunless Days* (1990), *Hu-Du-Men* (1996) and *a Queer Story* (1997). In 1986, he set up his own company, Shu Kei's Creative Workshop Ltd., to distribute art-house films. Up to date, its library has over 150 features. He is responsible for the translation of subtitles of most of his own releases. He was Artist-in-Residence of Sir Run Run Shaw Hall of Chinese University from 1998 to 1999 and has taught in both the Academy for Performing Arts and Hong Kong University. He also owns a film bookshop, the only of its kind in Hong Kong.

Janet TAURO is now working for the Ministry of Social Development in New Zealand after teaching at De La Salle University, Manila, from 1991 to 2007, where she completed her Doctor of Arts in Languages and Literature (D.A.L.L.) with distinction and outstanding dissertation awards in 2000. She has been teaching since 1991 at De La Salle University. Dr. Tauro has presented her research papers about translation and television studies at Miami University in USA, University of Leeds in UK and the Chinese University of Hong Kong. Also a journalist for more than ten years, she has written investigative reports for *Phil. Graphics, Starweek Magazine, Reporter Magasin* and *Village Voice*. In 1988, she was sent to London by Star Publications Inc. to investigate on the proliferation of mail-order brides syndicates, the plight of the Filipino workers which were used as reference for some of the related Congressional bills. In 1990, she wrote and produced segments for a major television network ABS CBN's *The Inside Story* on the situation of separated single parents, the

sufferings of the special children at Elsie Gaches and analysis of the country's educational system among others. As the head scriptwriter for Philippine Distance Education Corp., she has written and edited scripts for telecourses in education which were shown in PTV Channel 4. She was chosen as Writing Fellow for short story by the University of the Philippines PANULAT in 1997 workshop and Writing Fellow for drama by the National Commission on Culture and Arts in 1995 workshop.
(Email: jantauro@yahoo.com)

Jessica W. Y. YEUNG is Associate Professor of Translation Programme of Hong Kong Baptist University. She holds a B.A. (major in Translation), an M.Phil. in Comparative Literature and a Ph.D. in Performing Arts Studies. Her research interests include drama and literary translation, literary and critical theories and theatre studies. She is at present working on a research project on the works of Gao Xingjian, and another one on Cantonese productions of translated plays in Hong Kong. She has produced English surtitles for numerous *xiqu* productions and accompanied a *xiqu* troupe as interpreter and cultural mediator on a lecture tour to the U.K. She has also translated Chinese plays into English for the stage and radio broadcast. Apart from her academic and translation work, she also acts on stage and writes theatre and cultural criticism.
(Email: jyeung@hkbu.edu.hk, Address: Department of English and Literature, Hong Kong Baptist University, Waterloo Road, Kowloon, Hong Kong.)

ZHANG Chunbai, Professor of English, Dean of School of Foreign Languages and Director of Centre for Translation Studies of East China Normal University in Shanghai. He has been on the faculty of that university since 1984 when he received his Master's degree in English Language and Literature. He is executive director of China English Language Education Association and China Association for Comparative Studies of English and Chinese, and director of the Translators Association of China. His research focus is on translation studies. His publications include over 30 papers, 2 textbooks of translation, 3 English grammar books, 3 dictionaries, and a number of other textbooks. Since 1983 he has translated about 300 films and episodes of TV series for dubbing or subtitling, including *The Street*

Car Named Desire, The Rear Window, Hunter, The Colbys, Growing Pains and *Anna Karenina.*
(Email: cbzhang2@163.com)

Index

—⁓⁓—